Palgrave Studies in Literature, Culture and Economics

Series Editors
Paul Crosthwaite
School of Literatures, Languages & Culture
University of Edinburgh
Edinburgh, UK

Peter Knight
Department of English and American Studies
University of Manchester
Manchester, UK

Nicky Marsh
Department of English
University of Southampton
Southampton, UK

This series showcases some of the most intellectually adventurous work being done in the broad field of the economic humanities, putting it in dialogue with developments in heterodox economic theory, economic sociology, critical finance studies and the history of capitalism. It starts from the conviction that literary and cultural studies can provide vital theoretical insights into economics. The series will include historical studies as well as contemporary ones, as a much-needed counterweight to the tendency within economics to concentrate solely on the present and to ignore potential lessons from history. The series also recognizes that the poetics of economics and finance is an increasingly central concern across a wide range of fields of literary study, from Shakespeare to Dickens to the financial thriller. In doing so it builds on the scholarship that has been identified as the 'new economic criticism', but moves beyond it by bringing a more politically and historically sharpened focus to that earlier work.

More information about this series at
http://www.palgrave.com/gp/series/15745

Elaine Hadley • Audrey Jaffe • Sarah Winter
Editors

From Political Economy to Economics through Nineteenth-Century Literature

Reclaiming the Social

palgrave
macmillan

Editors
Elaine Hadley
University of Chicago
Chicago, IL, USA

Audrey Jaffe
University of Toronto
Toronto, ON, Canada

Sarah Winter
University of Connecticut
Storrs, CT, USA

Palgrave Studies in Literature, Culture and Economics
ISBN 978-3-030-24157-5   ISBN 978-3-030-24158-2 (eBook)
https://doi.org/10.1007/978-3-030-24158-2

Cover illustration: SOTK2011 / Alamy Stock Photo & vivacity.tv / Alamy Stock Photo

This Palgrave Macmillan imprint is published by the registered company Springer Nature Switzerland AG.
The registered company address is: Gewerbestrasse 11, 6330 Cham, Switzerland

This book is dedicated to the authors' families and our collaborative efforts.

Acknowledgments

The Editors would like to thank our editor at Palgrave, Allie Troyanos, editorial assistant Rachel Jacobe, and Meg Wallace, our indexer. Carrie Taylor preserved our sanity with her editorial efforts near the end.

We would like to thank the Franke Institute for the Humanities at the University of Chicago, the Public Discourse Project of the University of Connecticut Humanities Institute (UCHI), and the UCHI Humanities Book Support Award, and Paul Stevens, Chair of the University of Toronto's English Department, for supporting research for and publication of this volume.

The Editors extend special thanks to this volume's contributors, who submitted wonderful scholarship, received our collective input with good grace, and worked hard to meet deadlines during the thick of the academic year.

We would also like to thank our families for their understanding and support as we devised, compiled, wrote, and edited this volume.

CONTENTS

Notes on Contributors

Gordon Bigelow is a member of the English Department at Rhodes College in Memphis, Tennessee (USA), where he teaches courses on Victorian Britain and Ireland, contemporary theory, and the history of the novel. His research is focused on the problem of form in Anthony Trollope's Irish fiction and on the treatment of Atlantic slavery in Victorian economic thought. He is the author of *Fiction, Famine, and the Rise of Economics in Victorian Literature and Culture* (2003), as well as articles appearing in *Novel, ELH*, and *The Cambridge Companion to Anthony Trollope*.

Ayşe Çelikkol is an assistant professor in the Department of English Language and Literature at Bilkent University (Ankara, Turkey). She is the author of *Romances of Free Trade: British Literature, Laissez-Faire, and the Global Nineteenth Century* (2011). Her essays on nineteenth-century British and American literature have appeared in journals such as *ELH, American Literature, Victorian Poetry*, and the *Journal of William Morris Studies*. Her recent work explores links among ecology, capitalism, and Victorian literature.

Clare V. Eby is Professor of English at the University of Connecticut, Storrs (USA). She is the author of *Dreiser and Veblen, Saboteurs of the Status Quo* and *Until Choice Do Us Part: Marriage Reform in the Progressive Era*, as well as 30 articles and chapters. In addition, she edited the Norton Critical Edition of *The Jungle* and the Dreiser Edition of Theodore Dreiser's *The Genius*, and is associate editor of *The Cambridge History of the American Novel*. She is working on a monograph on corporate personhood in the twenty-first century.

Amanpal Garcha is an associate professor in the English Department at the Ohio State University, Columbus (USA). He is the author of *From Sketch to Novel: The Development of Victorian Fiction* (2009). His recent publications include "Forgetting Thackeray, Unmaking Careers," which appears in *Victorian Literature and Culture*, and "Imagining a Professional Future: Cognitive Criticism in Our Era of Information Work," which is published in *symploke*. He is working on a new book project titled "Preference: Nineteenth-Century Literature and Modern Forms of Decision-Making."

Elaine Hadley is Professor of English and Gender Studies at the University of Chicago (USA). She is the author of *Melodramatic Tactics* (1995) and *Living Liberalism* (2010). Her scholarship includes an essay on modern neoconservatism's roots in classical liberalism and a recent essay on statistics and Victorian war. She is working on a book about inequality, Victorian political economy, and neoclassical economics.

Audrey Jaffe is Professor of English at the University of Toronto (Canada) and author of several books, including *Scenes of Sympathy: Identity and Representation in Victorian Fiction* (2000), *The Affective Life of the Average Man: The Victorian Novel and the Stock-Market Graph* (2010), and *The Victorian Novel Dreams of the Real: Conventions and Ideology* (2016).

Deanna K. Kreisel is Associate Professor of English at the University of Mississippi, Oxford (USA). She is the author of *Economic Woman: Demand, Gender, and Narrative Closure in Eliot and Hardy*, published in 2012. Her articles on Victorian literature and culture have appeared in such journals as *PMLA, ELH, Representations, Victorian Studies, Nineteenth Century Literature*, and others. She is the co-editor, with Devin Griffiths, of an upcoming special issue of *Victorian Literature and Culture* on "Open Ecologies." She is working on a new project on utopia and sustainability in the nineteenth century.

Mukti Lakhi Mangharam is Associate Professor of English at Rutgers University, New Brunswick, New Jersey (USA). Her book *Literatures of Liberation: Non European Universalisms and Democratic Progress* (2017) explores local universalisms and associated traditions of democratic liberation in Indian and South African literatures. She has written widely on postcolonial and world literatures in journals including *ELH, Economic and Political Weekly, Journal of Commonwealth and Postcolonial Studies, Diacritics, ARIEL*, and *Safundi*.

Zachary Samalin is an assistant professor in the Department of English at the University of Chicago (USA). His research on British literature and culture of the nineteenth century has appeared in or is forthcoming from *New Literary History, Boundary 2 Online, Victorian Literature and Culture, Criticism,* and other venues.

Sarah Winter is Professor of English and Comparative Literary and Cultural Studies at the University of Connecticut, Storrs (USA). A scholar of nineteenth-century British literature and the history of the modern disciplines, she has written two books, *The Pleasures of Memory: Learning to Read with Charles Dickens* (2011) and *Freud and the Institution of Psychoanalytic Knowledge* (1999). Her research projects in law and literature focus on habeas corpus and the history of human rights, and on serial fiction and Victorian legal reform.

CHAPTER 1

Introduction: Reclaiming the Social

Elaine Hadley, Audrey Jaffe, and Sarah Winter

"It is possible," Gayatri Spivak argues, "to put the economic text 'under erasure,' to see, that is, the unavoidable and pervasive importance of its operation and yet to question it as a concept of the last resort" (85). This book seeks to realize just this possibility.

In George Eliot's *The Mill on the Floss* ([1860] 1914), a double Bildungsroman about the troubled growth into adulthood of two siblings, Tom and Maggie Tulliver, their progress into maturity is constrained by their father's bankruptcy. Business success and failure, and their determinative impacts on families, are a central thread in this tragic narrative. George Eliot, despite being a famously adept writer of free indirect discourse as a representation of her characters' thoughts, largely demonstrates economic thought through dialogue. When Tom seeks financial support from his uncle, Mr. Glegg, so that he might invest in some export goods that his old friend, the canny trader Bob Jakins, mentions, this is how Eliot portrays business:

E. Hadley (✉)
University of Chicago, Chicago, IL, USA

A. Jaffe
University of Toronto, Toronto, ON, Canada

S. Winter
University of Connecticut, Storrs, CT, USA

© The Author(s) 2019
E. Hadley et al. (eds.), *From Political Economy to Economics through Nineteenth-Century Literature*, Palgrave Studies in Literature, Culture and Economics, https://doi.org/10.1007/978-3-030-24158-2_1

1

"Ay-Ay," said Mr. Glegg, in an approving tone; "that's not a bad notion, and I won't say as I wouldn't be your man. But it 'ull be as well for me to see this Salt, as you talk on. And then—here's this friend o' yours offers to buy the goods for you. Perhaps you've got somebody to stand surety for you if the money's put into your hands?" added the cautious old gentleman, looking over his spectacles at Bob.

"I don't think that's necessary, uncle," said Tom. "At least, I mean it would not be necessary for me, because I know Bob well; but perhaps it would be right for you to have some security."

"You get your percentage out o' the purchase, I suppose?" said Mr. Glegg, looking at Bob. (319)

In the larger scene from which this passage comes, Eliot wishes to emphasize the way in which social relations infuse business relations, the sort of social relations where seeing, meeting, and knowing people are paramount. Tom assures his uncle that this deal is to be trusted precisely because he knows and trusts Bob who knows and trusts Salt, the shipman. And this might be, as well, one of the reasons why Eliot tends to prefer dialogue, the print instantiation of sociality, to make her point about the social nature of the economic relation.

Not long after this passage was written, the subdiscipline of neoclassical economics emerged from the classical economics of Eliot's own childhood, codifying axioms about the market that increasingly replaced this social exchange among known and knowable people with a market of pricing mechanisms only joined by people as isolated consumers. This book aims to think about the gains and losses of this story about the changing rules and outcomes of economics.

Economics has become one of the most dominant disciplines in the modern academy and, arguably, one of the most dominant discourses in political debate. Its consolidation over the past two and half centuries as one of the sciences—with all the authority that designation conveys—as well as its near-monopoly as the explanatory rubric for a wide range of policy debates in the social domain registers this dominance. The expanding authority of economics coincides, however, with what seems like a parallel contraction in the authority of humanistic inquiry. In using the tools of literary analysis and cultural criticism to reconnect economics to its historical context and roots in humanistic questions and concerns, we seek in this volume to recover the underlying assumptions of many ideas often accepted as givens: the result of what neoclassical economics, in its concerted efforts to be recognized as a science, presents as natural or normative laws. This context has often been neglected, forgotten, or simply overwritten by the impersonal assumptions that accompany mathematical models, which study markets and economic transactions as abstracted from the social domain in which they occur. Of course, this collection on its own cannot reverse this trend. We believe it shows, however, the crucial insights humanistic methods of analysis can add to the continuing debate about what constitutes economics, and suggests how that discipline might incorporate them. By looking both backward and forward, we hope to contribute to recent efforts within economics and in the interpretive social sciences and humanities to open economics once more to other disciplinary methods and insights, to alternative figurations of the human and its social environment. In so doing we also seek to reanimate the multiple motivations of society—beyond transactional self-interest—in order to ask questions about inequality, social justice, and environmental well-being.

Because of these goals, this book differs in several ways from previous collections and studies about economics and literature. First, it aims to demonstrate how humanistic inquiry can open up economic debates increasingly cast as specialist, taking advantage in particular of literary critics' ability to perceive narrative and rhetorical structures within economic theorizing. Second, the volume highlights dimensions of economics that the "science" of economics tends to ignore—putting a human face on discussions of (for example) labor, human capital, income inequality, and questions about the rationality or irrationality of economic behavior. Finally, in a deliberate effort to construct a narrative linking the present with its nineteenth-century assumptions and causes, our contributors look to the past, tracing a current concern to its nineteenth-century (or earlier) origins, and back to the present and future, exploring the development or persistence of nineteenth-century issues in the present day. In this way, the volume considers both the gains and losses in explanatory power, and the epistemological and moral blindness, which we see occasioned by the trend of economics toward abstraction and mathematical explanation. The book thus models a mode of historical inquiry that avoids both the strict constructionist version of new historicism, asserting radical differences between eras, and an ahistorical political philosophy that overlooks nuances in the development of concepts assigned to particular disciplines.

Our contributors seek to rediscover the social within the economic and thus create a more open encounter among disciplines. To this end, the volume is organized around a keyword format. Rather than short entries such as those in Raymond Williams's seminal volume *Keywords: A Vocabulary of Culture and Society* ([1976] 1983), our terms introduce full-length chapters oriented around a central concept that connects nineteenth-century political economy and economics to present-day issues. The chapters often analyze a case study or conceptual history, and frequently draw upon one or more literary texts as a way of illustrating and modeling the issues at stake. We use "keywords" as a clarifying element: not as mere definition, but rather as a way of formulating the humanities' ability to take the idea of economics in new directions by illuminating the concepts and values that have been associated with, and used to contest, the discipline's historical development.[1] The chapters in this volume show how the central categories of literary criticism—genre, narrative, character, plot, motivation, and setting—play an often unexamined role in economic theorization. They also, together, constitute an argument that humanistic inquiry can redefine the market as a field of social relations, reintegrating economics with the social sciences and exerting pressure on abstract economic articulations so that the social effects and histories of central "economic" concepts can become part of broadly shared discussions about the kinds of societies we desire for the future.

In defining the *Keywords* project, Williams explains that "the most active problems of meaning are always primarily embedded in actual relationships" that "are typically diverse and variable, within the structures of particular social orders and the processes of social and historical change" (1983, 22). Reflecting our similar concern with economic thinking as formed within and shaping specific social relations over time, our subtitle, *Reclaiming the Social*, draws on the Hungarian economic historian Karl Polanyi's influential critique in *The Great Transformation* ([1944] 2001) of the liberal ideology of self-regulating markets developed by Ludwig von Mises and Friedrich Hayek, based on an historical account of the social embeddedness of economic relationships. For Polanyi, industrialization in the eighteenth and nineteenth centuries gave rise to a new theory of the relationship between the economy and society as entailing a liberal "market economy," that is, "an economic system controlled, regulated, and directed by market prices," and derived from "the expectation that human beings behave in such a way as to achieve maximum money gains" (2001, 71). For such a market to be self-regulating, Polanyi explains, "demands nothing less than the institutional separation of society into an economic and a political sphere," through which society becomes subordinated to market requirements (74–75). Because the negations of the social relations of law and custom entailed in such a separation appeared unacceptable to many observers, however, a series of political reactions ensued to attempt to constrain and regulate market forces, giving rise to the oft-cited, dialectical "double movement" theorized by Polanyi between market forces and society.

Critics have called humanists' and social scientists' reliance on Polanyi's theory a kind of "fetishism" that treats the economy and markets as mere fictions, thus negating their materiality and complexity (Konings 2015). However, we emphasize that Polanyi's account is quite concrete because it is based on specific developments in Britain, as that nation took a leading role in the emergence of world-wide liberal and neoliberal markets. These included: free trade; the legal enforcement of the free market in labor (see also Steinberg 2016); the adoption of the gold standard; the maintenance of a favorable balance of trade through extraction of raw materials from colonies, followed by resale of manufactured goods to colonial populations; and the military enforcement of external debts. To re-embed the economy within society and to understand the sources of resistance to the dominance of market rationality, therefore, becomes in Polanyi's terms a fundamentally historical project: one that challenges us in the current volume to find new ways to understand both markets and the ways they have been described—in an arc from political economy to economics—within the larger global history of capitalism.

Nineteenth-Century British Literature and Economics

Reading literary texts "through" economics is no longer a new project; in fact, it has grown quickly since Mark Osteen and Martha Woodmansee organized a conference panel on this subject in 1991, and admitted "we were naming a phenomenon that we weren't entirely sure existed" (1999, 3). It is by now axiomatic to acknowledge publication of their 1999 collection, *The New Economic Criticism*, as establishing a new field and in exemplary fashion showing the way to its practice, relevance, and some of its methods. Some chapters dealt directly with specific texts and genres from a variety of historical periods, while others addressed the symbolic resonance of money and exchange—work begun previously by contributors such as Marc Shell, whose *Economy of Literature* (1978) carved out a space for an anthropologically oriented study of the symbolic nature of the relation between money and literature, and Jean-Christophe Agnew in his study of theater and the marketplace, *Worlds Apart* (1986). Economic criticism itself was showcased as part of the more general, and also rapidly expanding field of cultural criticism, demonstrating how the presence of cultural tropes from a variety of nonliterary disciplines had remained unnoticed in much-studied literary works and genres. Because the introduction to the Woodmansee/Osteen volume goes into detail about successive "waves" of economic criticism, we will not go over that material here, but will briefly demonstrate how this kind of work—its range, breadth, and quality—has come to define a major strand of Victorianist literary criticism.

Literary analysis at the intersection of economics and Victorian literature post-Woodmansee/Osteen took a new turn with work that focused closely on the narrative structure and rhetorical strategy of economic theory, and in doing so revised conventional assumptions about both economics and Victorian literature.[2] Just a few years before the Woodmansee and Osteen collection, Catherine Gallagher published an important article (1986) that overturned conventional understandings of Malthus's seminal *Essay on Population* (1798) by pointing out that health and vigor, in Malthus's analysis, did not contribute to a healthy society, but rather to one that was overtaxed and functioned beyond its capacities. Deanna Kreisel's chapter in this volume further illuminates the Malthusian roots of today's environmentalist debates over sustainability. Gallagher followed up in 1989 with her essay on Dickens's *Our Mutual Friend*, demonstrating a reversal of terms in which the health of the body politic relies on the "illth" of the individual body; both of these essays appear, along with chapters on Dickens's *Hard Times* and Eliot's *Daniel Deronda*, in *The Body Economic* (2009), an influential volume, which established the constitutive relation between early political economy and organicist conceptions of society.

Mary Poovey's several monographs over the past few decades have shown the kind of work that can be done when a literary critic directs humanistic interpretive tools to intellectual history and emergent disciplines. In *Making A Social Body* (1995), Poovey considered the moral implications that cling to economic concepts despite economists' insistence on their rationality, and in *A History of the Modern Fact* (1998), Poovey extended methods of literary analysis to economic history by studying the key role of accounting practices such as double-entry bookkeeping. In *Genres of the Credit Economy* (2008), she theorized how literary value was reconceived in relation to nineteenth-century credit markets. Gordon Bigelow's *Fiction, Famine, and the Rise of Economics in Victorian Britain and Ireland* (2003) also focused on disciplinary history in examining how neoclassical economics drew on Romantic philological conceptions of language to construct the subjectivity of the consumer.

Notable work has been published on the aesthetic and affective features of the nineteenth-century market as well, in particular Audrey Jaffe's *The Affective Life of the Average Man: The Victorian Novel and the Stock-Market Graph* (2010), which provided a focused account of the way Victorian novels make use of narrative and rhetorical forms associated with the stock market. Arguing for the importance of the transition within economics from production to consumption in the history of Victorian aesthetics, Reginia Gagnier's *Insatiability of Human Wants* (2000) proposed that the marginal revolution opened economics to discussions of the role of pleasure, taste, and aesthetics in commodity culture. An emphasis on emotions appears in several other works around this time: Tamara Wagner's *Financial Speculation in Victorian Fiction* (2010), Anna Kornbluh's *Realizing Capital* (2013), and Eleanor Courtemanche's *The 'Invisible Hand' and British Fiction* (2011). These critics and others have demonstrated amply that economic theory not only possesses narrative form, but that it can also serve as a tool of literary analysis, enabling new readings of some of Victorian fiction's own most influential texts.

As Tamara Wagner (2012) writes in a review of Courtemanche, in economics, "the 'invisible hand' of unknowable systems seems to pervade everything." Arguably many of the critical analyses mentioned above (and these are only a few, representative of a large and ever-multiplying field) were provoked by a growing awareness of the increasingly evident and often disruptive role of large and diffuse economic institutions (such as banks, the stock market, mortgage brokers, and the insurance industry) in twentieth- and twenty-first-century everyday life—a presence felt with greater urgency during and after the 2008 financial crisis, when some of these institutions were deemed "too big to fail," reinforcing a sense of their inevitability (and the presumed inability of ordinary citizens to live without them or resist their control). Few of these studies, however, make that connection directly.[3] It is the purpose of this volume to make such connections and to discuss explicitly the possible consequences of not recognizing the historical lineages and therefore contingent nature of these and other institutions.

Introverted Economics

A long inventive history of literary criticism has thus persuasively demonstrated the mutual imbrication of literary imagining and the crucial debates about political economy and economics of the nineteenth century. Much of this valuable scholarship shows that all types of literature—domestic fiction, moral fables, poetry, and drama, both within Britain and its empire—engaged emergent questions about wealth generation, distribution, and the workings of an increasingly industrialized marketplace. Less centrally, this criticism shows that political economists also turned to literature and related domains such as history to generate their arguments— as exemplification, as a hypothesis generator, as evidence. Malthus, for instance, relied on travel narratives to produce what we might call the data behind his famous formulation concerning the arithmetic increase of food failing to keep pace with the geometric increase in population. Marx's work relies at times on literary genre, on literary allusion and figuration. For instance, the famous line in *The Eighteenth Brumaire of Louis Bonaparte* (1852), "History repeats itself, first as tragedy, then as farce" (Marx n.d., 5) exceeds its aphoristic élan to observe with the help of generic literary categories how meaning is diluted through historical repetition. Moreover, many early political economists were more accurately described as men of letters, learned in several fields, as were John Stuart Mill and John Ruskin, both of whom wrote about the arts, history, and economics, and whose methodological approaches were inevitably hybrid.

By the time political economy largely transitions into what is now known as economics in the later years of the nineteenth century, however, the boundaries become nearly impenetrable between an economics discipline and a range of creative and critical writing practices only somewhat encapsulated by an academic imprimatur. One perhaps can broadly map the "two cultures" of C.P. Snow fame on this transition, since economics does increasingly purge itself of literary allusions and content, turning its attention away from historical perspectives and developing over time a highly technical, insistently quantitative language that becomes by the mid-twentieth century extraordinarily autonomous, resistant to interdisciplinary inquiry. The middle of the twentieth century marks the moment when neoclassical economics, first associated (somewhat inaccurately) with William Stanley Jevons, Carl Menger, Alfred Marshall, and Léon Walras in the second half of the nineteenth century and the early twentieth, established itself as the dominant form of economic practice. When undergraduates take microeconomics and macroeconomics today, they are largely learning the postulates, the mathematics, and indeed the suppositions of the neoclassical subfield. Moreover, a watered-down doctrinaire version of neoclassical economics—a superficial variety that James Kwak, among others, calls "economism": "this invocation of basic economics lessons to explain all social phenomena" (Kwak 2017, 6)—has permeated political and policy debates.

The increasingly esoteric nature of economic methods, steeped in a mathematical language of its own especial variety and in complex graphical models has made the task of interdisciplinary debate difficult. Literary criticism has understandably at times merely mined economics for associative resonance rather than trying to interrogate a field that has evolved into its own self-contained world. This segregation of neoclassical economics from the social sciences and humanities and its ambition to be scientific has shaped its methods and tools but also its arguments.

Indeed, neoclassical economics has formalized its domain as a self-enclosed world. At its origins, of course, political economy aimed to delineate a subject and a discipline. Practitioners were attempting to identify the patterns and rules of emergent capitalist markets, to specify what was distinctively economic action among people and, in turn, the nation. At the same time, they were laboring to demonstrate how their questions were unlike those posed by moral philosophy, natural religion, and stadial historiography. Establishing boundaries was thus foundational, but there was, even so, one open border. Throughout the nineteenth century, the oeuvre of political economy and later economics contains habitual references and constitutive analogies to the sciences, in particular mechanical physics. For most thinkers after the initial classical moment of Ricardo, Malthus, and Smith, markets were, if not precisely natural, mechanical and law-like, just as the physical universe showed itself to be. In this way, economics emerged from the nineteenth century with referential reverence for the mechanics, math, and status of physics, and by extension a firm sense of its estrangement from both the emergent social sciences and the humanities (Mirowski 1989). In what follows, we will provide a very short, admittedly schematic story about the consolidation of neoclassical premises that tries to foreground the discipline's circumvention of other disciplinary contributions in the humanities and social sciences.

Most modern economists do not draw on history nor do they formalize its forces in their theory: the markets of neoclassical economics exist in time but without history. These economists do not typically concern themselves with or employ the history of economic thought.[4] Their understanding of time is either presentist, such that, for instance, the equilibrium pricing point is understood to occur all at once, or future-oriented, hence the aim to predict future economic events. However, in both the present and the future temporalities, economics codifies rules that are not based on historical patterns but are assumed to be ahistorical, objective rules of a free market, akin to the physical forces in nature. Alfred Marshall, despite his interest in biological change and evolution, models temporal change in spatial terms in his theory of partial equilibrium, folding temporal events into a bounded, synchronic state (1895). Zachary Samalin's chapter connects such assumptions to the factory time management of early industrial capitalism.

Until very recently, with the emergence of behavioral economics, most neoclassical practitioners did not make use of psychology nor did they deploy its insights into human behavior. Neoclassical economics' "representative agent" acts rationally and has ordered preferences but no dimensional or consequential psychology. The impulses, affections, and habits of psychologized subjects are more often than not treated as distractions from or, to use economics' own term—exogenous to—the orchestrated actions of utility maximization, which are offered up as fully legible without recourse to the complex intentions, dispositions, or imaginings of actual persons.[5] If neoclassical economics draws its market subject from Bentham's utilitarianism (a much-debated proposition), then its actions matter rather than its intentions.[6] Acting to minimize pain and maximize pleasure, all men and women are alike; the varied pleasures and pains that might distinguish them or their experiences are not economically determinative. For Paul Samuelson (1938), who advanced a theory of "revealed preferences," one need only observe purchasing behavior to know all one needs to know about the consumer. Amanpal Garcha's chapter on consumer indecision in Victorian novels counters such a notion of clear and measurable preferences.

Neoclassical practitioners also posit a market in a society without sociological or anthropological density: exchanges of commodities through a pricing mechanism do not incorporate the complex dynamics of human social interaction or their possible embedded structures of meaning and causation. In neoclassical economics, André Orléan (2014, 25) argues, "'actors' relations with one another are thought not to matter, or at least not in any important way." The practices of aggregates, such as groups whose gender, race, class, or culture designate them as meaningful social groups, or other aggregates, such as social movements, political parties, or a mob do not substantively impact markets. Feminist economists and postcolonial theorists in particular point out the radical erasures of cultural particularity and meaning enjoined by neoclassical economics (Kayatekin 2009). Preferences enter the market already ordered, and their economic agents exchange commodities through a pricing mechanism that does not require their personal or institutional interactions.

These de-socializing (and perhaps anti-socialistic) tendencies emerged during the early decades when political economy started to morph into economics. They have continued in an uneven pace to the present day. The shift from political economy to economics has no single narrative but contains significant changes of subject and attention. Whereas political economy largely focused on the generation and distribution of wealth within the larger society, economics trains its singular attention toward market efficiencies. Less interested in questions of wealth distribution, economics arguably also turns away from questions of inequality. Audrey Jaffe's chapter in this volume on the transient nature of urban life in Dickens's early sketches underscores the central concerns with economic inequality that were sidelined by economics. Classical economics, a subset of political economy, considered supply the engine of the market, and thus oriented its observations toward labor and capital, while neoclassical economics turns toward demand, the action of the market fueled by discrete baskets of consumer preferences. Evaluating capital and labor in classical economics required more often than not a registration of class difference, if not a full-blown vision of social diversity and density. For Marx, the relation between capital and labor was a social relation. As James K. Galbraith (2014) observes: "To Karl Marx, [capital] was a social, political, and legal category—the means of control of the means of production by the dominant class." For neoclassical economists, Galbraith notes, "Capital was reframed as a physical item, which paired with labor to produce output." The central claim about capital made by Marx—that the relation between labor and capital was exploitative—is modified into a notion of capital's measurable share of profit as an investment in the productive process. Additionally, the shift to consumer preference and the representative agent in the market breaks up aggregate social groups like "labor" or "the working class," emphasizing instead abstract individuals operating largely autonomously, even within the macroeconomy.

Despite the conflation of freedom and the autonomy of the individual consumer undertaken by neoclassical economists, such as Milton Friedman and Gary Becker, the rational choice agent of neoclassical economics is not necessarily liberated, given the constraints of this more mechanical understanding of the market. As Thorsten Veblen observed, the physical mechanics underlying theorizations of the market in neoclassical economics removed the agency of the individual in society as much as it removed agency from social groups. Seemingly objective market forces and their states of equilibria were substituted for "the living items" implied in key classical economic terms, such as labor and production. Veblen (1898, 383) complains that an economist can "construct a theory of such an institution as money or wages or land-ownership without descending to a consideration of the living items concerned, except for the convenient corroboration of his normalized scheme of symptoms." Here the autonomous agent is a less a rational actor than a fully predictable "scheme of symptoms."

Recurring to physical mechanics and its authorization of mathematical and empirical fact further bestows on neoclassical economics the look of a value-neutral project. In the nineteenth century, there was for some practitioners a conscious turn away from what seemed like moralistic, religious, or indeed socialistic evaluations in the practice of political economy. As Veblen and a host of others realized, however, normative values lurked in what claimed to be a neutral taxonomic system. And from Adam Smith's seemingly benign but in fact extremely complex evocation of the "invisible hand," to Bentham's acclamation of the "greatest good for the greatest number," to Milton Friedman's celebration of free markets, political suppositions persist in neoclassical economics. Uncovering them, we see that the neoclassical project had many aims, including: to privilege free markets; to calculate away the conflict between labor and capital; to provide an alternative account of optimality that focuses on efficient allocation rather than wealth redistribution or social justice; to divert the legible power of labor and capitalists into reformulations of capital—machinery or human capital—to list some examples. Although it would be unfair and US-centric to say that most economists are Republicans, it does not seem unfair to suggest that the foundational building blocks of neoclassical economics embed conservative, classical liberal premises that often make arguments about human complexity, economic inequality, or class harder to mount effectively within the discipline. Although recent work in behavioral economics has taken on the rational-choice agent, showing its abundant capacity for irrational action, the singular focus on the consuming agent without any robust theory of social interactions, as, for instance, Veblen offered in his theory of "conspicuous consumption," suggests it may not produce a radical restructuring of economics.[7] The arrival of "the capability approach" in the domain of development economics, articulated by Amartya Sen (1977; see also Nussbaum 1997), also pushed back on some of these embedded suppositions. It attempts an ethical rerouting of marginal utility, in which its maximization is replaced by the maximal realization of lives worth living. Yet its embrace of market incentives and liberal models of cultivation does not fundamentally reimagine neoclassical premises. On the connections between neoclassical economics and Victorian liberalism, see Elaine Hadley's chapter.

Neoclassical economics treats the social domain represented and explored by the humanities and social sciences, then, as something exogenous to the market, which is not to say that economics is unconcerned with society, but rather that it formulates a society fully amenable to economic modeling. Since the middle of the twentieth century, neoclassical economics has returned to society fully armed with its asocial mechanics and suppositions in order to revise that world according to neoclassical models. A wide range of issues are now explicable in the terms of neoclassical assessment—climate change, crime, family dynamics—an imperial ambition initiated by Gary Becker and perhaps most popularly realized by Levitt and Dubner's *Freakonomics* (2005) and its podcast spinoff. In these turns to the social domain, then, interpretive social sciences and the humanities still play no role.

EXTROVERTED ECONOMICS

There may be signs of change in these tendencies. The 2008 financial crisis exposed neoclassical economics' predictive tools as woefully incapable: Ben Bernanke in government, and numerous economists in the academy and institutional settings across the country and the world downplayed the coming crisis, and in the aftermath were unsuccessful in explaining its causes.[8] There existed a percolating worry that economics had not only failed to predict the crisis but had fostered it. The crisis, fueled by complex financial instruments whose abstruse math was not well understood and by group behaviors inexplicable to the axioms of rational choice theory, rather loudly countered neoclassical economics' faith in market equilibria. It might well be seen in retrospect as a plausible historical turning point in the practice of economics itself, and in its availability for inquiry by the social sciences and humanities. This volume counts itself a participant in what it hopes will be a broadening in the theorization and practice of economics, in academia and beyond.

Not long after the crisis, Thomas Piketty's *Capital in the Twenty-First Century* (2014) reintroduced political economy to a broader academic public. Using mounds of historical empirical data and extended excursions into literary analysis, Piketty employed techniques of argumentation long eschewed by neoclassicists: the perspective of the long historical durée, the use of empirical data and thus an inductive method, and the animation of literary narratives as repositories of economic insight. This largely data-driven political economy has inspired, in part, new energies in economics proper, as evidenced for instance by the group Economists for Inclusive Prosperity (https://econfip.org/), whose members believe in the fundamentals of the profession but seek to extend its concerns to questions of equity and social welfare.[9] Sarah Winter's chapter studies the principle of equity in mid-nineteenth-century critiques of political economy. And there is the network, "Rethinking Economics" (http://www.rethinkeconomics.org), a group of students, academics, and professional economists whose mission statement declares: "Economics in universities is narrow, uncritical and detached from the real world. It is dogmatically taught from one perspective as if it is the only legitimate way to study the economy." Although there have been other subfields in economics throughout the twentieth-century—for instance, institutional, feminist, labor, Marxist, and development economics—they have often been treated as outliers, forced out of mainstream economics journals and obliged to create their own. In fact, feminist economists have long questioned the centrality of the rational choice agent of neoclassical economics, countering its vision of individualism and an historically deracinated society with alternative modes of sociality and exchange; but they have had a modest impact on the embedded gendered suppositions of the field (England 1993; Strassman 1993).[10]

Some of the very small number of economists who did predict the 2008 crisis are themselves advocates for revisions in economic methods, notably Steve Keen and Robert Shiller. Keen (2011), whose work incorporates a newer version of the evolutionary economics first described by Veblen, advocates for economics classes that teach advanced mathematics and physics, presenting them as far more sophisticated versions of the knowledge bases that have remained preserved in their more rudimentary nineteenth-century versions by neoclassical economics. These tools, Keen argues, better track and measure variability and chaos. Also inspired by Veblen, Geoffrey Hodgson in *Conceptualizing Capitalism* (2015) employs "legal institutionalism" when defining capitalism, an approach which takes both neoclassical and Marxist economics to task for ignoring the state's constitutive role in the historical formation and nurturance of capitalism. Clare Eby's chapter focuses on the role of the US Supreme Court in aggrandizing the constitutional rights of corporations.

Meanwhile, Robert Shiller's recent work (2017) has turned to narrative theory, seeking to articulate how hegemonic stories about economic events affect those events and the behaviors that respond to them. Like Piketty before him, Shiller shows himself uneasy with the status of literary form—to what extent it represents reality and thus is operable as evidence—but his perspective is nonetheless refreshing. Ayşe Çelikkol's chapter in this volume shows how narrative form can be enlisted to support assumptions in Victorian political economy about the potential for unlimited growth of the fossil economy. Peter Spiegler (2015) has taken on the presumptions of economic modeling so central to knowledge formation in economics, arguing for modeling enhancements, such as the integration of real-world data and ethnographic fieldwork. All these extensions beyond the narrow confines of neoclassical economics are promising.

In addition to this intradisciplinary ferment, scholars with diverse academic backgrounds have attempted to question neoclassical axioms and rethink economics theoretically. Economic historians have perhaps been the most persistent. Philip Mirowski's extensive oeuvre stands out, his scholarship extracting, in the magisterial *More Heat Than Light* (1989), the nineteenth-century skeleton of mechanical physics that still undergirds modern economics. Deirdre N. McCloskey's *The Rhetoric of Economics* (1998) has been key to a reevaluation of the rhetorical tendencies of economic theorizing, showing that the field incorporates literary modes and exhibits strong tendencies toward public advocacy of its own findings. Avner Offer and Gabriel Söderberg (2016) highlight the role that the Nobel Prize plays in authorizing and sustaining neoclassical economics' cultural and political dominance.

Interpretive social scientists, less inclined to rely on mathematical axioms, graphical modeling, and quantitative data, have published some of the most exciting work, seeking to affect foundational changes in understanding the economy and its markets. Both André Orléan in his *The Empire of Value* (2014) and Noam Yuran in *What Money Wants* (2014) argue that economics has long misunderstood the operational elements of the market, pushing for a re-centering of money as had Keynes and post-Keynesianism. Updating Marx, Orléan echoes Mirowski's claim that neoclassical economics fundamentally confuses value and substance, thereby relegating money to a formal rather than constitutive function as the densely social lubricator of exchange. Yuran, working with diverse social theorists from Freud and Lacan to Foucault and Marx, considers the implications of an economy of currency motivated by human desire, often working through his arguments alongside literary texts, including Charles Dickens' *Hard Times.*

Some postcolonial theorists have also turned their attention to early political economy and modern economics but not consistently so, often for the same reasons that humanists more generally often avoid this area: arcane mathematics and technical vocabulary. Culture and its disciplinary analogues, literature and anthropology, have traditionally been the objects of interrogation in postcolonial theory. Even so, the universalist and abstract assumptions undergirding neoclassical economics and development economics have been understood to be related to the assumptions operative in the broader imperialist tradition of Western knowledge formation. For instance, the developmental timeline of nations, drawn from stadial historiography, authorizes imperial conquest (Mehta 1999) and operates as a rationale for economic interventions under the guise of growth and development (Spivak 1985; Zein-Elabdin and Charusheela 2004). Such work often argues for the particularities of non-Western social communities and the evocation of alternative economies different from—not less than—modern global markets, as Mukti Lakhi Mangharam explores in her chapter. Drawing on both Giovanni Arrighi's study ([1994] 2010) of the longue durée history of capitalist expansion from the eighteenth through the twentieth centuries and Walter Benjamin's philosophy of history, postcolonial literature scholar Ian Baucom's *Specters of the Atlantic* (2005) illuminates the imbrication of the rise of finance capital with the Atlantic slave trade, demonstrating the unavoidable historical association of capitalism with the repeated atrocities perpetrated in the course of European colonial expansion. Gordon Bigelow's contribution to this volume also traces the longstanding scholarly discussion of the relationship between capitalism and slavery.

Sociable Economics

In the past few decades, some scholars have looked for synergy between economics and humanistic approaches, most notably the philosopher Martha Nussbaum in *Poetic Justice: The Literary Imagination in Public Life* (1997) and Gary Saul Morson and Morton Schapiro in *Cents and*

Sensibility: What Economics can Learn from the Humanities (2018). Nussbaum's book is an early interrogator of neoclassical economics' incapacity to grasp a fully dimensional human. She proposes a heightened role for the imagination as quantitative and rationalistic methods in the academy become increasingly dominant. *Cents and Sensibility*, authored by a literary critic and an economist, provides case studies of the benefits to be gained when economics opens itself to the humanities, with the stated goal of strengthening economics by enabling it to ask questions informed by humanistic concerns and enriched by a focus on narrative forms of explanation. One can quibble in the first instance with what are often liberal platitudes about the affective contributions of literature in Nussbaum. One can register the latter book's supposition that economics can learn something from humanistic methods even as it remains fully itself. We agree that Morson and Schapiro's recommendation for a "dialogue of approaches," rather than attempting a fusion of methods, provides one productive model for literary critics and economists to collaborate. They also offer useful critiques of certain reductive habits of economic reasoning.

We feel some dismay, however, that in Morson and Schapiro we see a worrisomely unequal accommodation. Although economists are not expected to change their methods but only to modify their deep expertise by learning from other disciplines, literature scholars are often urged, both by those outside their field and insiders defending the relevance of the humanities, to adopt the most generic forms of advocacy of literary study. For example, Morson and Schapiro ask us to restore the attractiveness of the humanities by helping students to "appreciate" works of "great literature" as sources of wisdom, empathy, and cultural and historical insight, but to avoid supposedly controversial or distracting claims about the ways that literary texts interrogate the political struggles of their day—a posture that would have been entirely foreign to such "great writers" as Milton, George Eliot, or Tolstoy. If such a reductive notion of literature becomes a key defense for the humanities, what happens to other humanities projects that can't so readily be bent toward primarily ethical purposes? We believe it is counterproductive for humanities scholars to negate their own methods and downplay their expertise, since other disciplines certainly will not, and probably should not, do so. But neither do we advocate that the humanities should turn inward and redefine their core specializations simply among themselves, in a defensive posture.

These works arguing for a rapprochement between the humanities and economics define a new interdisciplinary conversation that we hope will continue. Is it possible that just as the hard sciences and the biological sciences have seen themselves become increasingly "integrative" in the past generation, the social sciences and humanities are also due for a new era of integration? Mary Poovey's and finance expert and Wall Street veteran Kevin R. Brine's *Finance in America: An Unfinished Story* (2017) represents a deeply interdisciplinary collaboration focused on studying in detail the disciplinary history and rise of finance from the Great Depression to the global financial crisis of 2008. In their focus on financial models, or "simulations," which are "designed to approximate and simplify real-world situations so that something resembling experiments can be run" (9), we can see the benefits of combining Poovey's expertise in literary criticism and historical epistemology with Brine's knowledge of complex financial instruments. Piketty argues for a revival of twenty-first century political economy as a humanistic social science, while his multiple discussions of the way novels by Austen and Balzac represent inequality "with a verisimilitude and evocative power that no statistical or theoretical analysis can match" (2014, 2) also recognize in literature an analytical grasp on economic history and social relations under capitalism that corresponds to our approach. We are encouraged by the wide-ranging and cross-disciplinary conversations in *After Piketty: The Agenda for Economics and Inequality* (2017), but this collection does not include contributions by literature scholars. Our book begins to fill this gap.

ORGANIZATION AND CHAPTERS

Our contributors explore a range of questions: Could the resurrection of early political economy's notion of equity revise and/or enhance modern-day considerations of distribution? Could the Victorian conception of rent and renting, drawn into political economy of the time but always in excess of it, put productive pressure on the modern fixation on ownership? How can earlier understandings of labor during the era of political economy be brought to bear on the presumptions of human capital? How does a modern-day conception of rational choice in Chicago-school economics emerge from figurations of choice in Victorian notions of character? How have economic concepts and associated worldviews come to permeate the public sphere and everyday common sense about human aspirations and choices, as evidenced in today's popular journalism about economic globalization?

The chapters are organized into larger conceptual groupings. The first section focuses on the category of "Labor," spanning a spectrum from the abstract calculations of the economic benefits of investment in education described by the term "human capital," to the impact on workers' bodies of factory production in the nineteenth century, to the coerced labor of slavery. Tracking the ways that the twentieth-century concept of human capital construes education as an investment of mental labor to be maximized, Elaine Hadley (*human capital*) reads Thomas Hardy's novel *Jude the Obscure* (1895) as a narrative of the depletion of Victorian liberal ideals of individual cultivation that also illuminates neoliberal economic theory's covert efforts to retain in contemporary educational policy conservative values that constrain human flourishing and equality. Zachary Samalin (*exploitation*) draws a strong contrast between two distinct economic conceptions of time: the time-concept underpinning expectations of social progress by apologists for capitalism, such as Harriet Martineau, and Marx's theory of exploitation as the theft of value produced by workers' labor time. He shows how neoclassical economic theory excludes historical understandings of the variability of time's reckonings in industrial labor. Gordon Bigelow (*slavery*) studies the marginalization in economic history of British political economist John Elliot Cairnes's 1861 critique of the way free labor was being undermined by slavery in the Southern United States, uncovering how post-bellum economists' accounts of slavery as a remnant of feudalism obscured its imperial capitalist formation theorized by Cairnes and by many African American scholars of slavery.

In the next section, on "Growth," Ayşe Çelikkol (*expansion*) discusses the way Dinah Mullock Craik's novel, *John Halifax, Gentleman* (1856) both comments on and formalizes the principles of the steam engine's acceleration of industrial production. Grounding her contribution in the fossil fuel industry's tightening hold on the working classes in the 1840's, Çelikkol argues that the novel's character-population and plot reproduces and naturalizes for the reader the fossil economy's structure of unlimited growth. Exploring the consequences of such rampant growth for the environment, Deanna Kreisel (*sustainability*) traces the origins of the sustainability concept in nineteenth-century discourses of population and resource management, particularly Malthus and his successors and Victorian writings on coal exhaustion. She thereby highlights sustainability's derivation from industrial–capitalist fantasies and its contradictory affective economies of anxiety and hopefulness that continue to frame discussions today.

The third section considers the centrality of "Property," foregrounding continuities between ownership, identity, and space from the nineteenth century to the twenty-first. Drawing inspiration (and provocation) from Matthew Desmond's 2016 *Eviction: Poverty and Profit in the American City*, Audrey Jaffe's chapter (*rent*) focuses on the association between the transience of persons and that of property in Dickens, while contending more generally that nineteenth-century fiction links the solidity and permanence of character with the ownership of property. Clare Eby (*corporation*) turns our attention to US history and to the way the idea of the corporation links personhood to corporate models of perpetuity in property. Focusing on a series of landmark US Supreme Court cases from the late nineteenth century to the twenty-first, an 1885 novel by María Amaparo Ruiz de Burton, as well as Frank Norris's novel *The Octopus* (1901), and Richard Powers's 1998 novel *Gain*, Eby charts the corporation's progressive usurpation of constitutional rights accorded to human persons and how literary fictions counter these rulings by imagining corporate accountability.

The chapters in the final section on "Value" consider how modern economic concepts associated with market-based behavior such as "choice" and "freedom" emerged through political economy's reduction of competing understandings of social value, and have become normalized as descriptions of what should count globally as economic flourishing, rather than as signs of rampant economic inequality. Analyzing intriguing commonalities of method between Henry Mayhew's collection of data on the wages and rents paid by London's impoverished laboring classes in his 1849–1850 *Morning Chronicle* surveys and Thomas Piketty's study of the historical sources of inequality, Sarah Winter (*equity*) uncovers Mayhew's formulation in his published correspondence with his readers of an alternative theory to political economy called "social economy," based on the principle of equity and defining equal partnerships in profits between labor and capital. Amanpal Garcha (*choice*) draws attention to ongoing connections between the neoclassical economists' focus on marginal utility as the basis of rational choices made by consumers among a discrete set of goods in the market, and the frequent dilemmas of indecision faced by characters in Victorian novels. For these novelists, Garcha argues, characters' dithering over decision-making comes to represent a new version of modern subjectivity. Highlighting the role of popular journalism in depicting the twenty-first century global poor as predictable economic subjects, Mukti Lakhi Mangharam (*global inequality*) examines how political economy's rationalizations of imperial expansion still frame the economic assumptions of recent investigations in the *New York Times* focusing on global economic development. Mangharam pinpoints how this reporting on the contrasting career choices of two Indian sisters employed as garment workers incorporates their stories within a narrative of the economic ascendency of Western neoliberal capitalism.

Alternative groupings of chapters also emerge from shared lines of inquiry, such as the failure to account for racial discrimination traced in the chapters by Bigelow, Eby, and Hadley. Mobility counts as the human counterpart to neoclassical economics' foregrounding of growth; however, the ambivalence of economics toward mobility, whether in space or social status, can be traced in the chapters by Hadley, Jaffe, and Mangharam. Ambivalence about the potentially unlimited growth promised by a capitalist economy appears in Kreisel's account of sustainability and Çelikkol's discussion of Craik; both trace a narrative in which expansion is met by an anxiety about depleting natural resources. The permeation of workers' experience of time and colonization of life chances by liberal and neoliberal notions of free markets results in various forms of dehumanization analyzed by Samalin, Hadley, Eby, and Mangharam. Alternative conceptions of equality are explored by Winter and Mangharam. Hadley and Mangharam note the way the ostensibly expansive form of the Bildungsroman in fact relies on limited notions of what it means to be human. Instances where intellectuals and galvanized publics have participated in shaping alternative economic ideas and histories come to the forefront in Kreisel's, Winter's, and Bigelow's chapters. We invite our readers to formulate other conversations among these chapters, in hopes that they, too, will register "the unavoidable and pervasive importance" of economics and yet "question it as a concept of the last resort" (Spivak, 85).

Notes

1. For a different sort of approach to the critique of economics via the redefinition of keywords, see Leary (2018).
2. There is a sizeable body of work on economics and American literature, as well, which Eby's chapter in this volume gestures toward. Given the focus on the nineteenth-century British origin of economics and our field expertise, we will not provide an outline here of this growing archive. However, the chapters in this volume confirm that the boundary between nation-states means little for economics in particular, as it becomes in the twentieth century a transnational project with a mathematical lingua franca.

3. Many of the books written above are also by women, perhaps coinciden-
   tally, or perhaps intentionally responding in turn to the male-dominated
   discipline of economics. See also recent work by Çelikkol (2011) and
   Kreisel (2012).
4. Robert Fogel is credited with a form of economic history that depends
   heavily on data and math, which is labeled "cliometrics." It adopts econometrics in its interpretation of historical events.
5. Exogenous: "relating to or developing from external factors." See https://
   www.google.com/search?client=firefox-b-1-d&q=exogenous. A key term
   in economics drawn from the biological sciences.
6. Mirowski (1989, 205–207) questions what many others consider the
   strong genealogical relation between Bentham's utilitarianism and neoclassical economics.
7. Richard H. Thaler (2015) is the central figure of this trend. See related
   work by Daniel Kahneman (2011).
8. There were a few exceptions. Bezemer (2009) identifies Steve Keen, Dean
   Baker, Wynne Godley, Fred Harrison, Michael Hudson, Eric Janszen,
   Jakob Brøchner Madsen and Jens Kjaer Sørensen, Kurt Richebächer,
   Nouriel Roubini, Peter Schiff, and Robert Shiller.
9. The emphasis upon empirical data as a response to neoclassicism's deductive
   method is questioned by Steinbaum (2019). See https://bostonreview.
   net/forum/economics-after-neoliberalism/marshall-steinbaum-empiri-
   cism-wont-save-us.
10. Notable names are Ester Boseup, Diane Elson, Paula England, Marianne
    Ferber, Nancy Folbre, Ailsa McKay, Julie A. Nelson, Diana Strassman, and
    Marilyn Waring.

REFERENCES

Agnew, Jean-Christophe. 1986. *Worlds Apart: The Market and the Theater in Anglo-American Thought, 1550–1770*. New York: Cambridge University Press.

Arrighi, Giovanni. (1994) 2010. *The Long Twentieth Century: Money, Power and the Origins of our Times*. London and New York: Verso.

Baucom, Ian. 2005. *Specters of the Atlantic: Finance Capital, Slavery, and the Philosophy of History*. Durham and London: Duke University Press.

Bezemer, Dirk J. 2009. 'No One Saw This Coming': Understanding Financial Crisis Through Accounting Models. *Research Report 09002*. Research Institute SOM. Groningen: University of Groningen.

Bigelow, Gordon. 2003. *Fiction, Famine, and the Rise of Economics in Victorian Britain and Ireland*. Cambridge: Cambridge University Press.

Brine, Kevin R., and Mary Poovey. 2017. *Finance in America: An Unfinished Story*. Chicago: University of Chicago Press.

Çelikkol, Ayşe. 2011. *Romances of Free Trade: British Literature, Laissez-Faire, and the Global Nineteenth Century*. New York: Oxford University Press.

Courtemanche, Eleanor. 2011. *The 'Invisible Hand' and British Fiction, 1816–1860: Adam Smith, Political Economy, and the Genre of Realism*. Basingstoke: Palgrave Macmillan.

Eliot, George. (1860) 1914. *The Mill on the Floss*. Boston, MA: Ginn. Citations refer to 1914 edition.

England, Paula. 1993. The Separative Self: Androcentric Bias in Neoclassical Assumptions. In *Beyond Economic Man: Feminist Theory and Economics*, ed. Julie A. Nelson, 37–53. Chicago: University of Chicago Press.

Gagnier, Regenia. 2000. *The Insatiability of Human Wants: Economics and Aesthetics in Market Society*. Chicago: University of Chicago Press.

Galbraith, James K. 2014. Kapital for the Twenty-First Century? Review of *Capital in the Twenty-First Century*, by Thomas Piketty, trans. Arthur Goldhammer. *Dissent*, Spring. https://www.dissentmagazine.org/article/kapital-for-the-twenty-first-century.

Gallagher, Catherine. 1986. The Body Versus the Social Body in the Works of Thomas Malthus and Henry Mayhew. *Representations* 14 (Spring): 83–106.

———. (1989) 2009. The Bio-Economics of *Our Mutual Friend*. In *The Body Economic: Life, Death, and Sensation in Political Economy and the Victorian Novel*, 86–117. Princeton: Princeton University Press.

———. 2009. *The Body Economic: Life, Death, and Sensation in Political Economy and the Victorian Novel*. Princeton: Princeton University Press.

Hodgson, Geoffrey. 2015. *Conceptualizing Capitalism: Institutions, Evolution, Future*. Chicago: University of Chicago Press.

Jaffe, Audrey. 2010. *The Affective Life of the Average Man: The Victorian Novel and the Stock-Market Graph*. Columbus: Ohio State University Press.

Kahneman, Daniel. 2011. *Thinking, Fast and Slow*. New York: Farrar, Straus, and Giroux.

Kayatekin, Serap A. 2009. Between Political Economy and Postcolonial Theory: First Encounters. *Cambridge Journal of Economics* 33 (6): 1113–1118.

Keen, Steve. 2011. *Debunking Economics the Naked Emperor Dethroned?* Rev. and expanded ed. London: Zed Books.

Konings, Martijn. 2015. *The Emotional Logic of Capitalism: What Progressives Have Missed*. Stanford: Stanford University Press.

Kornbluh, Anna. 2013. *Realizing Capital: Financial and Psychic Economies in Victorian Form*. New York: Fordham University Press.

Kreisel, Deanna K. 2012. *Economic Woman: Demand, Gender, and Narrative Closure in Eliot and Hardy*. Toronto, ON: University of Toronto Press.

Kwak, James. 2017. *Economism: Bad Economics and the Rise of Inequality*. 1st ed. New York: Pantheon Books.

Leary, John Patrick. 2018. *Keywords: The New Language of Capitalism*. Chicago: Haymarket Books.

Levitt, Steven D., and Stephen J. Dubner. 2005. *Freakonomics*. New York: Harper Perennial.

Marshall, Alfred. 1895. *Principles of Economics*. 3rd ed. London and New York: Macmillan.

Marx, Karl. n.d. *The Eighteenth Brumaire of Louis Bonaparte*. Champaign, IL: Project Gutenberg. https://www.gutenberg.org/files/1346/1346-h/1346-h.htm.

McCloskey, Deirdre N. 1998. *The Rhetoric of Economics*. 2nd ed. Madison: University of Wisconsin Press.

Mehta, Uday Singh. 1999. *Liberalism and Empire: A Study in Nineteenth-Century British Liberal Thought*. Chicago: University of Chicago Press.

Mirowski, Philip. 1989. *More Heat than Light: Economics as Social Physics, Physics as Nature's Economics*. Cambridge: Cambridge University Press.

Morson, Gary Saul, and Morton Schapiro. 2018. *Cents and Sensibility: What Economics Can Learn from the Humanities*. Princeton: Princeton University Press.

Nussbaum, Martha Craven. 1997. *Poetic Justice: The Literary Imagination and Public Life*. Boston, MA: Beacon Press.

Offer, Avner, and Gabriel Söderberg. 2016. *The Nobel Factor: The Prize in Economics, Social Democracy, and the Market Turn*. Princeton, NJ: Princeton University Press.

Orléan, André. 2014. *The Empire of Value: A New Foundation for Economics*. Translated by M. B. DeBevoise. Cambridge, MA: The MIT Press.

Piketty, Thomas. 2014. *Capital in the Twenty-First Century*. Translated by Arthur Goldhammer. Cambridge, MA: The Belknap Press of Harvard University Press.

Polanyi, Karl. (1944) 1957, 2001. *The Great Transformation: The Political and Economic Origins of Our Time*. Boston, MA: Beacon Press. Citations refer to 2001 edition.

Poovey, Mary. 1995. Speculation and Virtue in *Our Mutual Friend*. In *Making A Social Body: British Cultural Formation, 1830–1864*, 155–181. Chicago: University of Chicago Press.

———. 1998. *A History of the Modern Fact: Problems of Knowledge in the Sciences of Wealth and Society*. Chicago: University of Chicago Press.

———. 2008. *Genres of the Credit Economy: Mediating Value in Eighteenth- and Nineteenth-Century Britain*. Chicago: University of Chicago Press.

Samuelson, Paul A. 1938. A Note on the Pure Theory of Consumer's Behavior. *Economica* 5 (17): 61–71.

Sen, Amartya K. 1977. Rational Fools: A Critique of the Behavioral Foundations of Economic Theory. *Philosophy & Public Affairs* 6 (4): 317–344.

Shell, Marc. 1978. *The Economy of Literature*. Baltimore: Johns Hopkins University Press.

Shiller, Robert J. 2017. *Narrative Economics*. Working Paper 2069, Cowles Foundation Discussion Paper, New Haven, CT: Yale University. https://cowles.yale.edu/sites/default/files/files/pub/d20/d2069.pdf.

Spiegler, Peter. 2015. *Behind the Model: A Constructive Critique of Economic Modeling*. Cambridge, UK: Cambridge University Press.

Spivak, Gayatri C. 1985. Scattered Speculations on the Question of Value. *Diacritics* 15 (4): 73–93.

Steinbaum, Marshall. 2019. Forum Response to "Economics after Liberalism: Empiricism Alone Won't Save Us." *Boston Review*, February 28, 2019. https://bostonreview.net/forum/economics-after-neoliberalism/marshall-steinbaum-empiricism-wont-save-us.

Steinberg, Marc W. 2016. *England's Great Transformation: Law, Labor, and the Industrial Revolution*. Chicago: University of Chicago Press.

Strassman, Diana. 1993. Not a Free Market: The Rhetoric of Disciplinary Authority in Economics. In *Beyond Economic Man: Feminist Theory and Economics*, ed. Julie A. Nelson, 37–53. Chicago: University of Chicago Press.

Thaler, Richard H. 2015. *Misbehaving: The Making of Behavioral Economics*. New York: W.W. Norton.

Veblen, Thorstein. 1898. Why Is Economics Not an Evolutionary Science? *Quarterly Journal of Economics* 12 (4): 373–397.

Wagner, Tamara. 2010. *Speculation in Victorian Fiction: Plotting Money and the Novel Genre, 1815–1901*. Columbus: Ohio State University Press.

Wagner, Tamara S. 2012. Review of *The 'Invisible Hand' and British Fiction, 1818–1860: Adam Smith, Political Economy, and the Genre of Realism*, by Eleanor Courtemanche. *Erudit*, July 29, 2014. 20. https://www.erudit.org/en/journals/ravon/2012-n62-ravon01483/1026012ar/.

Williams, Raymond. (1976) 1983. *Keywords: A Vocabulary of Culture and Society*. Rev. ed. New York: Oxford University Press. Citations refer to 1983 edition.

Woodmansee, Martha, and Mark Osteen, eds. 1999. *The New Economic Criticism: Studies at the Intersection of Literature and Economics*. New York: Routledge.

Yuran, Noam. 2014. *What Money Wants: An Economy of Desire*. Stanford, CA: Stanford University Press.

Zein-Elabdin, Eiman O., and S. Charusheela. 2004. *Postcolonialism Meets Economics*. London: Routledge.

PART I

Labor

CHAPTER 2

Human Capital

Becker the Obscure: Human-Capital Theory, Liberalisms, and the Future of Higher Education

Elaine Hadley

The dustjacket of Wendy Brown's 2015 *Undoing the Demos: Neoliberalism's Stealth Revolution* depicts a university lecture room in ruins, with paint peeling, water stains on the ceiling, graffiti on the walls, and abandoned lecture notes strewn on the floor. Part analysis, part lament about the neoliberal takeover of society, Brown's book treats the educational domain as a vivid instance of the damages wrought by what she calls "economization" (17). Brown describes the worrying rise of ROI (return on investment) measures, the rapid diminution of liberal arts learning in the college and university curriculum, and the rise of majors more closely linked to job-specific training. The book's interrogation of the educational field is far more than a toiling academic's self-indulgence, however. Brown knows well that a foundational concept of neoliberalism is "human capital," a concept formulated through the study and re-theorization of education and job training, or, what critics might suggest, is education *as* job train-

E. Hadley (✉)
University of Chicago, Chicago, IL, USA

© The Author(s) 2019
E. Hadley et al. (eds.), *From Political Economy to Economics through Nineteenth-Century Literature*, Palgrave Studies in Literature, Culture and Economics, https://doi.org/10.1007/978-3-030-24158-2_2

ing. In a paragraph headed, "Remaking the Soul," Brown espies a re-estimation of the human subject through the deployment of human-capital policy in education. "It is no news that European and North American universities have been radically transformed and revalued in recent decades" (22). She proceeds to provide a stark before and after narrative to sharpen the outlines of a lost educational past and the neoliberal present: "Once about developing intelligent, thoughtful elites and reproducing culture, and more recently, enacting a principle of equal opportunity and cultivating a broadly educated citizenry, higher education now produces human capital, thereby turning classically humanist values on their head" (24). Inspired by Foucault's fleeting but trenchant remarks on neoliberalism, Brown treats human capital not merely as a tool of economic modeling, not just as a quantitative measure of production in a growth economy, as economists and policy experts routinely do, but as itself a particular type of subject formed by neoliberal policies and institutions and one that takes the place of "elites" or "educated citizenry."

As a description of the present moment of education, Brown's sentences carry the force of truth, but her description of the past sounds elegiac, even nostalgic. What is the past she laments? Is it "classically humanist values" associated with Plato and Aristotle; is it classically liberal values associated with "thoughtful elites" and the "reproduction of culture," or is it classically democratic values, of "equal opportunity and a broadly educated citizenry"? These values are not all of a piece, but neither can one demarcate their boundaries cleanly—though there is a history that leads to this murky present. What Brown gestures toward, I believe, is the history of neoliberal human capital—the *liberal* history of human capital. Like a political progressive astounded at the rise of Donald Trump or the Brexit movement who finds themselves feeling almost warm and fuzzy for Ronald Reagan and Margaret Thatcher, there is here and elsewhere a certain unremarked liberal yearning leaking into our neoliberal moment. Just as Reagan and Thatcher parented the neoliberal revolution, liberalism has something to do with neoliberalism. Imbricated notions of the free market and of liberal education not only set the stage for human-capital theory and policy but also to some extent remain, albeit obscured, in neoliberal educational values.

To trace the relation between the liberal subject and the neoliberal subject of human capital, and then to espy liberalism's afterlife, I wish to turn to *Jude the Obscure*, Thomas Hardy's final novel, published in England in 1895.[1] A novel about a million things, it is also a novel about labor, education, and, in a deep and serious way, human flourishing. It is a novel that not only grasps with astonishing insight the trauma incurred by the false promise of liberal cultivation, of liberal freedom, but in the ashes of its liberal protagonist, Jude, shows that human-capital theory has its deep sources in the late Victorian period.

A story about a stone mason in the southwest of England whose love and work life take a sharp, tragic turn, *Jude the Obscure* is the very model of the over-determined novel, or, to put it another way, a novel that models all sorts of determinations. To say that it is a novel about the liberal history of human capital seems a reduction of its myriad aims, but it is this ample menu of determinations—Malthusian, Darwinian, Spencerian, ethnological, genetic, physiological, sociological, theological—that comments on the tragic delusions of the liberal Bildung and ultimately enables my account of the liberal subject's sneaky reformulation as incentivized human capital in the middle of the twentieth century. First, however, we must define human capital, and only then can we turn to its liberal history and prefiguring in *Jude the Obscure*.

THE HISTORY OF HUMAN-CAPITAL THEORY

Human capital "seems uncontroversial today" (White 2017, 1). "[W]e use the term as if it were always part of our lingua franca," the noted economist Claudia Goldin affirms, whose famous phrase "a race between technology and education" (Goldin and Katz 2008) derives from her human-capital research (2016, 55). Its naturalization has been especially successful in educational policy, as Clayton Pierce, among others, notes: "human capital theory has achieved nearly universal acceptance as the practical and ethical framework in which to view and judge educational health in the United States" (2013, 47).[2] Its ubiquity as an objective standard in education economics and policy attests to its conceptual centrality but also obscures its historical and sociological origins.

For many economists, "human capital" is a relatively recent innovation. The term itself is generally credited to the welfare economist Arthur Pigou (1928, 29), but its current analytical usage emerges with Jacob Mincer, at Columbia, Theodore Schultz, at the University of Chicago, and then flourishes there with Gary Becker in the 1950s and beyond. As B. F. Kiker outlines, however, a long list of thinkers in the eighteenth and nineteenth century wondered aloud whether a human's abilities and knowledge should be understood as capital. Adam Smith considered a human's abilities as part of what he called "fixed capital," since it could not be alienated ([1776] 1828, 12). Jeremy Bentham differentiated between the physical exertion of labor and the mental capacities applied in labor—not quite a full-throated notion of human capital but an attempt to register the added values that sometimes accrue to certain types of labor (1952, 53). J. S. Mill also makes this distinction but is quick to differentiate between a human and what he calls "wealth," since the economic valuation of a human could seem like commodification, whose analogue was enslavement, an association that haunts human-capital theory to the present day ([1848] 1909, 47).[3]

Some political economists who pursued the human-capital concept did so not to argue for the economic benefits of enslaved labor but in an effort to provide justifications for the care and maintenance of laborers, who if understood properly as capital, were worthy of sustenance and unsuitable for cannon fodder. Some of those most compelled by the human-capital concept used it to assess statistically the economic loss to the nation of war casualties (Boag 1916). It thus could function as one of the ways that capitalism could be seen as more quiescent in its culture of exchange than the culture of armed conflict and conquest that defined feudalism.

This early history of human capital should not be interpreted as humane, however. Especially in these earlier days of capitalism, the laborer was not a priori a human with rights; rather, some political economists, mathematicians, and actuaries turned to an ur-human-capital concept less to support a social agenda of care than to show capitalists it was sometimes economically wasteful to kill, maim, starve, or wantonly replace some employees and also to show statesmen that national wealth was increased by workers with skill and education attuned to the jobs they did; investment in workers paid dividends (Nicholson 1891; then later Dublin et al. 1946). The website *Investopedia* can provide us with this still popular usage in the practical world of business economics in which the capitalist's investment is paramount:

> Human capital is a measure of the economic value of an employee's skill set … The concept of human capital recognizes that not all labor is equal and that the quality of employees can be improved by investing in them; the education, experience and abilities of employees have economic value for employers and for the economy as a whole. (Kenton n.d.)

This definition also implies what some, like Gary Becker himself, take to be the inclusive, even sometimes politically inclusive, impulse in the human-capital understanding of capital—it is not just a valuation of education, but skills from on-the-job training or abilities gained over time. Although it may from some angles differentiate what was once undifferentiated in, say, Marx's abstract account of labor, human capital also has its own definitional capaciousness; it measures both on-the-job experience and education. I'll have more to say about value and equality in the human-capital concept later in this chapter.

Some version of human capital has been debated and valued over a long history of political economy, but the human-capital concept, as we now know it, also develops from a definition of capital that emerged gradually in the early twentieth century. In the wake of industrialization, economists late in the nineteenth century started to define capital proper as fixed physical stock, like machinery or railway lines from which income flows. By the twentieth century, economists began to observe that labor and capital seemed the same in this way: they were both physical stock which generated income (Hodgson 2014; Lewin and Cachanosky 2018). One can detect here an analogy between human bodies and machinery that might be the hidden genealogical origin for Foucault's phrase "abilities-machine" (2008, 226).

The mid-twentieth century, Nobel-prize winning work of Theodore Schultz and Gary Becker is marked by several notable revisions and added emphases. In both bodies of work, but especially in Becker, we see the complex mathematical modeling that was not present in earlier political economy; a representational language that for all its appearance as a neutral interpretive tool brings with it an assumption that the social phenomenon it seeks to explain is explicable as a mathematical relation.[4] We also see in their work the impact of the shift in emphasis that occurred in the latter half of the nineteenth century, the era of the marginal revolution, when the work of, among others, William Stanley Jevons and Alfred Marshall, relocated the focus of economics to consumption. With an emphasis on the consumer, and his exercise of demand as the engine of the market, they departed from Ricardo's and Malthus's understanding of production as the market's signal determinant. This shift may not be easily evident in the notion of human capital, given its valuation of the knowledge and skills of *the laborer* rather than a consumer per se, but a pithy quotation from Schultz should help us see this a bit better. Schultz writes: "Much of what we call consumption constitutes investment in human capital" (1961, 1). This is the moment when human capital can be delaminated from its value to the firm or the nation, leading to an emphasis on external investment in human capital, and can now be understood as an intrinsic feature of the human, who is now not only a consumer of education and of training, but is also an investor in him or herself who in Shultz's words, engages in "deliberate investment" (1) rather than, say, subsistence spending or impulsive purchasing.[5]

In this reformulation of labor, economics also captures what early political economy did not: the differentiation of labor that results in different incomes in the market. When a laborer receives an education, or on-the-job training, or works at a job for a certain amount of time and thus accrues experience, his value, economists would argue, is human capital. Like capital it results in profits (or wages). Like capital it contributes to production, ideally to increased productivity, and thus a better return on investment. Usually in calculations of human capital, the costs of training and of maintenance of life are set against the profits/wages gained over the long term. If the latter exceed the former, then human capital is a worthy investment.

Subsequent examinations of human capital, by Becker and others, wish to understand human capital from the perspective of this "deliberate" investor, a famous subject elsewhere known as the rational choice agent of modern Chicago-school economics, that twentieth-century version of *homo economicus*, who by definition reasons clearly insofar as his decisions seek to maximize utility, according to a stable set of preferences that remain unchanged over time. The self-interested behavior of this agent contributes to and manifests both the market's stability and the optimality of its resource allocation—both benchmark characteristics of the neoclassical theory of equilibrium. Becker's own words express well the ambition toward rigor invested in this understanding of economics: "The combined assumptions of maximizing behavior, market equilibrium, and stable preferences, used relentlessly and unflinchingly" (1976, 5).

Further characterized by his long view, by his willingness to invest with an expectation of profit (wages) only after a substantial expenditure of effort and time, the self-investor can be seen to be akin, but not direct kin, to the protagonist of a *liberal* Bildungsroman, as he sets out to find a job, according to an ordered set of preferences, enacting choices, making a claim on the future, or earning an income stream, as economists would call it. The agency of choice is one of the key ways that this self-investor sustains his conceptual connection to the consumer, as both are seen as expressing their market freedom through their consumption preferences. Some of the core questions asked and answered by human-capital scholarship posit this rational choice agent. Why do people spend so much time and money going to college? The answers lie in their "deliberate investments" in themselves, in their calculation of a return on those investments over the longer term of their work life. In the brave new world of human capital, everyone is engaged in a program of self-investment, competition with others, and what seems the complete attunement of human flourishing to the rhythms and rewards of the employment market.

IDEOLOGIES OF HUMAN CAPITAL

Because human capital is expressed as a measurable quantity and thus as having an objective status, economists and policymakers largely treat it as a politically neutral concept or at least as complimentary to a liberal agenda. Obama's Democratic educational policy was largely built on its assumptions (Pierce 2013), and the liberal political economist Thomas Piketty, who otherwise does not consider human capital in his estimation of wealth accumulation, concedes its efficacy as a concept (Kuehn 2018, 4).[6] Indeed, the apparent celebration of education in Becker and other Chicago-school economists (some of whom even support limited public-sector investment in education), alongside its seeming meritocratic formula, convinces many that human-capital theory is politically liberal or moderate and not just neoclassically liberal.[7] Even so, human-capital theory carries within it a host of what we might call conservative ideological assumptions, some of which reach back into nineteenth-century liberal values, such as unfettered markets, negative constructions of freedom, and the privileging of liberty over equality.

In its shift, as outlined above, from the valuation of human capital as a factor of production to Becker's self-investor, we see a characteristic move of neoclassical modeling. Pierre Bourdieu (1990) referred to this tendency in modeling as a "scholastic fallacy," which involves an error consisting, as Bernard Convert phrases it, "of taking the model built by the scientist to account for actions to be the very principle of those actions" (2003, 8). Human capital names a factor of wealth generation, but Becker then transfers that category within the model into an account of market behavior itself. This is one way of describing the process by which the ordinary human becomes the rational-choice human: the abstractions of modeling isolate market dynamics from the social domain, reformulate them as mathematical relations, and then re-insert those formulas into an economic agent who is now fully explicable through these quantitative economic terms. In this way, the social domain is reimagined as fully compliant with this neoclassically engineered human. With this assumption in place,

Becker and then Steven Levitt in *Freakonomics* can expand human capital's explanatory reach into all human behavior, since human behavior has become human-capital behavior (Levitt and Dubner 2006).[8] In *Accounting for Tastes*, Becker confidently asserts, "Fortunately, the methodology that has been developed to study the effects of investments in human capital on earnings is applicable to investments in personal and social capital" (1996, 5).[9] Marriage, family size, and crime can all be addressed through the formulas of human capital (Becker 1991; Becker and Tomes 1986; Becker, Murphy and Tamura 1989).

Human-capital theory also contains a normative valuation that goes unremarked by its practitioners, as critics have noted: "human capital is both our 'is' and our 'ought'" (Brown 2015, 36).[10] As a result, human capital carries a host of implicit behavioral prescriptions, including continual self-improvement—Foucault's "abilities-machine"—a life-long process that clearly now begins with children preparing through AP classes, music lessons, travel sports teams, and charitable efforts for that apex of their human-capital story: entry into higher education. If human-capital investment is exhausting, it can also be lonely. André Orléan, in his insightful alternative to neoclassical economics, elaborated in *The Empire of Value*, notes the radical social isolation of the human-capital agent, whose preferences are developed before market activity happens and without reference to others (2014, 23–26). The social domain consists merely of mechanical market operations devoid of substantive human interaction. Wendy Brown elaborates a moral feature of this isolation, which she labels "responsibilization" (2016, 6; see also Peters 2016, 300). As a free rational agent in the market, one invests to win but can also lose; the management of risk is thus one's own burden and not shared by a civic or social domain. Indeed, despite modest calls for public investment in early-childhood education, most human-capital economists prefer to remind us that human capital remains an investment source for firms as well, not just when investing in workers' training but also in providing the loans required by those investing in their own education. This is the macroeconomy of student debt, bank loans, for-profit universities, and the rising costs of tuition.[11] Invest you must but at your own peril.[12] Human-capital theory also evades the fact that other capitalists, when investing their capital, do not labor the way human capital requires: to obtain the anticipated returns, the self-possessor of human capital, unlike the owner of land or machinery, must continually labor throughout his or her adult life (Milanović 2015).[13]

In addition to the covert assertion of human norms, human-capital theory also cherishes embedded origin stories. In one, human capital develops from mere bodily effort into the rational investment in one's abilities, often mental, that transmutes that labor into capital over the long haul. This is a myth of modern capitalism, as man's mastery over nature and himself turns physical expenditure into mental and technological innovation, transforming necessity into choice. Another narrative seems to displace or erase both the classical economic and in turn Marxist premise that labor and capital are in an oppositional or exploitative relation. Human capital asserts the *shared* interests of labor and capital, since both interest groups are investors now. There is, finally, a positivist historical tale of the decline in aristocracy by birth and the rise of freedom and meritocracy. As Becker himself notes: "What the theory of human capital says is that people … can develop themselves in various ways" (Becker, Ewald and Harcourt 2012, 18).

The human-capital concept certainly includes both manual laborers and securities traders, both factory operatives and university professors, but the market does not value them equally. Indeed, much mid-twentieth century economics scholarship on human capital was trying to provide an explanation, or some might argue, a justification for the radical income and outcome differentials of these various groups, trying to find what might be considered the deeply endogenous rationales for inequality. "Endogenous" is a tellingly favored term in economics that is used to mean those factors within the economic event that produce particular results, but it is also used in the biological sciences where it means "caused by factors inside the organism". In these arguments, inequality hinges on learning, on skills, on aptitudes, on health, and all these are to be understood as, more often than not, intrinsic or at least partially intrinsic to the individual human agent, most often figured as that agent's "endowment" prior to investment in the market, or, as the result of "choices" made in the investment process. If these characteristics are endogenous to the human individual, and if some of these differential endowments are given prior to the market while others are "developed" in the market, then the ultimate distribution of incomes could be understood as not merely allocated optimally, as Pareto efficiency would deem it, but at the least inescapable and at best merited.[14] In this best of all possible worlds, the human-capital agent and his environment are so deeply compatible because they are engineered to work perfectly together. Humans may be free "to develop themselves in various ways," but the "various ways" must be fully responsive to market incentives. "Freedom," as Mirowski and Van Horn argue, "was redefined as a purely mechanical 'choice'" (2009, 163).

From this impoverished conception of freedom, one can now make better sense of why human-capital theory could never free itself from its close definitional connection to slavery—the dark shadow that gave Mill pause. If freedom is simply freedom in the market to act as the market commands, then slaves could also be "free" if it were shown they operated in a market. Perhaps they were even freer than non-slaves, since they could in fact alienate themselves. As Pierce observes: "slaves represented a pure form of human capital" (2013, 51). It was as if slaves were the ideal economic agent for neoclassical theory, who could enact pure economic rationality in a way that one could only wish for free laborers unable to sell themselves.

By the 1970s, the covert connection between slavery and human-capital theory was made manifest. In the watershed and controversial book *Time on the Cross*, from 1974, another Nobel winner, Robert Fogel, along with Stanley L. Engerman, develops a sub-field cliometrics (a statistically inclined economic history) by conducting an extensive study of plantation slavery through the lens of neoclassical human-capital theory. He concludes that slaveowners, responding to market incentives, invested in their slaves, who then, through that training and education, accumulated human capital themselves. Fogel understands himself to be giving credit to slaves. He describes the owner-slave relation as akin to the relation between capital and labor in a neoclassical frame; they are both engaged in parallel practices of incentive-seeking.

This explosive redefinition of slave life can only track if one excises the slaves' social, cultural, and psychological context, positioning the slave solely as an "abilities machine" in the market, whose particular wants and needs do not matter and if one avoids, as human-capital theory routinely does, the otherwise exploitive and unequal relations between owner and slave.[15] Slaves and their owners do not meet on equal footing in these exchanges but in fact arrive with differential endowments. "Inequality is not only the natural state of market economies, but it is actually one of its strongest motor forces for progress" (Mirowski 2009, 438). In this way, the free laborer and the capitalist conclude with differential capital stores. Through these bewildering inversions of terms and statistical data, the human-capital agent emerges from a rigorously purified economic domain where inequality is baked into the system and freedom is a kind of enslavement. "For all its rhetoric of freedom, neoclassical economics, at both micro and macro levels, is not comfortable with actual choice" (Offer 2012, 21). Rather than applauding the market liberation of the slave through human-capital theory, as Fogel attempts, one could instead espy the reversion of the laborer into servitude. This is just what *Jude the Obscure* will accomplish.

THE LIBERAL ORIGINS OF HUMAN CAPITAL

If what we are calling neoliberal formulations of human capital aim to conflate the laborer and capital such that humans in effect constitute their own investments, nineteenth-century liberal formulations of labor sought to draw strict demarcations between the practices of labor and the rest of human functioning, including capital formation. I rely in the following section heavily on Michel Feher's depiction of this division in his splendid essay, "Self-Appreciation; or, The Aspirations of Human Capital." Feher notes that nineteenth-century society increasingly assumed a market governed by natural laws, but that this free market was assumed to have borders, beyond which other forms of human activity ruled. He writes at length of the "free laborer" who is defined by this earlier, liberal, and classical moment of political economy:

> The free laborer, we have seen, is a split being. He or she is split between a subjectivity that is inalienable and a labor power that is to be rented out; he or she is split between the reproduction of a society of free laborers (i.e., its biological, social, cultural, and moral reproduction) and the production, circulation, and consumption of commodities. Last, he or she is split between spiritual aspirations and the pursuit of material interests: the former are necessarily specific to the individual and are thus incommensurable, while the latter are universal, or at least commensurable, and thus lend themselves to possible modeling and calculations. (2009, 30)

First, Feher understands the foundational subject in this modernizing society to be a laboring subject, but a *free* laboring subject whose freedom is to some extent defined by its freedom on occasion from market labor, not just its freedom *in* the labor market. Hence, this subject is at times a laborer in the market who "rents out" his labor—an employee, a factory worker, a solicitor, a teacher, an artist—but he is also an inalienable subject, what a Victorian liberal might call a man of character, or an individual, as J. S. Mill might describe it. As a free laborer at work, he or she is also thereby contributing to the various phases of the commodity market: he or she makes, exchanges, and then consumes those commodities. But, beside or outside that market, the subject of free labor also reproduces itself in the social domain, which means biological reproduction, to be sure, but also other forms of reproduction of a human society, through education, parenting, attending church, associating with friends and others, and voting. The market is distinct from these forms of human doing.

Feher then writes of the split between a spiritual life of priceless values and a material life of priced items. The liberal subject is depicted as having unique, even eccentric, qualities and tastes that are immune to market valuation, and he is equally an actor in the market, who, as laborer or as capitalist, engages in the measurable, countable, and regular practices of market exchange: note here that as a spiritual striver he is unique, individual, resistant to the comparisons that are necessary to arrive at a price, but as an agent in the material world, he becomes common, like others, subject to the uniformities of the newly emergent science of economics—a subject of statistics, of econometrics, of predictability and modeling. He may be free but insofar as he is free in the context of an abstracting labor market, each free man is identical to another, as each discrete quantitative unit is identical to another of the very same kind: the universality of sameness.

By contrast, modern human-capital theory manifests an "imperialist" ambition, as Ben Fine has described it (2010, 17). It has not only claimed, through the applications of some of its practitioners, a superior explanatory role in questions typically located in sociology, psychology, and anthropology, but it has also collapsed the strict liberal boundaries of valuation between the economy and the rest of human life that Feher describes above. Alfred Marshall, although credited as the first significant synthesizer of neoclassical economics, remained adamant that the study of economics concerned behaviors in the market only, a presumption that characterized the classical economics of Smith, Malthus, Mill, and Ricardo (Kiker 1966, 481). In this regard human-capital theory as it evolved in the twentieth-century appears to be a radical revision of the Victorian orthodoxy of separate spheres.[16]

Victorian novels often show the leakage of the commodity market into the ongoing social, domestic, and spiritual lives of Victorian subjects, but the prized division between those two realms is precisely the point of those stories: this leakage is portrayed as an outrage, an affront to the sacrosanct division of realms, as when Stephen Blackpool's rich romantic life in Dickens's *Hard Times* (1854) is diminished by his designation as a "hand." Or when Maggie Tulliver's complicated but domestically intact family life in George Eliot's *The Mill on the Floss* (1860) is forever exposed and ultimately decimated by bankruptcy.

Jude the Obscure also seems to organize its story along the lines of what I might call this liberal division within the free individual, but, as I will argue, the familiar policing of the private and the economic—the narrative strategies that either reinforce this boundary or treat its collapse as tragedy in these other novels—does not fully take shape in *Jude*. In this novel, after all, both Jude and Sue find much that structures the separate spheres culture antagonistic to their desires: they both, to differing degrees, resist marriage, conventional religion, and social conformism. Rather, in this novel, policing gives way to an attempt to envision the coming neoliberal formation and to struggle to acquire the proper terms of critique. This is not just a tragic narrative but also a dystopic one, in which extreme violence and allegory destabilize the familiar Victorian contours of the realist Bildungsroman.

FROM FREE LABOR TO HUMAN CAPITAL

Feher's definition of free labor under a liberal mandate at first seems to describe Jude's story well. In what follows, I will focus mainly on Jude, given that his story is the most explicitly framed as an *Erziehungsroman* (education Bildungsroman), but there will be something to say about the remarkable Sue as well. Jude is a stonemason, a good example of Feher's free laborer in the late Victorian period. Hardy notes:

> There was a stone-mason of a humble kind in Alfredston … he offered his services to this man for a trifling wage. Here Jude had the opportunity of learning at least the rudiments of freestone-working. Some time later he went to a church-builder in the same place, and under the architect's direction became handy at restoring the dilapidated masonries of several village churches round about. ([1895] 2017, 41)

A manual worker, Jude is nonetheless one with skills; he is also a freelancer, who rents himself out to building projects, evincing physical and economic mobility—a free laborer. Again Hardy: "he was out of his apprenticeship, and with his tools at his back seemed to be in the way of making a new start" (72). As a patently free laborer, Jude engages in the commodity process referenced by Feher by producing a tangible product, and he also quite clearly consumes commodities, as he sustains himself for additional days of work: "What was most required by citizens? Food, clothing, and shelter" (41). In this material realm, Jude is a measurable, calculating, and calculable subject—seeking out employment, weighing one job against another.

During his free time, and this freedom is the precise other to his status as laborer and commodity consumer, he is free to be unique, inalienable, incalculable—not like any other little boy in Marygreen. Hardy smartly portrays the split self of Jude the free laborer:

> Inside and round about that old woman's "shop" window, with its twenty-four little panes set in lead-work, the glass of some of them oxidized with age, so that you could hardly see the poor penny articles exhibited within, and forming part of a stock which a strong man could have carried, Jude had his outer being for some long tideless time. But his dreams were as gigantic as his surroundings were small. (31)

Sitting amidst his aunt's stock of small commodities, his "outer being" was stuck in a "long tideless time" of near-subsistence level material transaction, but his "dreams were as gigantic as his surroundings were small." Inchoate, indeed ill-formed, Jude pursues his spiritual life; he dreams ultimately of the ancient seat of learning at Christminster, and a life of the mind that in his earliest understanding has to do with reading and languages and a transcendence analogized in the ascending spires of the Gothic buildings he sees sparkling in the distance. As his reading proceeds, Jude fills out his dreams in terms of the liberal Bildung of vocation, which prizes self-perfection and disinterestedness. In the Christminster voices of bygone scholars he channels as he walks among the colleges, he hears the words: "Her ineffable charm keeps ever calling us to the true goal of all of us, to the ideal, to perfection" (75). And also, this vow: "I have exercised the powers committed to me from no corrupt or interested motives, from no desire to gratify ambition, for no personal gain" (76). This version of self-expression is, quite literally, priceless.

Jude's growing unconventionality, his free thoughts about sex, about marriage, about religion, though perhaps modest in comparison to Sue's, is nonetheless the most unique emblem of his maturing sense of freedom. In the mature Jude, Hardy seems to be pushing the terms of the liberal bargain and the Bildungsroman itself to their furthest boundaries, testing their capacity to fulfill the promises they extend concerning the division between one's incalculable spiritual life and the measurable rules of the market.

Most of us know how the novel ends, alas. However, I do not want to suggest it is simply a liberal ideal of freedom failing at its own ambitions, as many critics have suggested. Jude's sad fate enacts the collapse of this formerly balanced split self—not into some fractured psyche or broken self—but into another type of coherent identity—Jude as nascent human capital. Or, put a slightly different way, Jude's decline enacts the human drama of the collapse of the liberal subject into something veering toward the neoliberal subject that is human capital, but without the celebratory zest imagined by the neoclassical economists.

In what follows, the split self will be shown to be "reformed" into the human-capital subject but through a dystopic counternarrative to the neo-classical mythos. Turning upside down the mythic progress from manual labor to mental capital embedded in the human-capital theory, Jude none-theless reveals its presence. Jude's dream of Christminster, which com-mences in the realm of dreams and apparitions, rather quickly turns into various iterations of occupational training, as Jude turns from dreams of scholarly study, to ambitions within the church, and finally right back to the stonemason job with which he starts his adult working life.[17] In this turn, Jude's inalienable individuality, his spiritual ambition, succumbs to calculations of income, as he determines what sort of jobs can bring the best returns. Once he returns to this job, he cannot appreciate it as a kind of noble labor, as John Ruskin famously champions. At any rate, the imperatives of the market and his poor health require that he change jobs once more. The final recourse near the novel's end, when Jude "chooses" to sell "Christchurch" cookies rather starkly satirizes the "self-entrepreneur" of human-capital theory: this is not merely the tragic inva-sion of market values into a realm of priceless character cultivation, but instead a dystopic vision of the neoclassical version of freedom where one's creative aspirations are literally reshaped by market incentives into commodities.

Given that Jude's is a story of decline and not development, it also speaks to that which human-capital theory obscures. Rather than his employers and himself taking parallel investment paths, the exploitative quality of this directly conflictual relation between management and labor emerges in the steady breakdown of Jude's weakening body.[18] Rather than a story about an aspirational person failing to become the liberal self, then, the narrative arc tries to describe what Jude has become. He has not returned to his origins but become something else: the isolated worker, desperately in possession of preferences that have no job market (inchoate desires for sex, for beauty, for transcendence, for humanist learning) and emptied entirely of social relationality, as he and then Sue wander further away from family, home, and each other. Moreover, his losses cast as failed investments of time and money have exposed himself and his family alone to the kinds of risk that might otherwise be held in common by extended family or the community.

His efforts at reproduction, another of the separate selves to which Feher refers, are especially doomed but also harbor in their depiction penetrating insights into a dystopia that has co-opted Jude's Bildung. His course of study is shown to be useless, not only in its spiritual incapacity to transport Jude inside the walls of Christminster, but to operate as a reproduction of learning. Christminster, full of blind alleys, ghosts of quotations, and dead languages seems incapable of extending its authority into the future. His muddled understanding of learning shows him to be a naïve investor. But Jude's failure to tap into the substance of education and the novel's portrayal of the inside of Christchurch as skeletal and funereal raise substantive questions about whether there are both some "inside" to higher learning and some profits of any kind to be gained over time.

Human-capital theory emerged as a powerful explanatory construct and engine of educational policy in part because it demonstrated quantitatively that there was a "college premium" in the years after World War II, such that college-educated people made better money than those without a college degree, and that this increased income justified the cost of obtaining that degree.[19] Most purveyors of human-capital theory, Becker included, simply assume that the income premium gained from a college degree results from the "skills and learning" acquired in that education. However, in much of the quantitative work, there is no effort to confirm this assumption. Is it possible, some ask, that the college premium in their research simply marks a reduction of a complex set of variables into a single manageable variable? Or is it merely a crude mechanism used in hiring to differentiate broadly between candidates whose "skills and learning" are otherwise difficult to assess? Graham Pyatt asks, "is it that the labour market finds it convenient to use a dummy variable defined with respect to college education in place of the continuous variable 'ability'?" (1966, 636) Or does the "college premium" simply enact a deflection by numbers of a social exclusivity that sustains its value precisely because it operates as a form of class reproduction rather than a meritocracy? Scandals concerning celebrity parents' attempts to purchase entry into college for their children raise similar questions. As Pierre Bourdieu famously argues in his 1970 *Reproduction in Education, Society and Culture*, heritable privilege mostly defines entry to elite institutions, and the transmission of cultural capital, rather than a pattern of elective learning through self-discipline and the university disciplines, more accurately describes the reproduction accomplished by these institutions. In all these interrogations of the education premium, the character-forming function of education that inspired Jude has fallen away entirely. I am less interested in which of these questions accurately describes the function of education than in the idea that together they detect the purely formal status of education in the neoclassical model.

The disconnect between Jude's reading and language learning and his access to Christchurch can now be tentatively aligned with the obscured imperatives of neoclassical economics. What his acquired knowledge of the Biblical Greek may mean or how it affects his character matters not at all. As Mirowski observes in a more modern context, "the absolute validity of that knowledge is not the true motive or objective of the exercise, but rather subordination of the overall process to corporate strategic imperatives" (2009, 426). In the neoclassical formulation, Jude, Richard Phillotson, and aristocratic sons are all equally human capitalists, just as slaves and owners were, in Fogel's formulation. As the labor education market attains equilibrium, one can argue that each laborer in the market earns what is optimal for efficiency, but the content of that knowledge and training are subsumed into incomes flows. One cannot call the labor market a meritocracy, either. As Hayek admits, "the market order does not bring about any close correspondence between subjective merit or individual needs and rewards" (1967, 172). Inequality recast as "differences in human investment," human compromise with irremediable constraints recast as "choice," and freedom recast as the freedom to respond to market prompts provide a covert rationale for elitism.

In Becker's work this elitism operates in nearly full view. In a co-authored volume, Becker writes about how the rational-choice subject approaches another form of reproduction—the reproduction of children within the family. He espies a supply and demand formula in the deliberations: "higher fertility discourages investments in both human and physical capital. Conversely, higher stocks of capital reduce the demand for children" (1993, 325). With the reduction of family size, the family can devote more time to the "education and training" of their beloved human capital, who then provides a return on the capital invested. In this mathematized model, each rational-choice family may strategize in this way but no mention is made of the differential "endowments" each family brings to its calculation. The travel soccer, SAT tutoring, the music lessons, and foreign travel that enable students to distinguish themselves in the putatively meritocratic system of college admissions are defined as "choices" made in a field of like-minded human-capital investors.

Jude and Sue fail at this human-capital imperative, and, in turn, fail to reproduce optimally. Because their "higher fertility" discourages investment in human capital, because Jude continually recurs to his Christchurch dream rather than market prompts, the children suffer in a world in which all behavior is counted as investor risk. Indeed, Father Time, before he commits his murder-suicide, captures the dynamic between over-production, investment choice, and risk:

> How ever could you, Mother, be so wicked and cruel as this, when you needn't have done it till we was better off, and Father well! To bring us all into more trouble! No room for us, and Father a-forced to go away, and we turned out to-morrow; and yet you be going to have another of us soon! . . .'Tis done o' purpose!—'tis—'tis!" (Hardy 2017, 265–266)

Father Time, a dark knight of human capital, punishes the parents who do not become masters of their own futures, and who, unlike him, fail to think effectively about the longer-term outcomes of their choices. The horror of child-on-child multiple murder, not previously seen in a Victorian novel, captures the novel's registration that its generic conventions are inadequate. It evokes tragic conventions only to eschew the catharsis of tragedy and the developmental arc of the Bildungsroman for a modern dystopic morality play in which a little boy becomes an allegorized patriarchal figure—"Father Time"—for this brave new world where time is measured by maximal investments aimed at long-term returns. The rupture of moralism into a text so at pains to resist moral platitudes brings into relief the underlying normative claims of an ethos that its practitioners sought to bracket off as exogeneous to its scientific account of the market.

For all the myriad revisions effected by neoclassical economics of the Victorian tradition of classical economics, its early history in the first half of the twentieth-century shows that despite the merger of market spheres and non-market spheres and the redirection of economic theory to demand, human-capital theory was not as revisionary of Victorian social and moral norms as one might suppose. Indeed, *Jude the Obscure* reveals as much: Sue's inability to wrest herself from traditional gender roles and religious constructs especially after her children's deaths should now be viewed as compliant with the neoclassical program rather than a reactionary response to it. The stratification of social class, the hierarchy of economic prestige, the existence of profound inequality, the division of sexual labor, and the sequestration of religious belief to private life that characterizes British-Victorian society in the nineteenth century were never a problem and thus never a target for this theoretical project. Indeed, despite the co-optation of non-market life practices, human-capital theorists found a way to retain not only the elitisms of privilege in its formulations of education but also the exploitations of race, sex, and gender from this earlier era. In discussing his early twentieth-century understanding of human capital, John Bates Clark seems to be joining Father Time in his condemnation of the over-production and under-investment wrought by his parents. Here is Clark:

> Man does not add to his capital, when he spends money in training or educating himself for a useful occupation. He gets something, indeed, that increases his productive power, and in getting it he is obliged to practice abstinence. He deprives himself of pleasure, in order that thereafter he may produce more than he otherwise could. (1908, 116)

The acclamation of abstinence alongside the language of individual responsibility in this passage could easily be transposed to a Victorian sermon. Indeed, if one looks back to Father Time's castigation, he is not only defending human-capital temporalities but apportioning the blame to his mother rather than his father and declaiming the absence of the father from the household in a turn to patriarchal hierarchies and pieties—hence his name evokes both the temporality and power structure posited in the human-capital concept. This blame seems especially unjust to Sue who never much seems to desire sex, who indeed resists it precisely because it seems too much like alienable labor that renders her indebted to her partners (McGregor 2016). Despite a generations-long consolidation of our notion of *homo economicus,* as much trumpeted by its supporters as denigrated by its detractors, Sue reminds us that the notions of free labor and human capital rely on what Angela Mitropoulos calls "an oikonomics," a residual but fundamental linkage between free labor and the patriarchal household's normative values regarding the distribution of goods. This oikonomics enforces, even in the otherwise "free love" of Jude and Sue, an implicit authority concerning sexual supply and demand (2012, 28–38).

Human capital's version of this patriarchal household lies, for instance, in Gary Becker's assumption that, in so far as children require continual investment to maximize human capital, the mother should remain home to act as educator (Cooper 2017, 225).[20] One can see that an economic model has been superimposed on a nineteenth- and twentieth-century domestic arrangement without the domestic arrangement changing. There is in this argument a double move that should by now be familiar. Becker transposes domesticity into economic formulas even as he deems "exogeneous" to those formulas conservative social and moral suppositions that even so undergird the desiccated social domain imagined by neoclassical economics. The more things change, the more they stay the same.

Jude the Obscure exerts some pressure on these early lineaments of neoliberal human functioning while at other times seeming to succumb to them. The multiple determinations that circulate in the thematic ambiance of the novel could be understood as ripostes to the liberal and then neoliberal privileging of choice and the latter's narrowing of human flourishing to the rules of microeconomics. As Jude declines into ill-health, the novel registers his actual labor: its bodily consequences and exploitations. The novel also shows definitively that Jude, unlike a capitalist, does not own the means of production; his meager income is not merited due to the varied outcome of his rational choices; rather, inequality is built into the rules of the macroeconomy. If Father Time condemns his parents' behavior as a choice, the novel's Malthusian determinism reframes choice as human sexual inevitability. Moreover, the couple's inability to find sufficiently large lodgings for their growing family at the end of novel is depicted as a result of the immoveable forces of social convention. Even their struggles as a companionate couple are less about their own bad decisions and far more about some dark inevitability in their generational lineage. Jude, Hardy implies, never had a chance even if he had a choice.

IRRESPONSIBLE EDUCATION

It is time to return to that quotation of Wendy Brown's from the earliest section of this chapter, that passage where an elegiac "before" of higher education is placed alongside the dark corporatization of present-day colleges and universities. Brown herself carefully distinguishes between two moments, one a classical education for "developing intelligent, thoughtful elites and reproducing culture" and another a progressive education for "enacting a principle of equal opportunity and cultivating a broadly educated citizenry." She notably favors the latter. I want to suggest that my argument urges some caution in turning to either of these models without first taking the force of their integration into human-capital theory. Indeed, the easy adoption of human-capital theory by the Obama administration, the treatment of human capital as an objective measure in much educational policy, the widespread embrace of ROI calculations and pre-professionalization programs within graduate schools, and the largely quiescent response by the academic class to the economization of education suggests that there are many progressively aligned educators who misrecognize liberal humanist virtues and democratic values within the policies drawn from human-capital theory.

In this chapter, I have sought to show how human-capital theory has captured ideals of liberal development and mental autonomy as well as democratic principles of equality and meritocracy and reworked them for the better functioning of a neoclassical market structure that conceals its neo-Victorian cultural assumptions. No doubt these neoclassical economists are astute, but these wholesale revaluations of treasured educational ideals may not have required Nobel Prize winners to effect this brave new world in which we teach and learn. Some of the liberal ideals baked into our conception of the liberal arts were to some extent easily incorporated into human-capital theory: it was not an abduction but an adoption. Although human-capital theory may fundamentally displace the ideal of the disinterested pursuit of perfection, it fully revitalizes the liberal ideal of autonomy and its developmental life-course—the Bildung. The continued robustness of the Bildungsroman in our era may well provide literary evidence for this claim, despite Hardy's own decision to beg off writing them. It bears repeating that what many of us think of as freedom emerged in a co-dependent relation with capitalist free enterprise. Those who champion the liberal arts that still linger in our institutions should register the economic connections between this curriculum and the endowments of their institutions. As we debate among ourselves which texts to teach and how to reanimate our humanities' majors through curricular revision, is it possible our administrators and Boards of Trustees only treat "liberal arts" as a formal consumption function that names, to re-use Pyatt's words, "a dummy variable" that differentiates between one kind of self-investor and another? To put another way, it hardly matters what is learned or known in a liberal arts education; it simply matters that it happens. As we seek to teach and develop the minds of students in our classrooms, as we make a case for a literary education or the learning of Classical Greek, are the classrooms in which it happens simply storage facilities for cultural capital that is reproduced in the preceding admissions process? And is that admissions process in elite institutions a democratic meritocracy or one where differences in endowments are both taken as given and bracketed off so that all applicants are understood as independently investing in an efficient if unequal market? These are the presumptions that can, while admitting some small curated collection of "underserved populations"—note how consumption is implicit in the "service" verb—reproduce in a newer fashion some of the labor and gender hierarchies of the nineteenth century that have lingered long into the twentieth century and beyond.

Brown's commitment to democracy is in many ways a stronger riposte to human-capital educational policy than liberal arts rationales still saturated by Victorian presumptions. Defining democratic educational ideals that do not downdraft on traditional references to the liberal arts, drawn in part from Victorian traditions and now integrated into neoclassical human-capital policies, is not an easy task, however. In an effort to divest education from the market imperatives of human-capital theory, critics may seem blithely unaware of why most students seek education, revealing thereby their own privilege. As Jude himself notes, "What was most required by citizens? Food, clothing, and shelter." Furthermore, the most common response to what is denounced as a purely economic consumption of education recurs to the benefits of the liberal arts in ways that sound strikingly like the Victorian ideals parroted by Jude: students should seek "the ideal, to perfection" rather than engineering school; they should bypass a finance degree due to "no corrupt or interested motives, from no desire to gratify ambition, for no personal gain." If we embrace what seems to us a more appealing model of education that figures the student as an intellectual seeker, we may imagine we are snatching the educational model from the jaws of a purely instrumentalized notion of human effort in the human-capital era, but we may in fact be succumbing to the self-investment model unawares. Possibly, we will be turning away, as well, from a democratic model of education entirely. *Jude the Obscure* warns us of that delusion, for it situates the aspirational poor exactly outside the walls of education, condemning them to hopeless indebtedness as they vainly try to better themselves in ways that do them no good.

Without yet formulating admirable alternatives to the currently existing educational system, this chapter concludes. Its main aim has been to clarify the human-capital concept, describe its subtler operations and their indebtedness to Victorian economic and liberal ideology, and to show why today it is both accepted and embraced as politically progressive even as it erodes democratic impulses. The political crisis embedded in human-capital theory and neoliberalism more generally is, as Wendy Brown notes, a crisis of democracy. One need only listen to Milton Friedman, one of the patriarchs of neoclassical economics whose theories have been so thoroughly realized in the present day: "What I believe in is not democracy but in individual freedom in a society in which individuals cooperate with one another" (n.d.). Friedman, like his colleagues, has a talent for the obfuscatory phrase. Let me translate: he believes in cooperating with one another through a society fully permeated by the market. Jude and Sue showed us over a century ago how that story goes.

Notes

1. The author would like to dedicate this chapter to Mary Poovey, in honor of her retirement. Thanks also to Jonathan Levy. *Jude the Obscure* was composed around the time of some key publications of the neoclassical tradition: *The Philosophy of Wealth: Economic Principles Newly Formulated* by John Bates Clark, in 1888; the first edition of Alfred Marshall's *Principles of Economics*, 1890; Eugen v. Böhm-Bawerk's *Capital and Interest*, also 1890; J. S. Nicholson, "Capital and Labour: Their Relative Strength," 1892; and Philip Wicksteed's *An Essay on the Co-ordination of the Laws of Distribution*, 1894.
2. "Education health" is an odd term that Pierce presumably draws from the biopolitical approach of Foucault, which he adopts throughout his book. It is, however, a bit confusing or perhaps ironic that he uses it to define human-capital measures of education, which typically rely on mechanical rather than organic metaphors.
3. Mill's differentiation between human resources and wealth marks the moment that comes in nearly every discussion of human-capital theory up to its consolidation in the mid-twentieth century: its reckoning with slavery. Branko Milanović, among others, notes that in transforming labor into human capital, the concept ignores its difference from inhuman capital, which like property can be alienated (Milanović 2013). For Mill, as it proves to be so with Thomas Piketty 170 years later in *Capital in the Twenty-First Century*, the potential conflation between human capital and slavery renders it a persona non grata. Later economists were not so fastidious; most simply insisted on using the term anyway but noting this one difference from fixed capital. As will be argued later in the chapter, human-capital theory does not purge slavery as a topic nor as a conceptual girder.
4. Peter Spiegler, in his trenchant examination of mathematical modeling in economics: "the objects under investigation must plausibly be stable, modular, and quantitative, with no qualitative differences among instantiations of each type" (2015, 45).

5. Schultz's work addressed a quirk apparent in calculations of economic growth. In the twentieth century, economists noticed a sizeable residual, as Goldin defines it: "the residual is that portion of economic growth the researcher cannot explain by the increase in physical productive factors such as the capital stock, the number of workers and their hours and weeks of work" (Goldin 2016, 58). In other words, inputs of machinery and labor did not add up to the total sum of measured growth, indicating another factor of production was missing. Schultz demonstrated the missing factor was the skills and education of labor.

6. Not enough has been made of Obama's early years at UChicago's law school and the network of associations he made with business economists at the Booth School at UChicago.

7. Pierce (2013) guides my work on the modern "liberal" politics of human-capital educational policy. The scholarship of Kevin Murphy (Murphy and Topel 2016) and James Heckman (Carneiro and Heckman 2003) will give some taste of this scholarship. Also see the website of The Center for the Economics of Human Development: https://cehd.uchicago.edu/. In this context, of course, "liberal" refers to the American label of Democratic politics, not the Victorian liberal ideology of negative freedoms, laissez-faire policies, and a favoring of liberty over equality.

8. Foucault on Becker: "That is to say, any conduct which responds systematically to modifications in the variables of the environment, in other words, any conduct, as Becker, says which "accepts reality,' must be susceptible to economic analysis" (Foucault 2008, 269).

9. Mirowski and Van Horn (2009) also argue relatedly that the ambition of human-capital theory was an intentional component of its development.

10. See also Mirowski (2009) on its normative impulses.

11. Lazzarato writes well on the culture and economics of debt (Lazzarato 2012, 2015).

12. Bröckling quotes Becker: "Corresponding to the economic approach, *most* (if not all) deaths are to some extent suicides in the sense that they could have been postponed if more resources had been invested in prolonging life" (2011, 257).

13. Mirowski (2009, 436) seems right to suggest that these mid-century neoclassical economists were not classically laissez-faire; rather, they supported government measures that instantiated their vision of the market—student loans, corporate welfare, etc.—while denuding the domain of social supports. In its historical context, neoclassical economics seems a pointed political project.

14. Pareto efficiency or optimality occurs when a preference or individual can not be made better off without making at minimum another individual or

preference less so. In a state of equilibrium, Pareto efficiency is presumed to occur, but efficiency is not equality, nor necessarily justice.

15. Fogel was not defending slavery as an institution, but was defending the economics of the institution insofar as it responded to market forces, which only shows how he considers the "moral" considerations as something outside and independent of the institution's inner workings—exogenous. Efficiency is the fundamental value undergirding neoclassical economics. Pierce (2013) is helpful on the role of slavery in human-capital theory, and Gutman (1975) was the first thorough critique of Fogel's book. Caitlin Rosenthal (2018) also espies the early lineaments of the human-capital concept in the slavery era, but she emphasizes the ways in which slave owners valued their slaves as capital rather than the ways in which slaves could be implausibly imagined to be engaged in self-investment. See also Berry (2017). Fogel and Engerman did revise and respond to critics in a second edition.

16. I am not suggesting that "separate sphere" ideology is a synonym or exact equivalent for the division between free labor and the domains of social reproduction as Feher describes them (he rather fails to give gender its due), but that separate sphere ideology is perhaps a social elaboration of this theoretical description.

17. The narrative does appear to show a devolution into a human-capital framework, but it lurks close to the surface even early in the novel. When Jude's immature desire for Christminster is most idealistically naïve, it also shows him to be attempting utility maximization: he constructs a mechanism on his wagon so that he can deliver goods *and* study/train at the same time. And from the beginning, he appears to calculate quite often about long-term returns—years of patient learning and study culminating in the coveted entry to Christminster.

18. The employers in this novel are largely invisible, true to the way that market agents are not in direct contact in neoclassical exchange.

19. See Welch (1999) for a classic neoclassical study of the college premium that argues that education was the primary explanation for increasing levels of inter-class and inter-race equality at mid-century and beyond, without remarking on the impact of either the Civil Rights or Women's Rights movements.

20. Feminist economists Carolyn Shaw Bell, Marianne Ferber, Bonnie Birnbaum, and Isabel Sawhill noted the unchanged gender roles of Beckerian economics as early as the 1970s.

REFERENCES

Becker, Gary S. 1976. *The Economic Approach to Human Behavior*. Chicago: University of Chicago Press.

———. 1991. *A Treatise on the Family*. Enl. ed. Cambridge, MA: Harvard University Press. http://pi.lib.uchicago.edu/1001/cat/bib/11198854.

———. 1993. *Human Capital: A Theoretical and Empirical Analysis, with Special Reference to Education*. 3rd ed. Chicago: The University of Chicago Press.

———. 1996. *Accounting for Tastes*. Cambridge, MA: Harvard University Press.

Becker, Gary S., Francois Ewald, and Bernard Harcourt. 2012. 'Becker on Ewald on Foucault on Becker': American Neoliberalism and Michel Foucault's 1979 'Birth of Biopolitics' Lectures. Institute for Law and Economics Working Paper 614.

Becker, Gary S., Kevin M. Murphy, and Robert F. Tamura. 1989. *Human Capital, Fertility and Economic Growth*. Vol. 90-5 (PRC). Discussion Paper Series/ Population Research Center; Chicago, IL: Economic Demography Group, Economics Research Center, NORC/University of Chicago.

Becker, Gary S., and Nigel Tomes. 1986. Human Capital and the Rise and Fall of Families. *Journal of Labor Economics* 4 (3, Part 2): S1–S39. https://doi.org/10.1086/298118.

Bentham, Jeremy. 1952. *Economic Writings: Critical Edition Based on His Printed Works and Unprinted Manuscripts*. Edited by J. Stark. London: Published for the Royal Economic Society by Allen & Unwin.

Berry, Daina Ramey. 2017. The Ubiquitous Nature of Slave Capital. In *After Piketty: The Agenda for Economics and Inequality*, ed. Heather Boushey, Bradford J. De Long, and Marshal Steinbaum, 126–149. Cambridge, MA: Harvard University Press.

Boag, Harold. 1916. Human Capital and the Cost of the War. *Journal of the Royal Statistical Society* 79 (1): 7–17.

Bourdieu, Pierre. 1990. *Reproduction in Education, Society, and Culture*. Edited by Jean Claude Passeron. London: Sage in association with Theory, Culture & Society, Department of Administrative and Social Studies, Teesside Polytechnic.

Bröckling, Ulrich. 2011. Human Economy, Human Capital: A Critique of Biopolitical Economy. In *Governmentality: Current Issues and Future Challenges*, ed. Susanne Krasmann, Thomas Lemke, and Ulrich Bröckling, vol. 71, 247–268. New York: Routledge.

Brown, Wendy. 2015. *Undoing the Demos: Neoliberalism's Stealth Revolution*, Near Futures. Brooklyn, NY: Zone Books.

———. 2016. Sacrificial Citizenship: Neoliberalism, Human Capital, and Austerity Politics. *Constellations: An International Journal of Critical & Democratic Theory* 23 (1): 3–14. https://doi.org/10.1111/1467-8675.12166.

Carneiro, Pedro Manuel, and James J. Heckman. 2003. Human Capital Policy. SSRN Scholarly Paper ID 434544. Rochester, NY: Social Science Research Network. https://papers.ssrn.com/abstract=434544.

Clark, John Bates. 1908. *The Distribution of Wealth: A Theory of Wages, Interest and Profits*. New York: The Macmillan Company.

Convert, Bernard. 2003. Bourdieu: Gary Becker's Critic. *Economic Sociology: European Electronic Newsletter* 4 (2): 6–9.

Cooper, Melinda. 2017. *Family Values: Between Neoliberalism and the New Social Conservatism*. New York: Zone Books.

Dublin, Louis Israel, Alfred J. Lotka, and Mortimer Spiegelman. 1946. *The Money Value of a Man*. Rev. ed. New York: The Ronald Press Company.

Feher, Michel. 2009. Self-Appreciation; or, The Aspirations of Human Capital. *Public Culture* 21 (1): 21–41. https://doi.org/10.1215/08992363-2008-019.

Fine, Ben. 2010. *Theories of Social Capital: Researchers Behaving Badly*, Political Economy and Development. London: Pluto Press.

Fogel, Robert William, and Stanley L. Engerman. 1974. *Time on the Cross*. Boston: Little, Brown and Company.

Foucault, Michel. 2008. *The Birth of Biopolitics: Lectures at the Collège de France, 1978–79*. Translated by Michel Senellart. Basingstoke: Palgrave Macmillan.

Friedman, Milton. n.d. I Don't Believe in Democracy. Interview Transcript. Accessed March 13, 2019. http://hellocoolworld.ca/media/TheCorporation/Democracy.pdf.

Goldin, Claudia. 2016. Human Capital. In *Handbook of Cliometrics*, ed. Claude Diebolt and Michael Haupert, 55–86. Berlin, Heidelberg: Springer. https://doi.org/10.1007/978-3-642-40406-1_23.

Goldin, Claudia Dale, and Lawrence F. Katz. 2008. *The Race between Education and Technology*. Cambridge, MA: Belknap Press of Harvard University Press.

Gutman, Herbert G. 1975. *Slavery and the Numbers Game: A Critique of Time on the Cross*. Urbana: University of Illinois Press.

Hardy, Thomas. (1895) 2017. *Jude the Obscure*. With an introduction by Morton Dauwen Zabel. Digireads.com Publishing. Citations refer to the 2017 Digireads edition.

Hayek, Friedrich A.von. 1967. *Studies in Philosophy, Politics and Economics*. Chicago: University of Chicago Press.

Hodgson, Geoffrey M. 2014. What Is Capital? Economists and Sociologists Have Changed Its Meaning: Should It Be Changed Back? *Cambridge Journal of Economics* 38 (5): 1063–1086.

Kenton, Will. n.d. Human Capital. *Investopedia*. Accessed February 1, 2019. https://www.investopedia.com/terms/h/humancapital.asp.

Kiker, B.F. 1966. The Historical Roots of the Concept of Human Capital. *Journal of Political Economy* 74 (5): 481–499.

Kuehn, Daniel. 2018. Human Capital in the Twenty First Century. *European Journal of Comparative Economics* 15 (1): 3–9. http://eaces.liuc.it/default.asp.

Lazzarato, M. 2012. *The Making of the Indebted Man: An Essay on the Neoliberal Condition*. Vol. 13. Translated by Joshua David Jordan. Semiotext(e) Intervention Series; Los Angeles, CA: Semiotext(e).

———. 2015. *Governing by Debt*. Vol. 17. Translated by Joshua David Jordan. Semiotext(e) Intervention Series; South Pasadena, CA: Semiotext(e).

Levitt, Steven D., and Stephen J. Dubner. 2006. *Freakonomics: A Rogue Economist Explores the Hidden Side of Everything*. Rev. and expanded ed. New York: William Morrow.

Lewin, Peter, and Nicolás Cachanosky. 2018. Substance and Semantics: The Question of Capital. *Journal of Economic Behavior & Organization* 150 (June): 423–431. https://doi.org/10.1016/j.jebo.2018.01.024.

McGregor, Melissa. 2016. The Unwaged Labour of Love: Social Reproduction in Jude the Obscure. Paper presented at the Annual Meeting of the North American Victorian Studies Association, 1–5. Phoenix, AZ.

Milanović, Branko. 2013. OPINION: Junk the Phrase 'Human Capital.' *Al Jazeera America*, February 25. http://america.aljazeera.com/opinions/2015/2/junk-the-phrase-human-capital.html.

———. 2015. Globalinequality: On 'Human Capital' One More Time. *Globalinequality* (blog), February 19. http://glineq.blogspot.com/2015/02/on-human-capital-one-more-time.html.

Mill, John Stuart. (1848) 1909. *Principles of Political Economy, with Some of Their Applications to Social Philosophy*. London: Longmans, Green, and Co. http://hdl.handle.net/2027/mdp.39015002976382. Citations refer to the 1909 edition.

Mirowski, Philip. 2009. Postface: Defining Neoliberalism. In *The Road from Mont Pèlerin: The Making of the Neoliberal Thought Collective*, ed. Dieter Plehwe and Philip Mirowski, 417–455. Cambridge, MA: Harvard University Press.

Mirowski, Philip, and Rob Van Horn. 2009. The Rise of the Chicago School of Economics and the Birth of Neoliberalism. In *The Road from Mont Pèlerin: The Making of the Neoliberal Thought Collective*, ed. Dieter Plehwe and Philip Mirowski, 139–178. Cambridge, MA: Harvard University Press.

Mitropoulos, Angela. 2012. *Contract & Contagion: From Biopolitics to Oikonomia*. Brooklyn, NY: Minor Compositions.

Murphy, Kevin M., and Robert H. Topel. 2016. Human Capital Investment, Inequality, and Economic Growth. *Journal of Labor Economics* 34 (S2): S99–S127. https://doi.org/10.1086/683779.

Nicholson, J.S. 1891. The Living Capital of the United Kingdom. *The Economic Journal* 1 (1): 95–107.

———. 1892. Capital and Labour: Their Relative Strength. *The Economic Journal* 2 (7): 478–490.

Offer, Avner. 2012. Self-Interest, Sympathy and the Invisible Hand: From Adam Smith to Market Liberalism. *Discussion Papers in Economic and Social History* 101 (Aug.): 1–27.

Orléan, André. 2014. *The Empire of Value: A New Foundation for Economics.* Translated by M. B. DeBevoise. Cambridge, MA: The MIT Press. http://pi. lib.uchicago.edu/1001/cat/bib/10078409.

Peters, Michael A. 2016. Education, Neoliberalism, and Human Capital. In *The Handbook of Neoliberalism*, ed. Simon Springer, Kean Birch, and Julie MacLeavy, 297–307. New York: Routledge.

Pierce, Clayton. 2013. *Education in the Age of Biocapitalism: Optimizing Educational Life for a Flat World*, Variation: New Frontiers in Education, Culture, and Politics. New York: Palgrave Macmillan.

Pigou, A.C. 1928. *A Study in Public Finance.* London: Macmillan and Co., Limited.

Pyatt, Graham. 1966. Review of *Review of Human Capital: A Theoretical and Empirical Analysis, with Special Reference to Education; The Residual Factor and Economic Growth; Econometric Models of Education*, by G.S. Becker. *The Economic Journal* 76 (303): 635–638. https://doi.org/10.2307/2229541.

Rosenthal, Caitlin. 2018. *Accounting for Slavery: Masters and Management.* Cambridge, MA: Harvard University Press.

Schultz, Theodore W. 1961. Investment in Human Capital. *American Economic Review* 51 (1): 1–17.

Smith, Adam. (1776) 1828. *An Inquiry into the Nature and Causes of the Wealth of Nations.* Edited by J. R. McCulloch. Edinburgh: Printed for A. Black and W. Tait. http://pi.lib.uchicago.edu/1001/cat/bib/2440331. Citations refer to the 1828 edition.

Spiegler, Peter. 2015. *Behind the Model: A Constructive Critique of Economic Modeling.* Cambridge, UK: Cambridge University Press.

Welch, Finis. 1999. In Defense of Inequality. *American Economic Review* 89 (2): 1–17. https://doi.org/10.1257/aer.89.2.1.

White, Lawrence H. 2017. Human Capital and Its Critics: Gary Becker, Institutionalism, and Anti-Neoliberalism. GMU Working Paper in Economics No. 17-02. https://papers.ssrn.com/sol3/papers.cfm?abstract_id=2905931.

CHAPTER 3

Exploitation

On the Use and Abuse of the Nineteenth Century: Toward a Genealogy of Exploitation

Zachary Samalin

As a concept, exploitation remains moored to the nineteenth century. One reason for this enduring attachment is, of course, Karl Marx. Even after 150 years, Marx's theory of the exploitation of labor continues to exert the most influence on and demand the most robust engagement from contemporary critical theoretical discourse; and even after a century of debunking and dismissing, its claims continue to shape and influence economic discourse, socialist and Marxist no less than liberal and neoliberal. Marx was at once a product and a theorist of his times, and, for both of these reasons, which often can be difficult to distinguish from each other, the use of his theory of exploitation today remains attached by its roots to the nineteenth century.

Marx's theory of exploitation retains its centrality today, I argue in this chapter, partly because it has become an emblem of a broader set of unresolved questions about the historical difference between nineteenth-century and contemporary capitalist society. The theory of exploitation

Z. Samalin (✉)
University of Chicago, Chicago, IL, USA

© The Author(s) 2019
E. Hadley et al. (eds.), *From Political Economy to Economics through Nineteenth-Century Literature*, Palgrave Studies in Literature, Culture and Economics, https://doi.org/10.1007/978-3-030-24158-2_3

itself was built out of a description of a social and economic world that had in the 1860s only relatively newly come to be dominated by wage labor and its organizing temporal structures. Today's world is still dominated by wage labor, although the organizational effects of that domination are hardly felt as new anymore, while at the same time, there are also new structures and forms of domination waiting to be described. The theory still retains its strong claim to descriptive relevance, but we can also learn something by thinking about the way it has aged or needs to be renovated, or about our enduring attachment to it, or, conversely, about what it means to live in a world that has gotten used to aspects of capitalist life that were once legible as new social phenomena.

In its simplest form, Marx's theory of exploitation is as follows. Starting from the premise that in a capitalist economy workers are compelled to sell their labor, Marx asserts that workers produce value through their labor in the form of commodities. However, only some of the value produced by their labor returns to the workers; the rest of it belongs to the capitalists who have purchased their labor and own the production apparatus. In this schematic description, exploitation occurs, even if the workers are paid their due, and even if profits are minimal, because the capitalists reap a surplus value that was sown by the workers. The bulk of the vast literature of Marxist theory on exploitation lies in figuring out how to assert that this scenario is politically and economically wrong or untenable, but without grounding the theory in the appeal to moral right or fairness, which Marxism has tended to construe as ideology.[1]

My goal in this chapter is neither to critique nor to renovate Marx's theory of surplus value and exploitation, but rather to focus on a set of assumptions about time and history which are embedded in Marx's theory. One of Marx's most penetrating insights was that the formal economic relation of exploitation, which could be expressed statically as the rate of surplus over that of wages, was in fact a dynamic process that involved the subordination of workers to an external structure of "socially necessary" labor time. As Marx often put it, wage laborers work for themselves only for part of the day, after which point they work solely for the owner of their labor, who therefore can be said to exploit them. This transposition from the static terms of property and ownership into the dynamic terms of temporality was a crucial innovation. Most theories of exploitation acknowledge this temporal dimension in Marx's analysis, but do not go on to argue that the medium of exploitation itself in capitalist society is time.[2] That, however, is what I hope to show was one of Marx's key historical insights into the nature of nineteenth-century capitalist society. And by tracking how this insight emerged out of certain areas of Victorian political economy, and went on to function in Marx's work, I hope as well to shed light on more recent manipulations of the function of time in economic discourse.

The nineteenth century is the historical frame of reference for the concept of exploitation, rather than merely the origin of its most significant theorization. This frame of reference extends beyond Marxist theory, and in fact colors and influences the ways in which exploitation has been depicted in a variety of contexts over the last half-century. For instance, thinking about the violence of labor tends to involve the invocation of the Victorian scene of abuse. The opening section of Studs Terkel's *Working*, a compendium of interviews with America's laborers conducted at the close of the 1960s, is a notable example. "This book, being about work," the first sentence reads, "is, by its very nature about violence." Although Terkel's interlocutors describe scenes that are often quite specific to the complex economic landscape of 1960s American society—the Chicano labor struggle and the Vietnam War loom large—for Terkel, thinking about the violence of work often means thinking about Victorian exploitation. The "daily chore" of Chicago factory worker Grace Clements, he writes, "reveals to us in a terrible light that Charles Dickens's London is not so very far away nor long ago," though "Scrooge has been replaced by the conglomerate" (2004, xiii–xiv). In a similar vein, Terkel goes on to refer to Henry Mayhew's letters to the *Morning Chronicle* at the close of the 1840s, which endeavored, through interviews and analysis, to lay bare the exploitative conditions of London's working class and to excoriate the indifference of the British middle class. These references inscribe Terkel's project, as well as the scenes of labor the book depicts, within the horizons of a nineteenth-century cultural and economic landscape. Terkel even dedicates *Working* to Jude Fawley, the thwarted protagonist of Thomas Hardy's 1895 novel *Jude the Obscure*, who dies from a respiratory disease contracted through his work as a stonemason.

In a similar vein, the analysis of allegedly new forms of labor thought to be specific to late twentieth-century capitalism has also frequently been situated within a Victorian frame of reference. Arlie Hochschild's influential sociological study of "emotional labor," *The Managed Heart: Commercialization of Human Feeling*, begins with a nightmarish scene of child labor from "The Working Day," one of the two central chapters on exploitation in Marx's *Capital*. The sheer physical brutality of this opening foray is meant to contrast but also to bring out a hidden resonance with the book's principal focus on the way that the regulation and control of affect has been absorbed by the processes of value creation in the service economy. "At first glance it might seem that the circumstances of the nineteenth-century factory child and the twentieth-century flight attendant could not be more different," Hochschild writes, "But a close examination of the differences between the two can lead us to some unexpected common ground" (2012, 5). Focusing on Marx's account of alienation, itself closely related to his theory of exploitation, Hochschild sought to close up the imaginative and conceptual distance between an ostensibly post-industrial or deindustrializing scene of first-world late capitalism and a rapidly industrializing Victorian past.

In such attempts to use the nineteenth century in order to make sense of the violence of labor—including "emotional labor" and other forms of work which previously might have gone unrecognized—an ambivalent structure of historical feeling comes into focus.[3] In this structure of feeling, the acknowledgement that capitalist labor is violent has been thoroughly entangled with the ideology of progress. On the one hand, the expectation that exploitation has already been dealt with, relegated to the Victorian past, is a consequence of the presumption of economic progress, itself a living artifact of Victorian ideology that has been perpetually reanimated by modern economic discourse. On the other, the invocation of the past, the feeling that its violence continues to obtrude into and saturate the present, is meant to disrupt the smooth continuities of the ideology of progress. These articulations of ambivalence point to a readiness among contemporary thinkers to make use of the nineteenth century as an object, to put it to work, so to speak, whether as the scene of structural abuse that renders present violence sensible, as a vanishing point on a receding horizon that makes possible the imagination of progress, or in other ways that further imbricate the analysis of exploitation with the ideology of progress. What does one get, I am asking, from continuing to think exploitation by way of the nineteenth century?

This ambivalent structure of feeling also played an important role in the development of the theory of time that lies at the heart of American neoliberal economics, the work of Gary Becker in particular. Freed from thinking about labor time as a constitutive part of value production, Becker produced a theory of time allocation that can be seen as the distorted negative image of the Marxist theory of exploitation. In research published from the early 1960s onward, Becker argued influentially that non-working time was productive of a kind of value that he termed human capital, and that this productivity could be measured in quantitative economic terms. To recall, Marx had argued that a portion of working time was productive of value not for the worker, but only for the owner of capital. Critics of capitalism since Marx have thus in one way or another maintained that unremunerated working time is the basis of exploitation. Becker, by contrast, moved preemptively to invalidate this theory by insisting that *all* time was potentially productive of value in ways that had been occluded by traditional economic discourse's exclusive focus on labor. In fact, Becker argued, once the use of time is understood in this revised manner, it "not only [becomes] difficult to distinguish leisure from other non-work, but also even work from non-work" (1990, 100). The difficulty of maintaining these distinctions led to a more fundamental erosion of the difference between production and consumption, supply and demand, destabilizing even further the economic categories which had propped up critiques of the exploitation of labor.[4]

We will return to Becker's argument in greater detail below, but I want to emphasize from the outset the extent to which the new era of economic discourse and policy that neoliberal theorists have sought to usher in for half a century depended on an argument about the experience and usage of time. Indeed, one thing that Becker and Marx both understood about capitalism was that it derives much of its power as a social and economic system from the organizational, or disciplinary, control of time. Marx's insights into the power dynamics of temporality directly informed his critique of Victorian capitalism. For Becker, by contrast, the opening up of time, of the minute, to new horizons of productivity required keeping the individual utilization of temporality insulated from the careful analysis of historical change. Without this insulation, we will see, Becker would not have been able to maintain his commitment to the core neoclassical economic assumptions of market equilibrium and stable preferences on which he founded his analysis. In the world envisioned by Becker, time is an endlessly elastic resource waiting to be maximized by savvy self-investors, but there is also something static and undynamic about the neoclassical concept of time he relies on that keeps him from thinking about it as a social phenomenon subject to meaningful historical variation.

Significantly, however, Becker viewed his accounts of time allocation and human capital as the culmination of the major social scientific projects of the previous century. Asserting that his "economic approach provides a unified framework for understanding behavior that has been long sought by and eluded Bentham, Comte, Marx, and others," Becker stripped exploitation of its explanatory power as an economic concept by positing

his neoliberal theory of time as the ultimate solution to the social theoretical puzzles of the nineteenth century—a sharp break with the economic
thought of the past, but a tacit continuation of its regime of progress as
well (1990, 14).

"TIME AND THE HOUR": MANUFACTURING VICTORIAN TEMPORALITY

During the nineteenth century, the individual's relationship to time was
transformed. Marx was among the first observers of modern industrial
capitalism to recognize this, and one of the tasks of Marxist historiography, especially since the 1967 publication of E.P. Thompson's influential
essay "Time, Work-Discipline and Industrial Capitalism," has been to sub-
stantiate and deepen our understanding of the social experience of this
radical change. Thompson argued that "the transition to mature industrial
society entailed a severe restructuring of working habits—new disciplines,
new incentives, and a new human nature upon which these incentives
could bite effectively," while also documenting the many ways that workers mounted resistance to the new temporal regime (1993, 354).[5] In this
section, I describe the production of this new regime of temporality
through a brief discussion of Thompson, then turning to a short essay on
watchmaking by Harriet Martineau to see how time, exploitation, and
progress were intertwined in the Victorian sociological imagination.

Thompson showed how over the course of the eighteenth and the first
half of the nineteenth century "time-measurement [emerged] as a means
of labour exploitation" (1993, 389). Whereas prior to industrialization
time had in some contexts been measured *by* labor (i.e. a length of time
might be conceived in terms of how long a common task took), time now
became the primary medium through which exploitation occurred. The
factory owner did not merely purchase workers' labor for a given amount
of time, but subordinated them to the regular, rationalized time of the
factory clock, trained them to work according to it and to reorganize their
social lives around it. The apparent objectivity of clock time proved compatible with more inward-facing modes of subjective discipline as well.
Structuring work around the regular divisibility of the day into hours and
the hour into minutes can be understood as part of the moral and spiritual
dimensions of the long-term rise of capitalism that Max Weber associated
with the Protestant ethic. But this subjective conditioning in turn made

possible a consciousness of the novelty and historical contingency of the new temporal regime. Time was newly experienced as objective and unrelenting, but for many workers the newness of this experience only drew attention to the fact that time was itself a malleable, protean medium, and that the reorganization of the workday around the seemingly inexorable ticking of the clock could be resisted.

Firsthand accounts of Victorian factory life make abundantly clear these transformations in the temporal structure of the nature of work. Thompson's sources often evidence the extent to which control over time was explicitly understood by factory owners to be a versatile means of disciplining and subordinating workers. "When I went to a spinning mill I was about seven years of age," James Myles reports in his autobiography, *Chapters in the Life of a Dundee Factory Worker* (1850), "I had to get out of bed every morning at five o'clock, commence work at half-past five, drop at nine for breakfast, work until two, which was the dinner hour, start again at half-past two, and continue until half-past seven at night":

> Such were the nominal hours; but in reality there were no regular hours, masters and managers did with us as they liked ... The clocks at the factories were often put forward in the morning and back at night, and instead of being instruments for the measurement of time, they were used as cloaks for cheatery and oppression. Though this was known amongst the hands, all were afraid to speak, and a workman then was afraid to carry a watch, as it was no uncommon event to dismiss any one who was presumed to know too much about the science of horology. (1850, 12–13)

In framing exploitation as systematic cheating, Myles echoes the prevailing opinion of Victorian social critics, such as Henry Mayhew, who sought to expose the dishonesty and unfairness of factory and workshop owners. Yet by the same token, we glean from Myles's remarks that the factory clock functioned upon its introduction into the workplace not only as an opportunity for malpractice, but as an organizational system that workers had to absorb, and against which they would come to measure that malpractice normatively. Thus, it is the workers in this scenario who must insist upon "regular hours," and who had to become scientists of horology. The reclamation of stolen minutes could only become a form of protest against abuse once time had become the medium through which exploitation transpired. As Thompson writes, by the time the Ten Hour Act was passed in 1847, workers "had accepted the categories of their employers and learned to fight back within them. They had learned their lesson, that time is money, only too well" (1993, 389).

Against this backdrop of historical change in the constitution of temporality, I now want to examine the role of time in Victorian capitalist apologetics in order to pave the way for subsequent discussion of time in neoclassical economic theory. To the proponents of nineteenth-century capitalism, the dominance of the new disciplinary regime of time was a necessary part of the development of modern industrial society. For such apologists, the subordination of workers to the production schedule was simply the price of the ticket for civilizational progress. Indeed, the wager made by Victorian political economy was that under capitalism (and only capitalism), labor time and historical progress could be measured by the same standard, thus making it counterproductive for government to interfere with the industrial production process on behalf of workers. To reduce or augment the amount of time workers spent working, they argued, would either slow down or accelerate Britain's progress on the ever-extending stepladder of history.[6] There was in this respect a recognition that time was heterogeneous and elastic, something that could speed up or slow down. Yet by the same token it was argued that such volatile changes were now over, consigned to the past, since the mechanisms of time-measurement had been perfected. The temporality of the future was the homogenous time of the railway and the factory clock, even though the discovery of this time was evidence of the unevenness and historical variability of time itself.

Martineau's short piece can help illuminate what is significant about this collapse of temporal registers in Victorian political economy. Published in 1852 in Charles Dickens's *Household Words*, Martineau's "Time and the Hour" sought to take readers to the scene of commodity production, making the fabrication of watches serve as a symbol of the alleged rational and technological progress of human civilization.[7] Martineau begins the piece by describing the development of increasingly precise techniques of time measurement as humankind's successful capture of the sublimity of the heavens. "We cannot but marvel at the perfection that men have reached in recording the passage of time," she writes, going on to exclaim:

> We see that time is given out, as it were, from the magnitudes and motions of the stars; and in that view, it seems a deed almost beyond estimate, that man should have caught this product, and made it record its own lapse from moment to moment … But to receive the full impression, we should go into

the work-shop where scores of men and boys are busy in making and arrang-
ing the materials—the hard, dead mineral materials—which are to give out
something intangible, unutterable, as real as themselves, yet purely ideal in
its connexion with us. (1852, 556)

In this passage, Martineau describes time as an ethereal "product" that has
merely been "caught" by human technological ingenuity. The suggestion
is that time is something that exists naturally, objectively and independently of human culture, but that it is nonetheless rendered utile and even
produced by the latter. In this sense, the production process itself is pressed
into the service of a longer historical process of technological advance.
This narrative begins with sun dials and "the sharp line of the shadow
drawn on the glaring sands of the desert, by the mute and immovable
Pyramid of Cheops," but it ends with the manufacture of British watches
for export, such as "those made for the market of Alexandria" (556, 558).
The Egyptian references are meant as bookends; in Martineau's telling,
there is an unbroken line connecting the primeval discovery of time to the
production of time for a global market propped up by British imperialism.
    Invoking this *longue durée* of civilizational progress, Martineau strives
to abstract from the scene of production: "That men by putting together
brass and steel, and a jewel or two, and some engraved marks should present to us, as in a mirror, the simultaneous doings of the stars in the sky,"
she writes, "seems to raise the work-room into a place of contemplation or
eloquent discourse" (556). Yet although Martineau wants to describe the
watchmaking workshop as removed from the normal material conditions
of work, she does acknowledge the price labor exacts from the body. In
the production of watches, the particular physical cost of labor is the loss
of vision. Noting that "the eye is usually worn out in a much shorter time"
than the span of a career, she ends the short essay by observing that the
eyesight of her guide through the shop floor had already begun to fail. His
incipient blindness, she explains, was the result of squinting and straining
his eyes specifically in order to paint the minute marks, "with the utmost
exactness," onto the face of the watches. "We could understand,"
Martineau writes, "how the excessively small figures were done, though
hardly how human eyes could stand such a trial" (559). It is thus the eloquent, contemplative work involved in the very act of representing the
celestial substance of time as regularly measurable minutes that places the
greatest strain on the human body—a strain which renders the use of a
watch impossible.

Martineau's recognition of the violence of this labor is not meant as a critique of exploitation. To the contrary, she stresses only the compensatory nature of the manufacture of time. "It is sad to think how the senses and faculties of some are overstrained to minister to the luxuries of others," Martineau writes, in the essay's last paragraph. But ultimately this violence is offset by the gains its yields:

> If we could reconcile ourselves to this at all, it would not be in the case of any toys, be their beauty and the money value of them what they may; but in the production of this exquisite talisman, the watch, which can tell us, in the interval of tides and sunsets, where the stars are, and what they are doing, behind the veil of the noonday light and the midnight cloud. (559)

Not all production is worth the violence it enacts. But measured against the civilizational value of the use of time as a technology of measurement, the physical cost of labor for the worker is insignificant. The worker sacrifices his sight in order to make visible to others the momentous and otherwise hidden flow of time.

Martineau strives to bring the labor of watchmaking so completely under the sign of technological progress as to make plain to her reader that the violence of work is simply the natural cost of having access to time. However, here Martineau, seemingly unwittingly, describes a strange nexus of working time, exploitation and the movement of progress. Not only is it the case that the labor of watchmaking can be said to contribute to the forward momentum of civilization, but Martineau also implies that the violence of that work can itself be measured temporally, as the effect of an acceleration of time. Cementing this connection, Martineau observes of her guide that "by working in a blaze of sun-light he 'aged' his sight thirty years in a single fortnight [and] now requires strong magnifiers to work at all" (559). Time is, in this account, the medium through which the violence of work transpires. Work makes time move faster, makes it leave its marks on the body sooner. Whereas the strain on the body was the specific consequence of the rendering of time into regular units, these very same units are also used to measure the specific strain that this labor places on the body, which comes to look like a distortion of time.

Martineau's sketch offers a remarkably condensed account of the prevailing Victorian political economic justifications of exploitation. What sets her account apart from other more boilerplate apologias is the recognition that work, its violence, and the alleged progress it yields, are all comprised of the same rationalized units. These units become available as a medium of social organization with the discovery and dissemination of the clock, which Martineau equates with the achieved state of European modernity, itself seen as the high-water mark of the longer-term advance of techno-rational progress. Martineau wants us to understand the advent of clock time as the capture of a homogeneous temporal substance that was already there, waiting to be discovered. But in fact, she describes something quite different: the production scene of the technological implement of time measurement, which not only quantifies the length of the working day, but also its physical violence. The violence, however, reflects a temporal aberration, the acceleration of time, the squeezing of thirty years of "aging" into two weeks of hard work. "With increased productivity," Moishe Postone has observed, "the time unit becomes denser" (1993, 292). We wind up with the bizarre sense of time's simultaneous elasticity and its rigidity, the irregularity of its accelerations alongside the rationalized character of the punch clock.

EQUILIBRIUM ON THE PLATEAU OF PROGRESS

Martineau's description of the manufacture of time anticipates significant problems that the analysis of temporality would pose to neoclassical economic theory as the nineteenth century drew to a close. Like Martineau's account of the violent acceleration of temporality in the labor of watchmaking, the later difficulties derived from the entanglement of matters of time measurement with the more wide-ranging enthusiasm for civilizational progress. If anything, the increasing mathematical sophistication of economic methodology had the effect of exacerbating rather than allaying this confusion of temporal registers. The more precision and scientific credibility economics could claim for itself, the less its *fin de siècle* practitioners felt the need to interrogate their uncritical presumption that modern capitalist society represented the historical terminus of the progressive development of civilization. Indeed, economics understood both the development of capitalism and the emergence of its own disciplinary innovations as outcomes of the same civilizational processes, which were described in heavily racialized terms. The opening chapters of Alfred Marshall's influential *Principles of Economics* (1890) epitomize this self-confirming narrative: unlike members of allegedly "primitive" cultures, Marshall explains, members of modern and specifically white capitalist societies had developed capacities for "a deliberation and yet a promptness of choice and judgment, and a habit of forecasting the future and of shaping one's course with reference to distant aims" that made them especially suited for economic activity no less than for economic thought (1890, 5).[8]

Neoclassical economics imagined that the result of the forward march of progress would be the economic mastery over time and the subdual of the uncertainty of the future. In effect, it offered an unlikely model of historical development as a kind of steep plateau: with the uncertain process of scaling the edifice of modernity safely in the past, the future would now stretch out endlessly in plain view, protected from change. Yet this fantasy of a future known just as well as the past was extraordinarily difficult to square with even the most basic challenges that the nature of time posed to economic analysis. Marshall was acutely aware of these challenges, asserting in the opening paragraphs of *Principles of Economics* that "the element of Time … is the centre of the chief difficulty of almost every economic problem" (xxi). There was a fundamental friction between economics and time, Marshall observed, that arose from the methodological need to impose periods onto the dynamic flux of time. Although he could admit that "Nature knows no absolute partition of time into long periods and short," Marshall nevertheless saw that economics could not do without the convention of carving up of time into such segments, since the length of a given period is a basic constituent of economic calculation.

This tension between the "absolutely continuous" nature of time and the need to impose temporal divisions in order to make sense of economic phenomena was most pronounced in the context of the theory of general equilibrium. Articulated most fully by Léon Walras in the 1870s, the concept of equilibrium inspired in Marshall a mild skepticism. In order to determine equilibrium prices, one had to describe a specific duration of market activity, but, as Marshall recognized, this methodological dependency on the period had no real basis in the empirical reality of time. Indeed, the point of equilibrium theory was to postulate temporally static frames of given duration within which optimal prices could be derived from granular calibrations of supply and demand. If this was to have mathematically predictive value, it meant that rational choices about a given market had to be able to be mathematically reconciled in advance. Seen in practical terms, however, the pre-reconciliation of choices represented a kind of rejection of time, as G.L.S. Shackles observes, since it presumed that all the actors in a given economic scenario would make their choices simultaneously. "The world of pre-reconciled choice," Shackle writes, "must therefore be in effect timeless, it must have no 'earlier' or 'later' in respect of choice" (2017, 265).[9] A period of equilibrium was in this sense a length of time that had been constructed to serve as a repudiation of time.

Though he understood equilibrium thinking to involve a problematic abstraction from time, Marshall maintained that it nevertheless contributed to the general increase of scientific knowledge about the economy. His ambivalence is striking and, I would argue, represents part of the legacy of neoclassical economic thought. In a lengthy analogy, for example, Marshall compares the physical equilibrium reached by a falling stone dangling from a string to "the oscillations of the scale of production" of a market as it tends toward economic equilibrium. Yet this elaborate comparison to physics rapidly resolves into a rejection of the terms of the initial metaphor itself: "But in real life such oscillations are seldom as rhythmical as those of a stone hanging freely from a string; the comparison would be more exact if the string were supposed to hang in the troubled waters of a mill-race, whose stream was at one time allowed to flow freely, and at another partially cut off," he writes, adding, "These considerations point to the great importance of the element of Time in relation to demand and supply" (405).[10] In this repudiation of one analogy by another, one can see Marshall bumping up against the limitations imposed by the very disciplinary norms and premises that organized his inquiry. For time here comes to seem like an insurmountable obstacle to equilibrium theory, even though equilibrium itself was introduced into economics precisely as a way of understanding how markets behave over time. Thus, time is what reveals the metaphor of equilibrium to have been a mistaken figure or catachresis.

Marshall was an innovative thinker, whose response to encountering the limitations of economic theory was to introduce complexity and nuance when possible. Faced with the problem of the static nature of equilibria, he responded with the notion of different lengths of period. The idea of longer and shorter periods still abstracts from time, but the "long run" also allowed Marshall to introduce uncertainty more directly into the analysis of market calibration. An outbreak of disease among livestock might lead to a temporary rise in the demand for fish, he suggests, which might in turn contribute to a long-term distaste for meat; or it might also lead eventually to overfishing, or to fishing in deeper waters, or better organization of the fishing industry, and so on. The length of the period conditions the nature of the equilibrium a market reaches. What these examples show is Marshall's simultaneous eagerness and inability to accommodate the transformative and variable power of time in economic analysis: "Fragmentary statical hypotheses are used as temporary auxilia-ries to dynamical—or rather biological—conceptions," he writes, "but the central idea of economics, even when its Foundations alone are under discussion, must be that of living force and movement" (1977, xxi). Yet in these attempts to grapple with time, abstract time itself always remains constant, the invariant condition against which all other phenomena can be measured. In this regard, neoclassical economics could not account for the aberrant acceleration of time that becomes legible in the figural mar-gins of Martineau's sketch, where a man ages years in the course of a few weeks on the job. What is not just lacking but unthinkable in neoclassical economics is precisely that sense of the mutability of time itself—not merely of its inexorable forward march, but of its elasticity as a social stan-dard subject in its own right to "living force and movement."

Exploitation as the Usurpation of Time

Marx was the first critic of capitalism to theorize the exploitation of labor in terms of the transformation of the social usages of time.[11] He built his case on the substantial empirical evidence amassed by the Victorian factory inspectors, whose reports trumpeted on page after page that "moments are the elements of profit" (Marx 1977, 353). To reiterate, Marx's start-ing point was that time had come to function as the dynamic principle of social domination in the production of surplus value under the system of capitalist exploitation. However, he also understood that classical political economy was a formalist discourse that not only had no real means of representing social dynamism but rather was designed to exclude it. Consequently, Marx rolls out his theory of exploitation over the course of two methodologically distinct chapters of *Capital*. First, in chapter nine, "The Rate of Surplus-Value," he presents his theory in formal economic terms; in the following chapter, "The Working Day," he provides a histori-cal account of the increasing regulation of working time, before and after the passage of the Factory Acts. Marx was therefore able to account for exploitation from two seemingly incompatible perspectives: the dominant perspective of political economic discourse, in which exploitation could only appear as a static formal relation, and a socially critical perspective rooted in historical narrative and focused on the variability of time. The stark contrast between the two chapters allows Marx to address shortcom-ings in the way that political economy understood the social determina-tion of time, while also suggesting that the workers' struggle for control over the working day could itself be seen to resolve labor into a formal relation of exchange.

In chapter nine, Marx seeks to demonstrate that "the rate of surplus-value is … an exact expression for the degree of exploitation of labour-power by capital, or of the worker by the capitalist" (1977, 326–327). In these terms, surplus value is the quantity of value produced above and beyond what workers receive in payment for their labor. Therefore, if a worker produces as much surplus value in a day as she is paid, then the rate of exploitation is one hundred percent. To recall, this is where we encounter Marx's argument that a worker "works one half of the day for himself, the other half for the capitalist," which Marx also describes as a split between necessary and surplus time. Although the theory of the rate of exploitation as described in chapter nine forms the heart of Marxian economic doctrine, it was precisely this aspect of Marx's argument that was subjected to the most vehement repudiation by his late nineteenth-century marginalist critics. For these later critics, it was possible to derive a commodity's value from its marginal utility, and to show that labor only entered into the picture as one among other factors contributing to the supply side of equilibrium pricing. After all these additional factors were taken into consideration, the rate of exploitation would become negligible. Taken on its own, the theory of exploitation lacks the dynamism to forcefully answer these critiques. Yet neither did those critiques take into account the more substantial analysis of time that Marx develops in the very next chapter.

In "The Working Day," Marx assembles his readings of the factory inspectors' reports into a narrative detailing the decades-long struggle over the length of the working day. As David Harvey has observed, it is in this transition from the theory of surplus value to the discussion of the working day that Marx first raises the problem of "the command of the social nature of temporality itself" (2010, 134). Suddenly, the static quantities of labor time from the previous chapter give way to a grueling account of the funhouse distortions of working time. The limit to the working day, Marx asserts at the chapter's beginning, is "not a constant, but a variable quantity," which is "determined by the duration of the surplus labor" and conditioned only by the physical limits on human labor and "the general level of civilization"; "these limiting conditions," Marx adds, "are of a very elastic nature, and allow a tremendous amount of latitude." Here we encounter a catalog of cheating and abuse focused almost exclusively on what Marx refers to as the "usurpation" of time:

These "small thefts" of capital from the workers' meal-times and recreation times are also described by the factory inspectors as "petty pilferings of minutes," "snatching a few minutes," or, in the technical language of the workers, "nibbling and cribbling at meal-times."

It is evident that in this atmosphere the formation of surplus-value by surplus labor is no secret. "If you allow me (as I was informed by a highly respectable master) to work only ten minutes in the day over-time, you put one thousand a year in my pocket." "Moments are the elements of profit." (353)

Marx's analysis has significant consequences for our discussion. In the first place, Marx here forcefully asserts that control over time measurement is the power relation through which exploitation takes place, and that this form of social subordination is not reducible to a formal relationship. The capitalist class not only demands so many hours of work per day in order to maximize profit, but it also actively constructs and disfigures what counts as an hour for a worker, "hounding him hither and thither, in scattered shreds of time" (403). This deformation of time cannot be adequately contested through an appeal to formal rights or rules or fairness. Rather, it must be contested through "force": "Hence, in the history of capitalist production, the establishment of a norm for the working day presents itself as a struggle over the limits of that day, a struggle between collective capital, i.e. the class of capitalists, and collective labour, i.e. the working class" (344). In other words, the social constitution of time is the outcome of class struggle.

Moreover, once one admits the social constitution of time as a power relation, it becomes difficult to maintain the model of temporality inherent in the concept of economic equilibrium.[12] As we have already seen, equilibrium theory presupposes—however ambivalently—the stability of time as an unreactive given in order to avoid confronting the dynamism of time as a source of uncertainty and unforeseeable change. John Hicks puts it concisely: "A state of equilibrium, by definition, is a state in which something, something relevant, is *not* changing; so the use of an equilibrium concept is a signal that time, in some respect at least, has been put to one side" (1976, 140). Marx's argument that the socially necessary labor hour is constituted through class struggle, force and domination has implications for the theory of equilibrium and later economic doctrines premised on it that extend beyond this critique. In light of Marx's analysis, it becomes insufficient simply to fault equilibrium theory for neglecting the inexorable march of time as a source of uncertainty. Rather, Marx insists on the volatility of time. This volatility renders it inadequate even as an axis of measurement because its constitution as a measure depends on conflict inherent in the labor process. As Postone puts it, "the abstract temporal constant ... is both constant and non-constant" (1993, 292). Even if one accepts the marginalist critique of Marx's theory of surplus value, the elasticity of the socially constituted labor hour still introduces volatility into the equilibrium scenario. As Harvey notes, "If there is an equilibrium point for class struggle, it is not fixed, nor is it known" (2010, 159).

Marx's analysis picks up on precisely the variable aspect of labor time that Martineau's paean to Victorian progress registered but could only account for as a temporal aberration. The apparent contradiction that one might age thirty years from just two weeks of work expresses something that is actually very close to Marx's argument about the social basis of the hour. But for Marx, the irregularity of the hour is the norm, not the exception, even though it cannot be represented that way by the discourse of political economy. An hour will, under the capitalist temporal system, always remain an hour, a fixed unit of time unaltered by changes in its social composition.[13] As Thompson showed, the task of keeping regular hours fell not to Victorian factory owners, as one might assume, but to their workers, who had to surrender themselves to the new time structure in order to arrive at the basic scenario Marx outlines in chapter nine, in which surplus is generated out of the apparently commensurate exchange of wages for labor time. One of Marx's most singular accomplishments in theorizing exploitation was to recognize the violence, lived out by working people as a collective struggle with an uncertain outcome, inherent to this process of commensuration, in which the hour is made to run in order to stand still.

FLEXIBLE TIME AND PERSONAL EQUILIBRIUM

Over the last half-century, critics of late capitalism have suggested that current conceptions of time need to be fundamentally reimagined in order to keep up with new economic realities. Among these critics, Frederic Jameson has gone so far as to describe an "end of temporality," characteristic of late capitalist societies. "Older habits of clock time are ... eclipsed," Jameson writes of this historical transition, "the 'signifier' of the single day called into question," and "some new nonchronological and nontemporal pattern of immediacies comes into being." In Jameson's view, immediacy, simultaneity and other non-successive relations are the terms which best capture this transfigured economic present, such as the "displacement of old-fashioned industrial labor by the new cybernetic kind," the "opposition between 'Fordism' and a newly 'flexible' capitalism," as well as financialization and the shift to a globalized post- or neocolonial economy from one organized around Europe's exploitation of its colonies (2003, 707).

In this final section, I want to draw on the preceding discussion of time and exploitation in order to return to the broader questions raised in the opening section about the persistence of a nineteenth-century frame of reference in the present. Jameson's observations about the end of temporality might easily be described as an account of the disintegration of the very edifices of nineteenth-century capitalism I have been describing throughout—structures of exploitation and domination no less than the temporal structures on which they were founded. However, this compelling account of the orderly transition into disordered time raises more questions than it answers. Most crucially for my discussion, Jameson's metaphor of the "eclipse" of one regime of temporality by another highlights the need for contemporary critics of neoliberalism to spell out more precisely the linkages between historical and chronological modes of time measurement. For if the figure used to represent historical transition between phases of capitalism remains one of linear succession, then one might justifiably ask to what extent the temporal structure has been altered or disturbed. Conversely, given what I have characterized as the evacuation of time that sat at the heart of the neoclassical elaboration of economic progress, it becomes important to consider whether neoliberal capitalism has in fact ushered in the end of temporality or simply amplified some of the most enduring and characteristic ideological obfuscations in nineteenth-century economic discourse's treatment of time.

This question is best addressed by turning to the stories about temporality and the culmination of historical progress that have been spun and promulgated by neoliberal capitalist thinkers themselves. Becker's theory of time allocation would, he believed, provide closure to the social scientific problems that had stymied the great minds of the nineteenth century—a form of succession which I described earlier as both a repudiation of the nineteenth century and a tacit and uncritical prolongation of its regime of progress. However, for all its novelty, I remain skeptical that Becker's theory of time allocation represented the stark departure he claimed.

Becker anchored his new "economic approach to human behavior" in three specific neoclassical assumptions, namely, "maximizing behavior, market equilibrium, and stable preferences" (1990, 5). On the basis of this presumptively secure theoretical platform, however, Becker sought to reevaluate conceptual distinctions fundamental to economic discourse, such as those between work and non-work, as well as production and consumption. Becker's starting point is the realization of the extraordinary and unmined productivity of time. He writes:

> Economic development has led to a large secular decline in the work week, so that whatever may have been true of the past, to-day it is below fifty hours in most countries, less than a third of the total time available. Consequently, the allocation and efficiency of non-working time may now be more important to economic welfare than working time; yet the attention paid by economists to the latter dwarfs any paid to the former. (89)

This passage serves as the quasi-historical foundation to Becker's subsequent reevaluation of time and decentering of labor. Suggesting that the economic significance of non-working time has increased with the decreasing length of the work week, he attributes this important shift to "economic development" over a long period of market equilibrium stretching back into the previous century. Though Becker does not elaborate, the implication is that technological progress has driven this development, resulting in increased productivity and so shorter hours. Although Becker was not unique in his dismissal of the impact of collective political movements on labor conditions, what is unique to his work—and uniquely troubling—was its idiosyncratic and inconsistent manner of making use of progress in order to conceptualize the passage into a new regime of temporality.

The basic premise of Becker's theory of time allocation was that quantitative economic analysis could shed new light on the possibilities for optimizing the individual use of non-working time. Becker was in this regard acutely aware of the ways in which time measurement functioned under capitalism as a disciplinary force. Rather than being subject to the unyielding discipline of the factory clock, however, Becker construes the individual in its own right as a kind of factory or business venture—an enterprise of the self that produces its own satisfaction, as Foucault had already observed in the late 1970s.[14] It is around this complex point that Becker appears most clearly to make a break with earlier economic doctrines and to upend traditional economic categories. For if the individual is an enterprise engaged in producing and consuming its own utility in the form of human capital, then the line between working for oneself and working for someone else is effaced. Indeed, Becker seeks to blur the distinction between working and non-working time *per se*, arguing that most utilizations of time already hybridize work and non-work: "Is commuting work, non-work, or both?" he writes, "How about a business lunch, a good diet or relaxation?" In this light, Becker argues that most if not all forms of activity ought to be understood as commodities falling somewhere on a spectrum of "productive consumption." Even "pure work," he explains, can be understood as a commodity, albeit one "in which the contribution to consumption is nil," just as "pure consumption" is a commodity one consumes "in which the contribution to work is nil" (100).

Becker's analysis of time allocation and human capital seems to turn traditional neoclassical economic theory on its head: work becomes a commodity consumed by the worker, leisure becomes a form of productive and accumulative activity, and exploitation becomes unthinkable, since one is always first and foremost an employee of the firm of oneself. However, this argument also keeps in place the basic disciplinary function of time as a measure of economic productivity. The crucial innovation in Becker's account is that individual productivity is measured in terms of performance as a producer of human capital, which is to say, in terms of the optimization of time allocation. Here it becomes important to reflect on the function of Becker's commitment to equilibrium theory as one of the three axiomatic foundations of his thought. For if the individual is a firm, then the optimization of her allocation of time between production and consumption—her perpetually choosing how best to spend her time—is analogous to the reconciliation of a firm's economic choices within the hypothetical determination of market equilibrium. In Becker's theory of time, that is, the neoclassical idea of equilibrium is internalized, brought within the domain of individual activity, where it functions as a disciplinary norm conditioning behavior. Yet as I have argued throughout this chapter, equilibrium thinking is a means of conceptualizing time that nonetheless depends on the repudiation of time's social constitution and elasticity; and it was this renunciation of time in the service of predicting economic outcomes that was the central innovation of the nineteenth-century ideology of progress.

Martineau was able to regard the toll exacted on her working contemporaries and argue that the extraordinary violence of the nineteenth century was offset by gains that would be realized in the future. Historical expectation was the mechanism for alleviating the accumulation of damages caused by ever greater demands for labor to fuel the engines of progress. Yet even in her apologetics, Martineau could not help but report the lurid funhouse distortions of time that were caused by the process of economic development. The hour was not a fixed unit, but a ductile medium of exploitation, though Martineau and other proponents of capitalism after her have proved incapable of accounting fully for the dynamism of time. Since the nineteenth century, this dynamism has only been fully acknowledged by the analysis of exploitation. I have been proposing that this evasion and occlusion of time itself constitutes one of the most enduring contributions of nineteenth-century economic thought to that of the present, manifested in the nineteenth-century frame of reference that informs contemporary discussions of exploitation, no less than in the renunciation of time that lies at the heart of Becker's theory of time. Yet for Becker and other neoliberal theorists, historical expectation no longer serves as a mechanism for justifying exploitation, as it did for Martineau and other Victorians. Rather than looking forward, they look back, turning to the nineteenth century, making use of it, putting it to work, disfiguring it in the act of imagining a world in which exploitation not only did not happen but can never take place.

NOTES

1. Starting shortly after Marx's death in 1883, the labor theory of value was subjected to a series of critiques from which, in the eyes of most later economists, it would never quite recover. In the late 1970s, Anglo-American "analytical" Marxists attempted in particular to produce theories of exploitation that did not depend on the value theory, most influentially G.A. Cohen (1979) and John Roemer (1982). For related accounts of the continued relevance of Marx's theory of exploitation in the aftermath of the critique of the labor theory of value, see especially Diane Elson (2015) and Joan Robinson (1972).
2. Moishe Postone offers an important interpretation in *Time, Labor, and Social Domination* (1993) that has greatly influenced my thinking in this essay.
3. For an elaboration of the notion of the structure of feeling, see Raymond Williams (1977).

4. Becker recognized that his theory of human capital would be seen by many as a contortion of the Marxist theory of exploitation, but he flippantly dismissed such critiques: "It is easy to appreciate the problems created for this view by the human capital concept. For if capital exploits labor, does human capital exploit labor too—in other words, do some workers exploit other workers? And are skilled and unskilled workers pitted against each other in the alleged class conflict between labor and capital? If governments are to expropriate all capital to end such conflict, should they also expropriate human capital, so that governments would take over ownership of workers as well?" (Becker 1993, 16).

5. Similar to Thompson, Jacques Rancière argued that French workers' resistance to the transition to industrial capitalism involved the struggle "to take back the time that was refused them," and that "these gains in time and freedom were not marginal phenomena or diversions in relation to the construction of the workers' movement and its great objectives," but rather the very means by which political goals were realized (Rancière 2012, ix). Beyond the strictly European context, Chris Taylor has also argued provocatively that "Caribbean histories of slavery and emancipation constitute the political unconscious of [late twentieth-century] anti-work Marxism," suggesting that "alternative temporalities and modalities of sociality" are still to be recovered through the study of the resistance to labor time in post-emancipation Caribbean society (Taylor 2014, 2, 16).

6. In a lengthy invective in *Capital*, for example, Marx ridiculed the Victorian political economist Nassau Senior, who in fulminating against the reduction of the working day had insisted that factory owners' "whole net profit is derived *from the last hour*" (Marx 1977, 339).

7. Martineau was an ardent defender of industrial capitalism and a fierce opponent of economic regulation and workplace safety laws. In an 1855 pamphlet titled *The Factory Controversy: A Warning Against Meddling Legislation*, published by the National Association of Factory Occupiers, Martineau argued that government regulation of factory conditions constituted a form of "social oppression," a tendentious position over which she broke publicly and acrimoniously with Dickens. Prior to their falling out, however, Dickens had published over fifty pieces by Martineau. These pieces ranged widely in focus from studies of disability to current events, but a majority of them were episodic descriptions of various scenes of commodity production, such as "What There is in a Button," "How to Get Paper," "Cheshire Cheese," "Needles," and "Rainbow Making."

8. Marshall was unabashed about the white supremacism of his racial theory of economic progress. "There seems no reason to doubt," he asserts in the opening chapters of his *magnum opus*, "that nearly all the chief pioneers of progress have been Aryans who, in successive waves, have spread over

Europe and Asia from early homes in lands of frost and snow" (1890, 16). Attending to this distorted aspect of Marshall's thinking suggests that Hannah Arendt's landmark analysis of "race-thinking before racism" in nineteenth-century social thought ought to be extended further into the economic domain (Arendt 1979). On this topic, see Simon John Cook (2013).

9. Sharpening his polemic, Shackle writes elsewhere that "*all individuals simultaneously* must, if they are each to act rationally, have a knowledge, at the moment when each makes his choice, of what each other individual is choosing...If all such actions are simultaneous, it follows that the world we study must be deemed a timeless or momentary world. Rationality and time are alien to each other" (1988, 142). For related critiques of the inherent timelessness of equilibrium theory, see, among others, Nicholas Kaldor (1985), John R. Hicks (1976) and, more recently, Frank Ackerman (2002).

10. The analogy is also fruitfully read in light of Philip Mirowski's analysis of the role of the discourse of physics in the scientific development of classical and neoclassical economics in general, and in the notion of economic equilibrium in particular (1989, 238–241).

11. Even though time was widely recognized as a major axis of the industrial capitalist economy, no significant social critics before Marx had theorized exploitation in temporal terms. Instead, they tended to raise ethical–political questions of natural right and fairness. Pierre-Joseph Proudhon, for instance, argued in *What Is Property?* (1840) that the "laborer retains, even after his wages, a natural right of property in the thing he has produced" (1993, 88). Henry Mayhew, by contrast, argued that the abuses of the Victorian labor system could be understood as an organized structure of cheating that centered on the fairness or equity of wages (1851).

12. There is longstanding debate about the extent to which Marx's economic apparatus itself falls within the tradition of equilibrium theorizing. See, for instance, Kei Shibata (1933), Samuel Hollander (1981), Dušan Pokorny (1985) and Alan Freeman (1995).

13. Here I continue to draw on Postone's remarks concerning Marx's derivation of historical time, which Postone distinguishes from progressive abstract time as "the movement *of* time, as opposed to the movement *in* time." "In a sense," he elaborates, "changes in productivity move the determination of socially necessary labor time along an axis of abstract time: socially necessary labor time decreases with increased productivity. But, although the social labor hour is thereby redetermined, it is not moved along that axis—because it is the coordinate axis itself, the frame against which change is measured. The hour is the constant unit of abstract time; it must remain fixed in abstract temporal terms." Postone describes

this sense of the ongoing process of stabilizing the social labor hour as producing a "treadmill effect" in capitalist temporality (Postone 1993, 289, 292–294).

14. In a series of remarkably prescient lectures, Foucault influentially argued that Becker had ushered in a new conception of *homo œconomicus* as "an entrepreneur of himself," which had supplanted the previous liberal conception of *homo œconomicus* as "a partner of exchange" (Foucault 2008, 226). For a comprehensive and moderately critical take on Foucault's readings of Becker, see Wendy Brown (2015).

REFERENCES

Ackerman, Frank. 2002. Still Dead After All These Years: Interpreting the Failure of General Equilibrium Theory. *Journal of Economic Methodology* 9 (2): 119–139.

Arendt, Hannah. 1979. Race-Thinking Before Racism. In *The Origins of Totalitarianism*. New York: Harcourt, Inc.

Becker, Gary S. 1990. A Theory of the Allocation of Time. In *The Economic Approach to Human Behavior*. Chicago: University of Chicago Press.

———. 1993. *Human Capital: A Theoretical and Empirical Analysis With Special Reference to Education*. Chicago: University of Chicago Press.

Brown, Wendy. 2015. *Undoing the Demos: Neoliberalism's Stealth Revolution*. New York: Zone Books.

Cohen, G.A. 1979. The Labor Theory of Value and the Concept of Exploitation. *Philosophy and Public Affairs* 8 (4): 338–360.

Cook, Simon John. 2013. Race and Nation in Marshall's Theories. *European Journal of the History of Economic Thought* 20 (6): 940–956.

Elson, Diane, ed. 2015. *Value: The Representation of Labour in Capitalism*. New York: Verso Books.

Foucault, Michel. 2008. *The Birth of Biopolitics: Lectures at the Collège de France, 1978–1979*. Translated by Graham Burchell. New York: Picador.

Freeman, Alan. 1995. Marx Without Equilibrium. *Capital and Class* 19 (2): 49–86.

Harvey, David. 2010. *A Companion to Marx's Capital*. New York: Verso.

Hicks, John R. 1976. Some Questions of Time in Economics. In *Evolution, Welfare, and Time in Economics*, ed. A.M. Tang, 135–151. Lexington: D.C. Heath.

Hochschild, Arlie. 2012. *The Managed Heart: Commercialization of Human Feeling*. Berkeley: University of California Press.

Hollander, Samuel. 1981. Marxian Economics as 'General Equilibrium Theory'. *History of Political Economy* 13 (1): 121–155.

Jameson, Frederic. 2003. The End of Temporality. *Critical Inquiry* 29 (4): 695–718.

Kaldor, Nicholas. 1985. *Economics Without Equilibrium*. New York: M.E. Sharpe, Inc.

Marshall, Alfred. 1890. *Principles of Economics*. London: Macmillan.

———. 1977. *Principles of Economics, Eighth Edition*. New York: Prometheus Books.

Martineau, Harriet. 1852. Time and the Hour. *Household Words* 4 (102): 555–559.

Marx, Karl. 1977. *Capital, Volume 1*. Translated by Ben Fowkes. New York: Vintage Books.

Mayhew, Henry. 1851. *Low Wages: Their Causes, Consequences and Remedies*. London: Printed by the Author.

Mirowski, Philip. 1989. *More Heat than Light: Economics as Social Physics, Physics as Nature's Economics*. New York: Cambridge University Press.

Myles, James. 1850. *Chapters in the Life of a Dundee Factory Boy: An Autobiography*. London: Simpkin, Marshall and Co.

Pokorny, Dušan. 1985. Karl Marx and General Equilibrium. *History of Political Economy* 17 (1): 109–132.

Postone, Moishe. 1993. *Time, Labor, and Social Domination*. New York: Cambridge University Press.

Proudhon, Pierre-Joseph. 1993. *What Is Property*. New York: Cambridge University Press.

Rancière, Jacques. 2012. *Proletarian Nights: The Workers' Dream in Nineteenth-Century France*. New York: Verso Books.

Robinson, Joan. 1972. *An Essay on Marxian Economics*. London: Macmillan.

Roemer, John. 1982. *A General Theory of Exploitation*. Cambridge: Harvard University Press.

Shackle, G.L.S. 1988. Marginalism: The Harvest. In *Business, Time and Thought: Selected Papers of G.L.S. Shackle*, 136–150. New York: Macmillan.

———. 2017. *Epistemics and Economics: A Critique of Economic Doctrines*. New Jersey: Transaction Publishers.

Shibata, Kei. 1933. Marx's Analysis of Capitalism and the General Equilibrium of the Lausanne School. *Kyoto University Economic Review* 8 (1): 107–136.

Taylor, Chris. 2014. The Refusal of Work: From the Postemancipation Caribbean to Post-Fordist Empire. *Small Axe* 44: 1–17.

Terkel, Studs. 2004. *Working: People Talk About What They Do All Day and How They Feel About What They Do*. New York: The New Press.

Thompson, E.P. 1993. Time, Work-Discipline, and Industrial Capitalism. In *Customs in Common: Studies in Traditional Popular Culture*, 352–403. New York: The New Press.

Williams, Raymond. 1977. *Marxism and Literature*. New York: Oxford University Press.

CHAPTER 4

Slavery

Forgetting Cairnes: *The Slave Power* (1862) and the Political Economy of Racism

Gordon Bigelow

This chapter explores the following question: how has economic knowledge in the modern period been shaped by its relation to Atlantic slavery? My consideration will be a preliminary one, focused on an 1862 book by the Irish political economist John Elliot Cairnes. The broader question is striking and significant, however. Classical political economy emerged during the age of the slave trade and the development of the early tools of finance capitalism intertwined with it.[1] The passage from "political economy" to "economics" roughly coincides with the era of Reconstruction in the United States—W.S. Jevons's influential call for the renaming emerged in 1871 (Jevons 1957). The turn to neoclassical economics secured a methodological individualism that made it difficult to consider the social force exerted by groups.[2] One result was to obscure the economic and material legacies of slavery and the economic impact of racism in the present.

G. Bigelow (✉)
Rhodes College, Memphis, TN, USA

© The Author(s) 2019
E. Hadley et al. (eds.), *From Political Economy to Economics through Nineteenth-Century Literature*, Palgrave Studies in Literature, Culture and Economics, https://doi.org/10.1007/978-3-030-24158-2_4

A useful interpretive analogue for the project I have in mind can be found in Timothy Mitchell's 2011 book *Carbon Democracy*, which proposes that the shifting contours of democratic and anti-democratic politics in the twentieth century depended substantially on the concentrated energy sources tapped in fossil fuel deposits. I am interested here in a sub-claim of Mitchell's broader thesis: economics, as academic discipline and policy workshop, should itself be understood as a kind of "petroknowledge." "Like twentieth-century democracy," he writes, "twentieth-century economic expertise developed in a specific relationship to the hydrocarbon age" (Mitchell 2011, 139, 123). Nineteenth-century economics likewise developed in a specific relationship to the slave trade, enslaved labor, and the regimes of segregation that followed Reconstruction in the U.S. Cairnes's *The Slave Power* offers an illuminating passage in this history. Published in the second year of the American Civil War, it is a forceful attack on slavery and the moral and practical claims advanced in its defense. It was written quickly to respond to the pro-confederate voices dominating British coverage of the war, relying on information from recent books on American society (Blackett 2000, 27, 139; Weinberg 1968, 18–27). As a result, its impact was muted, and historians who discuss the book tend to focus on the limitations it inherited from its sources (Fogel and Engerman 1989; Smith, M. 2003; see also Maas 2015). However, the potential consequences of its argument are more sweeping than these accounts have recognized, offering pointed revaluations, for instance, of the relation between the market and society and between slavery and capital.

The Slave Power proposes that because of a variety of geographical and socio-cultural circumstances, production using enslaved labor had become highly stable and profitable in North America. Unsurprising as this insight might appear now, this conclusion by Cairnes overturned a century of mainstream thinking. It represented a crisis of method for Victorian political economy, since Cairnes's framing of the incentives at work in the slave states exploded the discipline's founding assumptions. The book demonstrates that the force of individual self-interest in a competitive marketplace has not exercised a liberalizing effect in American society but has instead built, and now sustains, a slave empire. The suggestion that arises in Cairnes's analysis is that slavery is a practice internal to capitalism, not a barbarous anomaly. Cairnes thus destabilizes the idea, axiomatic from Adam Smith forward, that the freely contracted activity of individuals will be more productive than coerced activity, and thus that capitalism will promote freedom and undermine coercion in society more generally.

This crisis never arrived for political economy, nor for its successor economics. Cairnes's insight was not taken up in any direct way, and the exclusion of similar questions about the profits of slavery has played a role not just in the history of economic thought but in that of a range of disciplines. It is possible that this pattern is beginning to shift. In the 2010s, detailed arguments about the wealth generated by slavery and its role in world history grew into a prominent debate (Parry 2016; Rockman 2014). Edward Baptist's *The Half Has Never Been Told* (2014) argued that the plunging price of raw cotton between 1810 and 1860, and the soaring profits that resulted, were produced not primarily by new machinery or new plant varieties but by the intensified torture inflicted on enslaved black workers. Sven Beckert's *Empire of Cotton* (2015) developed a vision of capitalism as a system built through war, not trade, through enslavement, not freedom.[3]

These arguments about slavery's role in capitalism were newsworthy, but they were not exactly new. The claim that racially-based slavery and anti-black racism were formative conditions of modern capitalism has been a persistent one in black scholarship across the twentieth century. It is a premise of W.E.B. Du Bois's sociological analysis in chapter 9 of *The Souls of Black Folk* (1903), an argument developed at length in his *Black Reconstruction* (1935) (Du Bois 1999, 1998). The specific hypothesis of Eric Williams's 1944 *Capitalism and Slavery* is that profits generated by slavery contributed to the concentration of investment wealth necessary for the early growth of industrialization. Walter Rodney's 1972 *How Europe Underdeveloped Africa* details the impoverishing effects of the slave trade on the continent, a dynamic he argues was reinforced in the colonial and postcolonial periods (Rodney 2018). Cedric Robinson's 1983 *Black Marxism* presents nothing less than a total reconception of modern economic history as "racial capitalism." For Robinson, a "Black radical tradition" of analysis, extending to Du Bois and beyond, develops a complex and evolving account of this system. This is a "Black movement," Robinson writes "whose dialectical matrix we believe was capitalist slavery and imperialism," but it can only be glimpsed once the student is able to set aside the "imperatives that have so long plagued Western scholarship" (167).

In this chapter, I do not intervene in the debate over Beckert's and Baptist's conclusions.[4] Instead I want to observe that their questions about the relation between slavery and capitalism have been present all along, and so their visibility in mainstream—i.e. predominantly white—academic and press circles confirms the pattern of these questions' earlier exclusion, and the possible shifting of this pattern. These and other revisionary histories of capitalism emerged in a period when anti-black violence and its long history in American institutions was also receiving renewed attention, and new accounts of the theft of black wealth prompted renewed calls for reparations. Studies of household net worth showed that median wealth among US white families exceeds that of African American families by a factor of at least 10—a gap that has not changed substantially in the past 40 years and is largely resistant to educational attainment (Hamilton and Darity 2015; see also Baradaran 2017). Prominent attention to these studies in media and public policy, along with the new trends in American history I noted above, suggest that we are entering a period of epistemological disruption, when configurations of knowledge disaggregate and scramble, and facts once repeatedly dismissed are brought into view. Cairnes's book can contribute to this realignment. To make this point I will look first at the treatment of slavery in earlier economic and abolitionist discourse; I focus here on Adam Smith, who set the program for the following century by suggesting that enslaved labor was not just morally wrong, but economically inefficient. I then turn to Cairnes, who tried to explain why the tendency of capital to seek high returns will not, in itself, break the power of slavery's New World empire.

Profit and Violence

Race and racism arguably serve a constitutive role in Adam Smith's political economy, given the way *The Wealth of Nations* sets off its formative analysis of the division of labor in western Europe with the supposed counterexample of Africa and its "naked savages" (Smith 1994, 13). Still, blackness in Smith's subsequent analysis functions less as the dark other of white wealth than as a term that must be excluded. While he addresses slavery in early works on moral and political philosophy, *Wealth of Nations* treats it mostly as secondary matter. The effect of this is to produce Atlantic slavery as a relatively small and marginal feature of a general account of trade and statecraft.

Smith's 1759 *Theory of Moral Sentiments* includes a stern moral condemnation of slavery, one that proved influential in subsequent debates on abolition (Ross 1995, 171; Swaminathan 2007, 491–507). The stadial model of history Smith develops there, relying in particular on popular accounts of indigenous North America, ascribes virtues of martial self-denial to the "rude and barbarous nations," where life is led "in continual danger." As a result, he concludes, "there is not a negro from the coast of Africa who does not… possess a degree of magnanimity which the soul of his sordid master is too often scarce capable of conceiving" (Smith 1976b, 205–206). The attack was severe enough to be recognized as a threat by British West Indian planters, one of whom in a 1773 pamphlet assailed the "totally ignorant" speculations of a certain "Scotch lecturer" (Martin qtd. Swaminathan, 494).

Smith first hints at an economic analysis of slavery in university lectures at Glasgow in the 1760s. He argues there that slavery is an irrational practice stemming from a "love of domination and authority over others" (Smith 1976a, 186). It is this failing, Smith argues, that leads proprietors to prefer enslaved labor to wage labor, even though "cultivation of land by slaves is not so advantageous as by free tenents [sic]," given that the "cost and the expence of their maintenance[e]" will be greater (185).

This sets the pattern for the mentions of slavery in *Wealth of Nations.* In the book's most direct treatment, Smith repeats the maxim that "work done by slaves … is in the end the dearest of any," reasoning that "a person who can acquire no property, can have no other interest but to eat as much, and to labour as little as possible" (Smith 1994, 418). It is only "the pride of man" that "makes him love to domineer" and urges planters to adopt this expensive system. The plantations of the British West Indies are mentioned explicitly here. Still, the chapter containing these passages is focused not on the political economy of enslaved cultivation, or New World colonies more generally, but rather on the history of Europe after the end of the Roman empire. It leads directly to Smith's famous argument on the waning of feudalism, which blasts the stupidity of the aristocratic proprietors who "for a pair of diamond shoe buckles perhaps, or for something as frivolous and useless" bargained away their land to a rampant bourgeoisie (444). The tension between the vain brutality of slave owners and the supposedly weak profits of their enterprise is less an issue in itself than an instance offered in support of Smith's primary story about the decline of feudal tyranny in Europe.

Slavery is addressed in his extensive chapter on colonies; however, it doesn't figure in the analysis of colonies per se but rather in a discussion of government. Enslaved people, Smith suggests there, are likely to be treated better in societies governed by "arbitrary" authority than in "free" societies. In despotic states planters are subject to magistrates who can enforce an ordinance—should one happen to exist—safeguarding the enslaved from violence. In a "free" society, planters will use their franchise to influence the justice system and insure their absolute rights as property owners (634). This hypothesis, which pushes Smith well away from his original subject, leads him to the point he seems bent on making, which has to do with the consequences of protecting the enslaved from violence. "The protection of the magistrate," he writes,

> renders the slave less contemptible in the eyes of his master, who is thereby induced to consider him with more regard, and to treat him with more gentleness. Gentle usage renders the slave not only more faithful, but more intelligent, and therefore, upon a double account, more useful. He approaches more to the condition of a free servant, and may possess some degree of integrity and attachment to his master's interest, virtues which frequently belong to free servants, but which never can belong to a slave who is treated as slaves commonly are in countries where the master is perfectly free and secure. (634)

What emerges here is the hint of an incentive structure that will—though this is nowhere clearly affirmed—price slavery out of the market. Leaving aside the device of the "arbitrary" government Smith uses to conjure this speculation, planters who allow enslaved persons to "approach to the condition of a free servant" will win more efficient and productive service, suggesting plainly that violent compulsion is a more expensive means of production than "gentle usage." The better enslaved workers are treated, the more productive their labor, until presumably any legal compulsion will be obviated, in the same way that the arbitrary violence of the old nobility was brought to book by a class of clever merchants in the passage above.

Nowhere does Smith consider Atlantic slavery as a subject in its own right, nor work through the significance of his counter-intuitive and, it turns out, counterfactual assertion that slavery is inefficient. Slavery stands to one side of the theory *The Wealth of Nations* proposes and the object of study it discerns. In earlier work on Smith, I focused on the transition from classical to neoclassical political economy, emphasizing the deep historical and social investments of Smith's theory of market life, in contrast to the ahistorical and radically subjectivist method that gained ground from Jevons forward (Bigelow 2003). I remain sympathetic to this vision of Adam Smith as a figure unconstrained by disciplinary boundaries that hardened after Jevons, and who envisioned economics as an outgrowth of moral philosophy, linguistics, and history. But there are continuities in modern economic thought as well as breaks, and the study of slavery requires that we see these continuities clearly. In the passages discussed here, there is an overriding faith in the power of individual self-interest, which can break the bonds of tyranny wherever they may be found. Smith's assertions about the political economy of slavery derive less from socio-historical analysis than from the non-empirical premise that economic life is governed by a "system of natural liberty" (1994, 745), one that will in itself tend to produce the best outcomes.[5] As Christopher Taylor observes in his *Empire of Neglect*, the focus in Smith's analysis, and in the classical school that follows him, is not on slavery but on empire (Taylor 2018, 42–43). The end point in *Wealth of Nations* is thus an attack on colonies as noxious products of sovereign administration, which will prevent a naturally ordered system of exchange from flourishing. Smith's emphasis on the "natural liberty" of economic agents in the marketplace thus results in, but also depends upon, the absence of slavery in his broader analysis.

Smith's backhanded argument about the inefficiency of slavery would become an article of faith in nineteenth-century British abolitionist discourse. Liverpool merchant James Cropper, a major anti-slavery figure in the 1820s, predicted that the superior profitability of wage labor would gradually drive down the value of slaves. Slave production would then "become burdensome," he argued, and "slavery will cease" (qtd. Taylor 2018, 82; see Davis 1975, 62–63). Harriet Martineau dramatized this argument in her story "Demerara" (1832), in which the son of West Indian planters studies political economy and conducts an experiment to compensate enslaved laborers for their work. These accounts follow the deductive epistemology grounding Smith's work, which holds that the self-interest of individual actors will eventually triumph over any local obstacle or inherited practice. Or as Marx would put it in 1848, "venerable prejudices" will be "drowned … in the icy water of egotistical calculation," carried away in a rising tide of productivity (Marx 1998, 37).

However, faith in this deductive logic, with its unwavering insistence on the power of free trade in all things, was diminishing in this period, questioned from all sides by Christian opponents of utilitarianism, pro-slavery opponents of abolition, and radical liberals who questioned the orthodoxy of free trade (Snyder 2006, 279–299; Taylor 2018, 83; Klaver 2003, 137–141). John Stuart Mill, in the latter camp, moved political economy away from strict deductivism, in a subtle compromise that would define the discipline for a generation (Klaver 2003, 139). Cairnes, a friend and follower of Mill's, would push the question further. Mill's *Principles of Political Economy* (1848) set strict limits on Smith's "system of natural liberty," arguing that while the competitive activity of self-interested individuals might, in the abstract, produce observable economic laws, these were always subject to contingent "human institutions" (Mill 1965, 21). Mill's brief chapter on slavery notes the "truism ... that labor extorted by fear of punishment is inefficient" but does little to consider how "human institutions" might subvert this tendency (Mill 1965, 247). Cairnes will do so, but in such a way as to show the "system of natural liberty" itself to be highly contingent, not a founding truth.

THE SLAVE POWER

If slave production is an embarrassment in Smith, shuttled off to the edges of the analysis and treated glancingly, it remains at the center of Cairnes's field of vision: it is not simply the subject of his volume, but the determining force that, in his analysis, governed the colonization of the Americas and all their subsequent history. He does maintain that there is a natural tendency for wage labor to be most efficient, but this rule is more or less irrelevant, he will argue, for understanding the North American situation. "It is said," he writes, "that free labour (regarded from a purely economic point of view ...) [is] superior to slave labour." As a result "there are those who anticipate the growth of a liberal policy in the South from the gradual operation of economic causes in ultimately identifying the interests of planters with those of the general community" (Cairnes 2003, 158–159). "Liberal policy" here would mean not just a free market in wage labor, but also the range of social and political freedoms thought to follow when the engine of economic self-interest is let loose. In fact, however, conditions current at that time already made it clear that the profits of the planting class were not being widely shared, and thus that the liberalizing force of the profit motive had been broken. "Slavery has not merely thwarted the general prosperity of the South," Cairnes argues, "it may even be shown to have operated to the special detriment of the particular class for whose exclusive behoof it is maintained" (159). That slavery has damaged the prosperity of regions enforcing it, Cairnes writes, "appears to me as demonstrable as any proposition in Euclid" (160).

The analogy to geometry—a paradigm of deductive logic—is telling in the passage. The damaging effects of enslaved production would seem to confirm the premise established in Smith, and with it the methodological faith that political economy could derive solutions to particular problems by reasoning from its *a priori* foundations. But as Cairnes has suggested, this general tendency has been undone in the United States. If the efficiency of free labor is demonstrable by logical proof, still, he writes, "it is vain to hope that the question of slavery will ever find its solution in economic motives," and thus "it is idle to argue this question on purely economic grounds" (162). With this drastic turn, Smith's faith in the natural efficiency of free labor is left behind, and Cairnes's analysis moves forward in a different direction, one signaled starkly on the book's first page. "In selecting the subject of North American slavery," he writes there, "I was influenced … by considerations of a purely speculative kind [… specifically,] to show that the course of history is largely determined by the action of economic causes" (lxxxvii). What he means by "economic causes," as he develops the argument, turns out not to be the "natural liberty" at work in Smith, but rather the material activities of production and exchange themselves, in their specific configuration at a given time, which he demonstrates through an extended analogy with empirical methods in natural science:

> The comparative anatomist, by reasoning on those fixed relations between the different parts of the animal frame which his science reveals to him, is able from a fragment of a tooth or bone to determine the form, dimensions, and habits of the creature to which it belonged; and with no less accuracy, it seems to me, may a political economist by reasoning on the economic character of slavery and its peculiar connexion with the soil, deduce its leading social and political attributes, and almost construct, by way of *a priori* argument, the entire system of the society of which it forms the foundation. (69–70)

The reference to comparative anatomy is a casual one, not fully developed here or elsewhere in the book, but the gesture is significant. Cairnes recommends a form of *a priori* reasoning, but not one not based on any preexisting principle of natural law. Instead, the method begins with an empirical study of "tooth or bone"—for the political economist, the "economic character" of a society—as these material structures or arrangements are said to give evidence for understanding more complex features of the object of study, since they function as the determining "foundation" for all other phenomena. There is no divine or natural law governing the rise or fall of the slave system. Instead, that system itself produces the social habits and political structures that keep it in place.

As the analysis develops, the economic arrangements of slavery encroach further and further upon the supposedly natural principles of human behavior that formed political economy's original basis. Once the conditions of enslaved production become established in the Atlantic economy, Cairnes argues, they determine specific "social and political results—as the means of upholding a form of society in which slaveholders are the sole depositaries of social prestige and political power" (162). He returns to detail these "social and political results" in a number of key passages. "Slavery in the South," he writes, "is something more than a moral and political principle: it has become a fashionable taste, a social passion" (169), embedded in "the habits and tastes it may have engendered" (68). In the closing pages of the book, Cairnes winds up this aspect of the argument: "The grand difficulty to be encountered in any scheme of emancipation which proposes to convert suddenly a *régime* of forced into one of hired labour, is the state of feeling which slavery leaves behind it in the minds of those who have taken part in its working" (341). Cairnes is searching here for a sociological vocabulary that will allow him to identify the inertial force of slavery—the "Slave Power" of his title—which is entrenched so deeply in the "feelings" of white society. It is this force, he suggests, that has prevented the otherwise irresistible trend of "natural liberty" from advancing. The Slave Power, he says more than once, is both "retrograde and aggressive" (17–18, 311); that is, it retards the advancement of the civic and economic freedoms that had been, and still were, the dream of political economy as a science. In this way, he writes, "the whole system of slavery tends to thwart the purposes of nature" (150).

The "social and political results" of enslaved labor prevent the engines of self-interest from powering the expansion of what Cairnes calls "liberal policy" in the South. Part of this economic and political matrix, in Cairnes's assessment, involves northern banks and investors who supply capital to finance the expansion of western plantations. The flow of profits within this financial system results in a "community of interest" between northern and southern wings of the Democratic party (199). Self-interest, in the search for profit, fails to serve the "purpose of nature" here, as it entrenches the practices of slave trading and slave labor all the more deeply in social and political life, rather than spurring the "liberal policy" that should in theory follow.

Cairnes thus explains why the common idea about slavery's inefficiency turned out to be so disastrously wrong. Smith suggested clearly, though somewhat carelessly, that slave production would be driven out of the market by the force of natural law, implying that the most efficient and least disruptive way to promote a free society is simply to wait until the capital flowing to slave production dries up. While Cairnes still subscribes nominally to such "purposes of nature," his task is to demonstrate how such purposes, if they can be relied on at all, have been permanently arrested.

The Irish perspective Cairnes brings to his analysis begins to become evident in these passages, with the twisted logic he follows in order to preserve some faith in the metaphysical core of his discipline. It may well be that in theory or in conventional markets "nature" tends in the direction of individual freedom, he argues, but in practice slavery arrests this natural force. Cairnes here assigns to slavery the same position that many assigned to the land system of pre-Famine Ireland. In several influential accounts, the Famine of the 1840s resulted from a perversion of the natural course of economic growth, imposed by a greedy oligarchy of planters who kept their tenants at the level of mere subsistence.[6] What was needed during and after the Famine, they argued, was a new instauration of political economy, a way to restore the natural field of agency and exchange that would become self-replicating and self-governing. The most thoughtful and sympathetic of these accounts came from Mill, whose proposal for relief involved a massive land reform program to transform landless laborers into what he called "peasant proprietors." "Property in the soil," Mill wrote in 1846, "has a sort of magic power of engendering industry, perseverance, forethought in an agricultural people."[7] Once established as owners of their own small plots, Mill suggested, the Irish poor would be subject to all the benign incentives thought to drive economic behavior in a *laissez-faire* market, as opposed to the corrupt and illiberal incentives set up to benefit the Anglo-Irish gentry. They would then undergo a moral revolution, embracing the virtues Mill names (See Zastoupil 1983). Cairnes uses Mill's phrase "peasant proprietors" liberally to describe the salutary force that could be gathered as northern whites are encouraged to settle alongside the formerly enslaved on land liberated in the south. But the overriding emphasis in Cairnes's argument is not on the natural force of *laissez-faire* but on the social and cultural power of habit, feeling, and taste which renders *laissez-faire* conceptually worthless.

Cairnes and Marx

Marx relied on *The Slave Power* in his discussion of Atlantic slavery in *Capital,* but Marx uses Cairnes as a passage to more general discussion rather than open an analysis of slavery per se, and in this way his treatment of the subject ultimately resembles Smith's more than Cairnes's. Marx quotes a key passage where Cairnes argues that the internal slave trade, growing in the southern states in the decades before the War, affected the labor practices in the largest plantations:

> The rice-ground of Georgia, or the swamps of the Mississippi, may be fatally injurious to the human constitution; but the waste of human life which the cultivation of these districts necessitates, is not so great that it cannot be repaired from the teeming preserves of Virginia and Kentucky … It is accordingly a maxim of slave management, in slave-importing countries, that the most effective economy is that which takes out of the human chattel in the shortest space of time the utmost amount of exertion it is capable of putting forth. (Cairnes 2003, 122, qtd. in Marx 1977, 377)

In Cairnes's discussion the passage works to refute the common assertion that plantation owners were motivated by self-interest to nourish and sustain the lives of enslaved workers. This is the theory implied in Smith's discussion of "gentle usage," and it featured explicitly in pro-slavery arguments.[8] But it also presses a systemic view of the political economy of slavery, showing the interdependence between a violent system of labor extraction and a violent trade in human bodies. After quoting this passage, however, Marx races ahead to transpose this dynamic onto the process of industrialization in Britain, where mill owners regard workers as interchangeable and easily replaceable. He glosses Cairnes's passage as follows: "For slave trade, read labour-market, for Kentucky and Virginia, Ireland and the agricultural districts of England, Scotland, and Wales" (Marx 1977, 378). As historian Stephanie Smallwood observes in a 2017 essay, slavery is rendered here into a convenient analogue with which to describe the demographic pressures of British industrialization. It allows Marx to describe precarious industrial labor as a figurative enslavement. "Throughout most of Marx's work," Smallwood writes, "slavery's chief function is heuristic: it is an ahistorical foil against which to set capitalism's unique and singular excesses and inhumanity" (Smallwood 2017, 80).[9] As in Smith, New World slavery sits apart here, conceptually distinct from the central elements of capitalism.

In her essay Smallwood restores a passage from Cairnes that just precedes the one highlighted by Marx. "My object at present" Cairnes wrote there, "is to direct attention, not so much to the barbarous inhumanity of the slave trade, whether foreign or domestic, as to what has not been so often noticed—the mode in which it operates in giving increased coherence to the system of which it is a part" (Cairnes 2003, 121, qtd. in Smallwood 2017, 79). Cairnes is arguing here that slave production on the newer plantations of the deep south and west relied on a traffic in enslaved workers, and thus that the Confederate states, if their independence were granted, would inevitably move to reestablish the trans-Atlantic slave trade. His emphasis here is not on slavery as an alternative to or analogue for industrial capitalism, but rather on the way the slave economy functions as part of a broader commercial "system," with market forces and price signals that urge particular decisions about labor management. The endemic violence of the slave economy shouldn't distract from its function within modern commercial society. It is not the remnant of a primitive stage of history, nor an analogy for modern capitalism, but rather an integral part of modern capitalism.

Forgetting

Cairnes pursued the conceptual implications of this finding in later work, becoming increasingly skeptical that free markets would naturally promote human freedom. A collection of essays from 1873 analyzed the stagnation of Irish agriculture after the Famine, explicitly rejecting both the idea of land as an exchangeable commodity, and the axiom of *laissez faire* itself (Cairnes 1873). Keynes cited it approvingly, calling Cairnes "the first orthodox economist to give frontal attack on laissez-faire" (qtd. in Boylan and Foley 1983, 111). Veblen would praise Cairnes in a paradigmatic essay from 1898, explaining well how Cairnes departs from his discipline even as he remains within it. Tracing the history of political economy across the nineteenth century, he writes:

> [T]here is less of an exercise of faith in Cairnes's economic discussion than in those … writers that went before him. The definitive terms of the formulation are still the terms of normality and natural law, but the metaphysics underlying this appeal to normality is so far removed from the ancient ground of the beneficent "order of nature" as to have become at least nominally impersonal … [I]t is no longer conceived to exercise its constraint in the interest of certain ulterior human purposes. (Veblen 1898, 385)

In other words, with Cairnes the "system of natural law" that provided the foundation for Smith's theory can no longer be understood as guiding human history toward prosperity and virtue.

However, faith in the "order of nature," as we know, roared back in the twentieth century. The metaphysical confidence that Veblen smirks at here would spin around to reemerge in the second half of the twentieth century in the neoliberalism of Hayek and the Chicago school. For this new economic faith to be sustained, however, the consequences of Cairnes's work on slavery had to remain suppressed. In the discipline of American history, Cairnes is dutifully cited in scholarship on slavery and abolition, but with little attention paid to the larger implications of his argument. *The Slave Power* remains in print in a university press edition, but with a scholarly introduction that focuses on the book's flawed sources and its limited analysis (Smith, M. 2003). Robert Fogel and Stanley Engerman's 1974 book *Time on the Cross* handles Cairnes in a similar way. Their ambitious recounting of data on the economic productivity of the slave states argues that slavery *was* profitable, and that the abolitionists who sought to prove the contrary were relying on faulty data. The authors spend considerable time rehearsing Cairnes's mistakes and those of his sources. Famously, however, they ignore the biggest question raised by Cairnes's argument, and their own, namely, what does it mean to say that slavery was good capitalism? Fogel and Engerman largely discounted the implication and, as a result, seemed to be ignoring this mass unfreedom and murder within the history of modern capitalism. As they acknowledged in a later edition of the book, "we seemed to be diminishing the moral horror of slavery" (Fogel and Engerman 1989, 274). This is perhaps why historians in the current moment, seeking to foreground slavery's role in the making of the modern global order, have largely avoided citing *Time on the Cross* and the ensuing controversy over its methods and presumptions.[10]

In economics, the suppression or forgetting of Cairnes is more complete. Cairnes again is dutifully praised in the major histories of the discipline, described as a distinguished but dismissible exponent of the classical school, a diligent Victorian mired in the imprecise methods of his age. Joseph Schumpeter's *History of Economic Analysis*, the definitive historical study of the mid-twentieth century, observes of Cairnes that "though most of his contributions have been sterile, his work, both analytical and methodological, marks an important stage." If "sterile" here means that few took up and extended Cairnes's findings, the assessment is hard to quarrel with. Schumpeter offers a telling, though presumably sympathetic, explanation: "the bulk of his working hours went into practical problems … [I]t was his 'factual' contribution (in particular his *Slave Power*, 1862), which accounts for his reputation with the English public of his time" (Schumpeter 1954, 534). Put another way, this otherwise talented logician was so caught up in the "facts" of slavery, colonialism, and the economics of extraction that he strayed from the path of pure theory.

What did outlive Cairnes and carry over into twentieth-century economics is the proposition he set himself against in *The Slave Power*: that the incentives of a competitive market would on their own function to combat the inherited prejudices that justified slavery and segregation. The modern adaptation of this thesis was offered by Gary Becker, whose 1957 book *The Economics of Discrimination* built a model to demonstrate that competitive markets in themselves provide the most effective means of lessening racial inequality. The assertion was established as neoliberal orthodoxy in 1962 by Milton Friedman, who cited Becker's "brilliant" study to show that "a free market separates economic efficiency from irrelevant characteristics" such as "color of skin" (Friedman 2002, 109, 117). Becker's thesis remains a powerful though not universally accepted element of the discipline (Darity et al. 2015), and his book is still cited as proof that competitive markets militate against racial prejudice.[11]

A version of this argument also appears in the related field of the history of economic thought. David Levy has argued that Victorian political economy served as a bastion of anti-racist progressivism (Levy 2002). Particularly in the popularized versions of Levy's work, written with economist Sandra Peart and published online, the account holds that the socialist and communalist assumptions of capitalism's critics fueled Victorian racism and eugenicism. In this argument Ruskin and Carlyle are exhibits A and B.[12] The free market thus stands as the heroic agent of human freedom, against the tyrannical musings of an old guard (Levy and Peart 2001–2002). However, political economists lined up on both sides of the slavery question. The American slave states produced their own pro-slavery branch of political economy, adapting Smith's doctrine of "natural liberty" easily to their own purposes (Carlander and Brownlee 2006, 402).

What is remarkable in all this theorizing about discrimination is the disciplinary isolation that characterizes it. The upshot in this body of work—that the best means to combat racism is market deregulation, and that white deregulators have done the most to advance racial equality—unfolds with little reference to research on African American history, studies of black wealth or income levels, or the work of black theorists. The pattern is comparable to the one Cedric Robinson described, wherein a full account of racial capitalism is developed in a black radical tradition, but this work is not generally consulted in mainstream academic research on race and economics. The marginalization of Cairnes's argument about the entrenched nature of the profit-structure and culture of American slavery is thus of a piece with a larger denial of slavery's formative role in the history of American capitalism.

If slavery and its material legacies have been scanted in much of mainstream economic thought, that pattern may be starting to change, in parallel with the new developments in the field of American history I mentioned at the start of this chapter. An increasingly self-aware sector of the discipline of economics is working to delink neoclassical methodology from neoliberal policy positions, building a movement toward what one group calls "inclusive prosperity." They argue in part for an economics equipped to confront the "racial disparities in wealth and well-being" that "remain stubbornly persistent" (Rodrik et al. 2019). Still, as economist Marshall Steinbaum remarked in a caustic though ultimately sympathetic response, this new effort has a long history to overcome: "Economists have drawn and re-drawn disciplinary boundaries to exclude anything that challenged incumbent wealth and power … The result was to turn the field into a safe space for rich white people to justify and naturalize the status quo" (Steinbaum 2019). Steinbaum is a Fellow at the Roosevelt Institute, a network of scholars that also includes Darrick Hamilton and William Darity, whose research on the racial wealth gap has given rise to its own call for a reform of the discipline (Darity et al. 2015).

Cairnes's work still has a role to play in our current debate, not least because it encourages an approach that connects up the separate disciplinary revisions going on in history and economics. Cairnes argued forcefully that the labor stolen from enslaved workers generated tremendous profit, and that this concentrated wealth in turn stabilized the "habits and tastes," the "state of feeling" that normalized the theft in the minds of many American whites. This affective matrix of racism continued to normalize the theft of black wealth throughout the twentieth century. Black property was routinely appropriated or destroyed in race "riots" and lynchings, from reconstruction forward (Ash 2013; Hirsch 2002). Aspiring black homeowners were excluded from the mortgage subsidies established in the New Deal—the program that arguably did the most to produce a white middle class in the United States. Left out of federal mortgage programs, black borrowers were serviced by a new ecosystem of predatory lenders who extorted above-market rates (Satter 2009). State and federal prisoners, disproportionately black, are compelled to work for a wage that is often effectively zero (Alexander 2012). These structures, increasingly well-known from the work of figures like filmmaker Ava DuVernay or writer Ta-Nehesi Coates, effect the transfer of black wealth into the hands of a disproportionately white class of managers and shareholders. Economic knowledge in a predominantly white academy and policy sphere has been distorted by the denial of these acts of violent appropriation. For those of us caught up in this history of denial, reading Cairnes now may help us to perceive this distortion and to know the violence of the present.

NOTES

1. This convergence is the subject of Baucom (2005).
2. As Regenia Gagnier writes, "The object of neoclassical economics under the Marginal Revolution after 1870, was to maximize individual choice and preference without comparing or ranking needs intersubjectively" (Gagnier 2010). See also Fullbrook (2004).
3. On response to Beckert and Baptist's books, see Parry (2016) and Hilt (2017).
4. Parry (2016) is a good introduction. See also Hilt (2017).
5. It is this premise that economist Duncan Foley (2008) calls "Adam's Fallacy," a category error that elevates markets onto a plane distinct from social and political institutions.
6. A good exemplar is Charles Trevelyan's lengthy *Edinburgh Review* essay of 1848, "The Irish Crisis." This line of thinking also runs ambivalently through Anthony Trollope's letters about government Famine relief efforts in the Sunday *Examiner* (Trollope 1965).
7. Qtd. in Gray (1999, 157). Mill is writing here in the *Morning Chronicle*, part of a series of articles on the Famine that appeared that year and the next.
8. South Carolina essayist Louisa McCord contended in 1856 that "It must be more profitable to [a master] to have healthy and happy slaves than sick and wretched ones" (qtd. in Carlander and Brownlee 2006, 399).
9. Smallwood's essay appears in a special edition of the *Boston Review* dedicated to the memory of Cedric Robinson, who died in 2016.
10. Neither Beckert (2015) nor Baptist (2014) reviews this literature in any detail in their studies, signaling their departure from this earlier conversation rather than an incremental advance upon it. Beckert and Rockman's introduction to the volume *Slavery's Capitalism* (2016) outlines Fogel and Engerman's argument, as well as Fogel's subsequent corrective, *Without Consent or Contact* (1989).

11. "As Gary Becker first explained systematically, the free market contains automatic penalties for the odious practices that most people have in mind when they deplore 'discrimination'" (Murphy 2010). Empirical studies aiming to test Becker's thesis include Charles and Guryan (2008).
12. For example, Carlyle (1849) and Ruskin (1893). The latter is a pamphlet published by a Liverpool tabacconist, with extracts from Ruskin's work and a racist cover illustration.

REFERENCES

Alexander, Michelle. 2012. *The New Jim Crow: Mass Incarceration in the Age of Colorblindness.* Rev. ed. New York: New Press.

Ash, Stephen V. 2013. *A Massacre in Memphis: The Race Riot That Shook the Nation One Year after the Civil War.* New York: Hill and Wang.

Baptist, Edward. 2014. *The Half Has Never Been Told: Slavery and the Making of American Capitalism.* New York: Basic Books.

Baradaran, Mehrsa. 2017. *The Color of Money: Black Banks and the Racial Wealth Gap.* Cambridge: Belknap.

Baucom, Ian. 2005. *Specters of the Atlantic: Finance Capital, Slavery, and the Philosophy of History.* Durham: Duke University Press.

Becker, Gary. 1957. *The Economics of Discrimination.* Chicago: University of Chicago Press.

Beckert, Sven. 2015. *Empire of Cotton: A Global History.* New York: Vintage.

Beckert, Sven, and Seth Rockman. 2016. Introduction. In *Slavery's Capitalism: A New History of American Economic Development*, 1–28. Philadelphia: University of Pennsylvania Press.

Bigelow, Gordon. 2003. *Fiction, Famine, and the Rise of Economics in Victorian Britain and Ireland.* Cambridge, MA: Cambridge University Press.

Blackett, Richard J.M. 2000. *Divided Hearts: Britain and the American Civil War.* Baton Rouge: Louisiana State University Press.

Boylan, T.A., and T.P. Foley. 1983. John Eliot Cairnes, John Stuart Mill and Ireland: Some Problems for Political Economy. *Hermathena* 135 (Winter): 96–119.

Cairnes, John Elliott. 1873. *Essays in Political Economy, Theoretical and Applied.* London: Macmillan.

———. 2003. *The Slave Power: Its Character, Career, and Probable Designs* (1862). Reprint ed. Columbia: University of South Carolina Press.

Carlander, Jay R., and W. Elliot Brownlee. 2006. Antebellum Southern Political Economists and the Problem of Slavery. *American Nineteenth Century History* 7 (3, Sep.). 389–416.

Carlyle, Thomas. 1849. Occasional Discourse on the Negro Question. *Fraser's Magazine for Town and Country* 40: 670–679. https://babel.hathitrust.org/cgi/pt?id=inu.30000080778727;view=1up;seq=690

Charles, Kerwin Kofi, and Jonathan Guryan. 2008. Prejudice and Wages: An Empirical Assessment of Becker's *The Economics of Discrimination. Journal of Political Economy* 116 (5): 773–809.

Darity, William Jr., Darrick Hamilton, and James B. Stewart. 2015. A Tour de Force in Understanding Intergroup Inequality: An Introduction to Stratification Economics. *Review of Black Political Economy* 42: 1–6.

Davis, David Brion. 1975. *The Problem of Slavery in the Age of Revolution, 1770–1823*. Ithaca: Cornell University Press.

Du Bois, W. E. B. 1998. *Black Reconstruction in America* (1935). New York: Free Press.

———. 1999. "Of the Sons of Master and Man." In *The Souls of Black Folk* (1903), ed. Henry Louis Gates, Jr. and Terri Hume Oliver. Norton Critical ed., 105–119. New York: Norton.

Eric Hilt, (2017) Economic History, Historical Analysis, and the "New History of Capitalism". The Journal of Economic History 77 (2):511–536

Fogel, Robert William. 1989. *Without Consent or Contract: The Rise and Fall of American Slavery*. New York: Norton.

Fogel, Robert William, and Stanley L. Engerman. 1989. *Time on the Cross: The Economics of Negro Slavery*, with New Afterward. New York: Norton.

Foley, Duncan. 2008. *Adam's Fallacy: A Guide to Economic Theology*. Cambridge, MA: Belknap.

Friedman, Milton. 2002. *Capitalism and Freedom*. 40th Anniversary ed. Chicago: University of Chicago Press.

Fullbrook, Edward. 2004. Descartes' Legacy: Intersubjective Reality, Intrasubjective Theory. In *The Elgar Companion to Economics and Philosophy*, ed. John Bryan Davis, Alain Marciano, and John Runde, 403–422. London: Elgar.

Gagnier, Regenia. 2010. *Individualism, Decadence, and Globalization: On the Relationship between Part and Whole*. Houndmills, UK: Palgrave Macmillan.

Gray, Peter. 1999. *Famine, Land and Politics: British Government and Irish Society, 1843–50*. Dublin: Irish Academic Press.

Hamilton, Darrick, and William Darity Jr. 2015. The Political Economy of Education, Literacy, and the Racial Wealth Gap. *Federal Reserve Bank of St. Louis Review* 99 (1): 59–76.

Hirsch, James S. 2002. *Riot and Remembrance: The Tulsa Race War*. New York: Houghton Mifflin.

Jevons, William Stanley. 1957. *The Theory of Political Economy* (1870). Reprint ed. Edited by H. Stanley Jevons. New York: Kelly.

Klaver, Claudia. 2003. Rewriting Ricardo/Renewing Smith. In *A/Moral Economics: Classical Political Economy and Cultural Authority in Nineteenth-Century England*, 134–160. Columbus: Ohio State University Press.

Levy, David M. 2002. *How the Dismal Science Got its Name: Classical Economics and the Ur-Text of Racial Politics.* Ann Arbor: University Michigan Press.

Levy, David M., and Sandra J. Peart. 2001–2002. The Secret History of the Dismal Science. 6 Parts. *The Library of Economics and Liberty*, January 22, 2001–May 13, 2002. https://www.econlib.org/library/Columns/LevyPeartdismal.html?highlight=%5B%22peart%22,%22levy%22%5D.

Maas, Harro. 2015. Olmsted, De Bow, and the Weight of Evidence on the American Slave South. *Journal of the History of Economic Thought* 37 (2): 171–185.

Martineau, Harriet. 1832. Demerara. In *Illustrations of Political Economy, No. IV*. London: Fox. https://oll.libertyfund.org/titles/1690.

Marx, Karl. 1977. *Capital: A Critique of Political Economy*. Vol. 1. Edited by Ernest Mandel and translated by Ben Fowkes. Vol. 1. New York: Vintage.

———. 1998. *The Communist Manifesto: A Modern Edition*. London: Verso.

Mill, John Stuart. 1965. Principles of Political Economy with Some of Their Applications to Social Philosophy. In *Collected Works of John Stuart Mill*, vol. II and III. Toronto: University of Toronto Press.

Mitchell, Timothy. 2011. *Carbon Democracy: Political Power in the Age of Oil*. London: Verso.

Murphy, Robert P. 2010. The Economics of Discrimination. *The Library of Economics and Liberty*, August 2. https://www.econlib.org/library/Columns/y2010/Murphydiscrimination.html.

Parry, Marc. 2016. Shackles and Dollars. *The Chronicle of Higher Education*, December 8. https://www.chronicle.com/article/ShacklesDollars.

Robinson, Cedric. 1983. *Black Marxism: The Making of the Black Radical Tradition*. Chapel Hill: University of North Carolina Press.

Rockman, Seth. 2014. What Makes the History of Capitalism Newsworthy? *Journal of the Early Republic* 34 (3, Fall): 439–466.

Rodney, Walter. 2018. *How Europe Underdeveloped Africa* (1972). London: Verso.

Rodrik, Dani, Suresh Naidu, and Gabriel Zucman. 2019. Economics after Neoliberalism. *Boston Review*, February 15. http://bostonreview.net/forum/suresh-naidu-dani-rodrik-gabriel-zucman-economics-after-neoliberalism.

Ross, Ian Simpson. 1995. *The Life of Adam Smith*. Oxford: Clarendon.

Ruskin, John. 1893. *Ruskin on Himself and Things in General*. Edited by William Lewin. Cope's Smoke-Room Booklets 13. Liverpool: Cope's.

Satter, Beryl. 2009. *Family Properties: Race, Real Estate, and the Exploitation of Black Urban America*. New York: Metropolitain.

Schumpeter, Joseph. 1954. *History of Economic Analysis*. Oxford: Oxford University Press.

Smallwood, Stephanie. 2017. What Slavery Tells us about Marx. In *Race, Capitalism, Justice*, ed. Walter Johnson and Robin D. G. Kelley. *Boston Review*: 78–82.

Smith, Adam. 1976a. *Lectures on Jurisprudence*. Edited by R. L. Meek, D. D. Raphael, and P.G. Stein. Glasgow Ed. of the Works and Correspondence of Adam Smith. Oxford: Oxford University Press.

———. 1976b. *The Theory of Moral Sentiments*. Edited by D. D. Raphael and A. L. MacFie. Glasgow Ed. of the Works and Correspondence of Adam Smith. Oxford: Oxford University Press.

———. 1994. *The Wealth of Nations*. Edited by Edwin Cannan. New York: Modern Library.

Smith, Mark M. 2003. Introduction. In *The Slave Power: Its Character, Career, and Probable Designs* (1862), ed. John Elliott Cairnes. Reprint ed., xvii–lvi. Columbia: University of South Carolina Press.

Snyder, Laura. 2006. *Reforming Philosophy: A Victorian Debate on Science and Society*. Chicago: University of Chicago Press. https://doi.org/10.7208/chicago/9780226767352.001.0001

Steinbaum, Marshall. 2019. Response to Rodrik et al. *Boston Review*, February 28. http://bostonreview.net/forum/economics-after-neoliberalism/marshall-steinbaum-empiricism-alone-wont-save-us

Swaminathan, Srividhya. 2007. Adam Smith's Moral Economy and the Debate to Abolish the Slave Trade. *Rhetoric Society Quarterly* 37: 491–507.

Taylor, Christopher. 2018. *Empire of Neglect: The West Indies in the Wake of British Liberalism*. Durham: Duke University Press.

Trevelyan, Charles. 1848. The Irish Crisis. *Edinburgh Review* 87 (176, Jan.): 229–320.

Trollope, Anthony. 1965. Trollope's Letters to the *Examiner*. Edited by Helen Garlinghouse King. *The Princeton University Library Chronicle* 26: 71–101.

Veblen, Thorstein. 1898. Why Is Economics Not an Evolutionary Science? *The Quarterly Journal of Economics* 12 (4, July): 373–397.

Weinberg, Adelaide. 1968. *John Eliot Cairnes and the American Civil War*. London: Kingswood.

Williams, Eric. 1944. *Capitalism and Slavery*. Chapel Hill: University of North Carolina Press.

Zastoupil, Lynn. 1983. Moral Government: J.S. Mill on Ireland. *Historical Journal* XXVI: 707–717.

PART II

Growth

CHAPTER 5

Expansion

Expansion in the Fossil Economy and Craik's *John Halifax, Gentleman*

Ayşe Çelikkol

In Dinah Mulock Craik's novel *John Halifax, Gentleman* ([1856] 2005), the eponymous hero and his wife, together with their dear friend Phineas, sit around the fire one cold night. John has just refused the Earl of Luxmore's corrupt offer that he run for the Parliament in the Earl's borough. John and his wife converse:

> "John, if you have a weakness, it is for fire. You're a regular salamander."
> He laughed—warming his hands at the blaze. "Yes, I would rather be hungry than cold, any day. Love, our one extravagance is certainly coals. A grand fire this! I do like it so!" (269)

This passage revolves around domestic bliss, but it also evokes the ways in which interior space is linked to its exterior.[1] The coal that feeds the fire conjures commercial and industrial contexts that extend into Britain's past

A. Çelikkol (✉)
Bilkent University, Ankara, Turkey

© The Author(s) 2019
E. Hadley et al. (eds.), *From Political Economy to Economics through Nineteenth-Century Literature*, Palgrave Studies in Literature, Culture and Economics, https://doi.org/10.1007/978-3-030-24158-2_5

and stretch across the world. "English coal production," notes the environmental historian Jason W. Moore,

> rose from 50,000 tons (1530) to 210,000 tons (1560) to 1.5 million tons by 1630. By this point, most of England's important coalfields were being exploited .... English coal's rapid ascent after 1530 directs our attention to the relations of primitive accumulation and agrarian class structure, to the formation of the modern world market, to new forms of commodity-centered landscape change. (2016, 95)

As coal production and consumption in England takes place in a "modern world market," the hearth in *John Halifax, Gentleman* is hardly self-contained. It signals the family's participation in the fossil economy, a system in which capital accumulates as increasing amounts of fossil fuels are consumed. Historically, the definitive rise of the fossil economy was concurrent with the industrial revolution, although, as Moore states, coal consumption was not negligible during the period of primitive accumulation in England. The hearth to which the trio retires is thus haunted by political and economic questions. Coal consumption is most relevant to the novel as a whole because John implements a steam-engine in his cloth mill, and by depicting John's ever-increasing wealth alongside his fondness for the fire in the hearth, the novel points toward the link between economic expansion and the consumption of fossil fuels.

This chapter attends to the use of coal in *John Halifax, Gentleman* to argue that the novel formalizes and naturalizes the structure of expansion that governs the fossil economy. To pursue this argument, I consider the economic theory that informs Andreas Malm's *Fossil Capital: the Rise of Steam Power and the Roots of Global Warming* (2016) alongside the novel. My chapter takes as its point of departure the principle, articulated by Malm and others, that the intrinsic expansiveness of capitalism is ecologically problematic, and it highlights the ways in which the economic dynamics of the fossil economy find thematic echoes and structural corollaries in a work of fiction that was produced and consumed during the heyday of the steam engine.[2] The novel translates the accumulation of capital into a narrative structure of sprawling plotlines and sets up a homology between economic growth and the establishment of a large family. The novel shows the way in which a historically contingent development could be rendered "natural" not just by the emergent study of the economy but by literary fiction that recasts production as biological reproduction.

By drawing attention to the cultural salience of expansion, this chapter aims to contribute to the growing body of literary scholarship attending to the rise of the fossil economy in Britain. As critics have argued, fossil capital motivated new inquiries about spatial scale and temporality that became manifest in fiction.[3] Following this lead, I examine the Victorian fascination with economic expansion in the age of coal by investigating Craik's fantasy of ongoing capital accumulation and relating it to Victorian and twenty-first-century economic thought.[4]

As the scene by the hearth indicates, when it comes to the burning of coal, the more the better, even for a middle-class family of limited means—the Halifaxes are not yet rich when the exchange takes place. This moment of domestic bliss gestures toward the industrial uses of coal that the novel will soon depict, which also operate according to the principle of the more the better. The growth of the family fortune after the installation of steam-based power at the cloth mills virtually knows no limit. John's deep-rooted desire for fuel, even, it seems, his sexual and/or familial desire, befit the expansive structure of the fossil economy, under which, with the introduction of coal-fired steam-power, capital accumulates swiftly. The novel devises a subject whose desires are in complete alignment with the prompts of this new market. The self-possessed stability of bourgeois life depends on a desire for limitless resource extraction and economic growth.

Historically, the accumulation of capital in the fossil economy implied that "increased quantities of biophysical resources [were] withdrawn from nature and, after being used up and degraded, discharged back into it" (Malm 2016, 284). The fossil economy gave rise to ecological degradation in the form of air and water pollution in the Victorian period, just as it is responsible for climate change today. We must revisit the early history of the fossil economy if we are to challenge our dependence on fossil fuels and reduce carbon emissions: the appeal of fossil fuels was in part ideological, and the critical examination of that ideology can assist us in our effort to reverse our preference for them. My goal in reading Craik's novel is to show that the fossil economy relied on middle-class domestic ideology to naturalize economic growth. As *John Halifax, Gentleman* familiarizes the structure of expansion that governed the accumulation of capital, it also manifests its limits and contradictions, for example, through subtle hints at John's suppressed sense of guilt—a remnant of an older form of socialization—and the treatment of capitalist crisis as external to the system.

Displaying the ideological appeal of fossil fuels, *John Halifax, Gentleman* works to naturalize an accumulative, ever-growing system based on the consumption of coal.[5] It thematizes the expansiveness that not only marked the industrial revolution but also provided a central paradigm around which classical economics organized itself. Even as it consolidates an ideology of growth, the novel, like all good ideologies, harbors contradictions clashing with the classical economic law of diminishing returns, and emergent neoclassical notions of scarcity. Craik's fantasy of boundless accumulation responds to ideas by classical economists such as Adam Smith and David Ricardo, who agreed on the desirability of growth even as they considered threats to it.

Although the dominant estimation of the growth economy was positive, an alternative to what the environmental economist Herman Daly calls "growthmania" was available in the nineteenth century (1974, 149) and is worth renewed attention: John Stuart Mill asserted that progress was possible within a stationary state in which the accumulation of capital would be suspended. Mill's alternative to perpetual growth can provide, as I argue at the close, some guidance to contemporary discussions, since it draws attention to the need for equitable distribution.

EXPANSION AND ITS ECONOMIC CONTEXTS

John Halifax's wealth is owed largely to his adoption of the steam engine, outlined during a central moment in the plot.[6] He is obsessed with that technology even as a poor young man. Before he becomes a manufacturer and has the opportunity to install the steam engine in his mill, he comments on the lucrativeness of steam power: "I do believe, by common patience and skill, a man might make his fortune with it at those Enderley cloth mills" (244). Yet despite the emphasis on his agency, steam-based profits appear self-generating: once the protagonist invests in the engine, they increase exponentially over time.

Craik is attuned to one of the dominant characteristics of capitalism: the tendency for capital to expand. It is telling that John's increasing reliance on fossil fuels coincides with the making of his fortune. The steam-operated mill guarantees increasing profits. Malm defines the fossil economy as: "an economy of self-sustaining growth predicated on the growing consumption of fossil fuels, and therefore generating a sustained growth in emissions of carbon dioxide." Malm indicates that growth in the fossil economy is a "progression propelled by its own inner forces" (11). "The fire" of growth "ignites … more growth," with "the loop reinforced anew on a grander scale" as the process grows, resulting in the emission of more and more carbon dioxide. Malm's rhetoric closely follows that of Marx, whose *Capital* often refers to the "self-expansion" of capital,[7] identifying it as "the very root of the capitalist mode of production," taking place "by means of the 'free' purchase and consumption of the labour-power" (Marx 1906, 487).[8]

In the late eighteenth and early nineteenth centuries, the conditions under which growth would take place had preoccupied Smith and Ricardo. The latter, for instance, had postulated that profits would decline as fertile agricultural fields became scarce. Reflecting the classical preoccupation with growth, *John Halifax, Gentleman* remains centered on the accumulation of wealth, offering a fortune that grows persistently, becoming "grand" like the fires that the protagonist admires. In this, it assuages those anxieties about profitability surfacing in such theories as Ricardo's law of diminishing returns, which Ricardo himself countered through the suggestion that trade would restore growth.[9]

Growth, of course, remains a goal in mainstream economic thought today; yet, because of the coupling of growth with carbon emissions, a green branch of political economy questions the unqualified celebration of growth, and asserts the "need to abandon the cornucopian myth of 'endless material goods'" (Barry 2009, 94).[10] As the political theorist John Barry writes, "Rather than focusing our energies on increasing the ecological and energy efficiency of capitalist production and orthodox economic growth, what we need to be doing is exploring ways of increasing the ecological and energy efficiency of human flourishing." If we "free up … 'growth' from its reduction to material wealth or capital accumulation," then "more, not less, innovation and creativity … will be the result, … rather than stagnation or regress" (2016, 312, 311). Ecological economists who advocate a steady state today seek a system in which the lack of an increase in output does not imply stagnation.[11] As they do so, they confront a powerful and resistant tradition of economic thought that treats growth as a solution to existing class stratification, as if increased GDP would automatically assure equitable distribution. Part and parcel of that tradition, *John Halifax, Gentleman* suggests that the accruing of capital remedies working-class suffering, though not without hints of underlying unease about that capacity.

RIPARIAN CONFLICT AND THE SHIFT TO STEAM POWER

As the novel portrays John's profitable switch to fossil fuels at the mill, it assumes that the laborers' troubles, and thus class conflict, will be easily resolved through growth. At first, John worries about the consequences of installing the steam engine, specifically the possibility of "hav[ing] all the country down upon [him] for destroying hand labour" (328). This fear of the workers' reaction wanes when John's wife decides to sacrifice her income, settled on her by John himself in case of "possible non-success in his business" (329); the workers can thus be fully paid even during the period of transition when the machinery is being installed. Mrs. Halifax's monetary input is hailed as a solution, impossible as that may be.

The *causes* of the installation of the steam engine are dual, one involving an aristocrat's whimsical punishment of John, and the other having to do with John's desire for more profit. The novel first elaborately sets up an external reason for the switch to the fossil economy: "Lord Luxmore has turned out of its course the stream that works my mill," complains John, at the very point when he is about to benefit from this seeming misfortune (326). "The waterpower being greatly lessened, I must either stop the mills, or work them by steam," he notes. His riparian problem is similar to that of his more famous counterpart, Mr. Tulliver of George Eliot's *The Mill on the Floss* (1860), who repeatedly asserts the "principle that water [is] water" when his supply is threatened by a neighbor (2015, 149). The first cause for the adoption of steam power in *John Halifax, Gentleman* is that John does not have access to water any more. The second is that the steam engine is more profitable than water power. John's double justification of his adoption of the steam engine betrays a sense that the fossil economy needs legitimation, and he finds this legitimation through the joining together of natural (lack of water) and market (increased production) necessities. The overdetermined switch to steam power, however, also communicates an underlying sense of unease about the fossil economy that casts doubts on its capacity to serve all classes at once.

The novel momentarily hints at the onerous uses of steam power when John exclaims with chilling earnestness: "steam-power once obtained, I can apply it in any way I choose" (341). However strongly he may identify as a friend of the working people, as owner of the business, he is at liberty to choose courses of action beneficial to himself, even if they prove detrimental to those he employs. Malm quotes John's emphatic declaration to highlight that, from its inception in the early 1800s, the combustion of fossil fuels in industrial settings tightened the capitalists' grip over working-class lives, dictating where the laborers lived and how they worked. "Steam," he writes, "arose as a form of power exercised by some people against others" (36). While Malm's comment on John's declaration is insightful, his brief engagement with the novel, which focuses on the fetishization of the steam engine, neither pinpoints the novel's obsession with self-sustaining growth nor traces the relevance of that obsession to the form of the novel. Whereas Malm evokes the ways in which John and the laborers ascribe agency to the steam engine, I turn to the ideology of growth that is implicit in this novel, arguing that the inherent expansiveness of industrial capitalism is naturalized in it, in ways that largely displace questions of equitable distribution with scenes of expanding biological reproduction. In what follows, I investigate the novel's treatment of the "self-expansion of capital" as spontaneous and turn to the parallel that the novel offers between the self-expansion of capital and the growth of the protagonist's family.

Self-Sustaining Growth and the Circuit of Capital

The Victorian middle-class ideology of the self-made man requires that John obtain his wealth by working hard, and the novel registers this necessity: "Twenty-five years of labor have won for me the position I desired," comments John (366). However, we see his labor only prior to the installation of the steam engine. Once the machinery is installed, the novel skips twelve years in the lives of its characters, resuming narration when the wealth has multiplied. The money seems to accumulate on its own: the increase in wealth, observable only through the signs of taste, takes place beyond what the narrative gaze can see: "For Mr. Halifax, a prosperous man now, drove daily to and from his mills, in as tasteful an equipage as any of the country gentry between here and Enderley" (356). John appears to play no role in the process of accumulation, but appears after the accumulation has taken place, to enjoy the fruits of his invisible labor.

Repeatedly, the novel treats accumulation as automatic, portraying it as a commonplace occurrence, a general feature of the economy rather than the singular lot of John Halifax:

> The Manor house family brought several other 'country families' to our notice, or us to theirs. These when John's fortunes grew rapidly—as many another fortune grew, in the beginning of the thirty years' peace, when unknown petty manufacturers first rose into merchant princes and cotton lords. (357)

There is a whole set of fortunes "gr[owing] rapidly" with no apparent cause, as if by magic. The text reflects the nineteenth-century assumption that "the growth of production, and especially manufacturing output" was guaranteed by the "accumulation of capital" (Piketty 2017, 228). Craik foregrounds a large-scale historical event rather than individual agency when it comes to explaining the cause of the growth, implying that this was an epoch of economic expansion. Whether the growth simply coincided with the thirty years' peace, or whether it was caused by it, remains unclear. The stretch of time was long enough for a wholesale class transformation to take place, with the bourgeoisie accumulating enough wealth to begin to supplant the aristocracy, manifest in the narrative's sudden staging of this scene in which John now literally occupies the vehicle of the "country gentry."

In an economy of self-sustaining growth, expansion is continual and appears unstoppable. Increasing productivity, however, comes with anxieties about consumption and a suppressed registration of the role Halifax plays in cementing class stratification. With his deep sense of responsibility for others, he avoids, together with his wife, a luxurious lifestyle. John captures the logic of the fossil economy perfectly as he points out, "Sometimes I fancy my life is too easy—that I am not a wise steward of the riches that have multiplied so fast" (358). The comment most directly expresses John's suppressed sense of guilt about his wealth. More interestingly for my purposes, the grammar of this statement ascribes to wealth a life of its own. Riches "multipl[y]" as if by magic, embodying the self-expansion that Marx ascribes to capital. The wealth is both the subject of the action (it does the multiplying) and its end-result. It simply accumulates, effacing the capitalist's responsibility in engendering a world of inequality. John thinks that he is unable to control the money itself, thus ascribing to it the capacity to exist independently beyond human agency and moral will.

Within a few decades of the publication of *John Halifax, Gentleman*, Marx was to elaborate the "self-expansion" of capital. While he does not seek to shed light on the increase in carbon emissions, he does help us understand why the economic setting for climate change is capitalism: as capital expands, so would the amount of fossil fuels required to turn capital into profits. Malm slightly modifies the expanded version of Marx's famous M-C-M' (money turned into commodity form begets more money) to express the biophysical stakes of the "self-expansion" of capital. In Marx's formula, P stands for production, L for labor power, and MP for the means of production. Malm in addition affixes an F, which represents fossil fuels, to the means of production. The circuit consists of

$$M-C\big(L+MP(F)\big)...P...C'-M' \quad (283)$$

Money first buys labor power and the means of production as commodities; production then transforms this combination into a new commodity, which will subsequently bring profits. The whole process involves an intake of fossil fuels. The second circuit brings more profits and burns more fossil fuels:

$$M'-C'\big(L'+MP'(F')\big)...P...C''-M'' \quad (284)$$

Malm notes:

> The cycle is by its constitution unlimited. Returning with a profit after every circuit, capital "ignites itself anew" like a driving fire that never goes out, so that the general formula can be extrapolated in perpetuity. (284)

Just as the increased amount of money starts off its own cycle to end up with even more money (M-C-M' → M'-C'-M''), one cycle of CO_2 emission is followed by another cycle in which even more CO_2 is emitted. As "capital recognizes no boundary in nature" (287), the fire grows and grows, in a way that might satisfy John Halifax, "the regular salamander" whose wife wants to convert the whole house into fuel. The self-sustaining growth pattern results in the chemical byproduct which has today reached a level close to the point of no return, with a narrowing window of opportunities to slow down anthropogenic climate change.

While, as Marx explains, the tendency to expand is inherent to the system, sooner or later, expansion must come to an end. Resource scarcity, if not economic crises, stall it, but not before pollution or climate change affects the planet and its residents. In the fossil economy the carbon footprint gets larger as time elapses. Approximately a decade after the publication of *John Halifax, Gentleman*, William Stanley Jevons (1865) was to assert that coal scarcity would suspend growth. Historically, however, the use of other kinds of fossil fuels, such as petroleum, allowed the accumulation of capital to continue, up to this day when expansion in the fossil economy has resulted in a decisive climate crisis.

Ecologists today who look for an alternative to this economic pattern and imagine a steady-state economy confront a challenge: while growth is unsustainable, "de-growth is unstable," as it is associated with "rising unemployment … and a spiral of recession" (Jackson 2017, 83). In an effort to conceptualize a steady state that would not be unstable, Tim Jackson first highlights why in the present system de-growth would imply collapse. Quoting Richard Douthwaite, Jackson focuses on the dependence of capital expansion on debt, claiming, "the fundamental problem with the debt method for creating money is that, because interest has to be paid on almost all of it, the economy must grow continuously if it is not to collapse" (Douthwaite 2006, qtd in Jackson 179). The conclusion that Jackson draws is that "a post-growth economy simply could not live inside any recognizable form of capitalism" (2017, 179). If self-sustaining growth is intrinsic to capitalism, within that system it has no alternative. Malm emphasizes the historical contingency of capitalist expansion: "Marx wants us to defamiliarize growth: however familiar it might appear to someone born and bred in an advanced capitalist society, it has to be seen for what it really is: a quirk of history, an eccentricity of the present" (286). Recently, Thomas Piketty has underlined the peculiarity of nineteenth- and twentieth-century economic growth in his examination of income inequality. Why and how does growth appear even to us today to be the default state of affairs rather than a historically specific, peculiar pattern?[12] As I have begun to demonstrate, such growth has been normalized in part through the ideology that marks Craik's novel, in ways that its narrative structure also makes explicit.

Beyond "Our Little World"

John Halifax, Gentleman is self-conscious about its expansive structure, with the narrator recounting the enlargement of John's circle of interaction and influence. Early on, the narrator, John's friend Phineas, notes, "[John] was indebted to no forefathers for a family history: the chronicle commenced with himself, and was altogether his own making" (41). The novel singles out John as the origin of what turns out to be a large family. In this patriarchal model the wife is reduced to a faint mirror image or a secondary echo of the paternal authority, so that the origin is singular rather than dual. Prior to John's marriage, he and Phineas are the sole characters whose actions provide suspense and drive the plot. Before the establishment of the Halifax family, Phineas speaks of "our little world" to refer to their narrow circle of interaction (91). By the end of the novel, that world will no longer be little, not only because John Halifax's influence grows, but also because he establishes a large household, whose members include his most intimate connections—his friend Phineas and wife Ursula—as well as his children. "[N]ow that our children are growing up, and our income is doubling and trebling year by year, we ought to widen our circle of usefulness," comments John, once they have established their large family (363). In this sentence, biological reproduction coincides with the multiplication of riches, signaling the way in which the novel provides psychological and biological analogues and indeed authorizations to growth.

The accumulation of capital takes place alongside other kinds of growth that are sanctioned by society and religion. The novel's fallen aristocrat Lady Caroline, who commits adultery, lacks children, and the intimation is that she is immoral precisely because she has no children who would induce a conscience in her. Producing offspring is a moral act in this expansionist novel.

By suggesting the interchangeability of economic production and biological reproduction (John excels in both), *John Halifax, Gentleman* dispels the threat of scarcity, which the birth of neoclassical economics would soon foreground. In biological terms, human reproduction is not an economy of depletion, in the sense that the birth of a first child does not make it less possible to conceive a second child. Production in the fossil economy, on the other hand, runs into scarcity as it depletes resources. However different procreation and economic growth may be for this reason and others, the plot structure of the novel is such that the family and the fortune mirror one another as fantasies of untroubled expansion.

John Halifax, Gentleman converts self-sustaining growth into a narrative structure that expands to integrate the experiences of the Halifax children into what at first appeared to be a Bildungsroman. Toward closure, the novel is no longer tracing the trajectory of a single character, but has become a compilation of coming-of-age-stories for multiple characters. The narrative spins out into multiple plots, which are not tightly connected one to another. This sprawling plot is the narrative corollary of John's swiftly multiplying riches, not simply because the parallel naturalizes expansion but because it provides a positive if notably conservative representation of equitably distributed wealth. What allows the novel to expand is the participation of the grown children in marriage plots. Guy and Edwin fall in love with the same young woman, and she returns the latter's love, to the former's devastation. The novel traces Guy's and Edwin's trajectories while at the same time communicating a young daughter's romantic attachment to an aristocrat who abandons his title. These courtship rituals point to the way in which capital reorganizes society, as it is redistributed to the bourgeoisie and flows through marriage. The urge to exchange and circulate that is associated with capitalism develops through the marriage plots, as money is transmitted through kinship and marriage. The marriage plots allow the novel to branch out, resembling the structure of expansion proper to the fossil economy. To the extent that heterosexual reproduction within marriage was normative at this time, its superposition with capital's "self-expansion" (M-C-M') in the plotline results in the naturalization of the latter.

The contemporary response to the novel registered the peculiarity of its expansiveness. One reviewer wrote: "*John Halifax* would have been unquestionably better in two volumes. We can give our interest to the hero and heroine; but when asked to transmit our affections to a second generation, we feel that the author is drawing too heavily on our good nature" (Anonymous 1856, 85). The reviewer seems eager for the narrative to provide an individual's Bildung, which would be in line with the novel's ideological embrace of the self-made man. Yet by its final third, the novel focuses on multiple characters connected by blood and the circulation of family money. For the bourgeoisie, the imagined root of wealth may be a self-made man, but as the money accumulates, the family becomes involved, as is evident in the novel in the establishment of a family firm, "Halifax and Son" (375). The proliferating plotlines of family members betray the impossibility of confining the story of wealth to a single generation—the children partake of the accumulated wealth. This narrative structure is loyal to the historical circumstances of nineteenth-century Britain, which constituted what Piketty calls an "inheritance society," "characterized by both a very high concentration of wealth and a significant persistence of large fortunes from generation to generation" (351). Capitalism did not hinder the centrality of inheritance, even though it claimed to replace aristocracy: hence, wealth is distributed but not redistributed.

THE TREATMENT OF CRISES AS EXTERNAL

The only stumbling block to expansion within the novel is the panic of 1825, which historically manifested itself through a series of bank failures. The novel's original audience had gone through another crisis approximately a decade before the year of publication, in the aftermath of the railway mania (Turner 2014, 72–75). With the growth economy presented as self-perpetuating, the novel must present the 1825 crisis as external to capitalism. The novel reassures its audience that such crises are the effect of individual moral failure and manageable through goodwill rather than technological innovation and/or capitalist expansion. In the coming years, neoclassical economics would deem crises exogenous, as if the market economy on its own would preserve equilibrium. For Jevons (1878), crises were rooted in as independent a phenomenon as fluctuations in solar rays, which affected crops.[13] Lacking such an explicit neoclassical framework, *John Halifax, Gentleman* nevertheless suggests the externality of crises, which it ascribes to an individual urge to speculate.

While John's fortune doubles and trebles without obstacles, other ventures overgrow. Phineas explains: "War having ceased, commerce, in its worst form, started into sudden and unhealthy overgrowth. Speculation of all kinds sprung up like fungi, out of dead wood, flourished a little, and dropped away" (377). The fungi-like growths in the system are the work of those who have not yet become rational actors of the kind neoclassical economics will presuppose. The solution to the problem lies in the personal merit of a select few. When the local bank seems doomed to fail as a bank run looms large, John, who has astutely invested in land rather than speculative commerce, prevents the collapse by depositing a large sum. The wisdom of his investment strategy ascribes a moral dimension to a market whose amorality was perceived as a threat. Individual goodwill can constitute a universal panacea, according to the narrator. Phineas comments, "I knew, almost by intuition, what [John] had done—what, in one or two instances, was afterwards done by other rich and generous gentlemen, during the crisis of this year" (391). The consolation that John is not one of a kind implies a trust in the money market whose contours are not foregrounded as a market per se but a little club of nice men. Such beneficent actors can compensate for the shortcomings of the masses of misguided investors, suggests the novel. John's actions counter the immorality of the market, which many Britons such as John Ruskin lamented. Through John's intervention, the novel imagines a paradoxical entity that pulls us outside classical and neoclassical assumptions of market mechanics: a market-economy in which individuals' actions are moral, not just rational. The novel recurs to an imagined moral economy, asserting John's ability as an individual actor to control the market, so as to humanize it.

The novel's economics also contradicts neoclassical principles by ignoring the issue of resource scarcity. Perhaps the most famous discussion of resource scarcity and depletion in the Victorian period was by Jevons, who identified a correlation between economic growth and the increase in coal consumption:

> Attention then is drawn [in this work] to the rapid and constant rate of multiplication displayed by the iron, cotton, shipping, and other great branches of our industry, the progress of which in general is quite unchecked up to the present time... The consumption of coal, there is every reason to suppose, has been similarly multiplying itself at a growing rate. (1865, xv)

The acceleration that Jevons makes explicit here is what Craik thematically raises and formally engages in her novel almost a decade before the publication of Jevons's *The Coal Question* (1865). Yet Jevons's central claim in this work, that "[w]e cannot long continue at our present rate of progress," by which he implies that the coal would not last (xvi), finds no equivalent in Craik's novel. Jevons writes, "the growth of production cannot go on *ad infinitum*; natural limits will ultimately be reached" (313). This acknowledgment of resource scarcity and natural limits to growth, which was in some ways already present in classical economics,[14] is absent in the account of the growth of the Halifax fortune.

Unlike neoclassical economists, Ricardo had not placed scarcity at the center of his theory of value, yet, he, too, recognized resource scarcity as a factor in economics. Nature, he wrote, "limited the productive powers of the land" (1819, 132). At the same time, his views were relatively optimistic, especially when compared to Malthus's bleak vision that the population grew faster than the supply of food: Ricardo "d[id] not assume any absolute limits but only admit[ed] that resources decline in quality and are therefore relatively scarce" (Barbier 2013, 1). Ricardian scarcity "implies that economic growth may lead to a temporary, increasing relative scarcity of a particular stock of resources, but this does not lead to an absolute constraint on growth" (4). Ricardo's preoccupation with the question of when and how growth would be possible is typical of classical economics, but by the mid-nineteenth century there was an exception to this tendency to seek growth: John Stuart Mill praised what Adam Smith called the stationary state. This alternative to the desirability of ongoing expansion is what I will briefly explore next. For all the strategies of naturalization and externalization apparent in Craik's novel, its wider context also harbors an ongoing worry about growth that becomes explicit in Mill's work. In Mill's notion of a stationary state, we can perhaps see an alternative formulation to that foregrounded in *John Halifax, Gentleman*.

THE IDEOLOGY OF GROWTH AND ITS DISCONTENTS

Craik's naturalization of growth is aligned with political–economic treatments of the topic by Smith and Ricardo. Smith had postulated that societies are in "advancing, stationary, or declining" conditions (Smith 1843, 26). The advancing state was the only desirable one:

> It deserves to be remarked, perhaps, that it is in the progressive state, while society is advancing to the further acquisition ... that the condition of the labouring poor, of the great body of the people, seems to be the happiest and the most comfortable. It is hard in the stationary, and miserable in the declining state. The progressive state is in reality the cheerful and the hearty state to all the different orders of the society. The stationary is dull, the declining, melancholy. (34)

Economic growth is associated with the happiness of the masses in Smith's model. Similarly, for Ricardo, the stationary state, which was inevitable if prohibitions on importation persisted, was undesirable. It was imminent because "the growth of capital and population leads to extension of cultivation to less fertile and less accessible land and to decreasing returns on cultivated land" (Blaug 1958, 6). The solution, according to Ricardo, was the repeal of the corn laws.

The approach to growth that Mill introduced in 1848 in his *Principles of Political Economy* ([1848] 1896) differed from Smith's and Ricardo's in that he found the stationary state desirable. He assumed that in Britain in the future "the rate of profit would speedily attain the minimum, and all further accumulation of capital would for the present cease." Yet this situation was not unwelcome. He declared, "I am inclined to believe that it [the stationary state of capital and wealth] would be, on the whole, a very considerable improvement on our present condition" (1896, 336). While capital and population are stationary, economic progress would not come to an end. Mill describes a state of society in which there is a "better distribution of property," "a system of legislation favoring equality of fortunes," "a well-paid and affluent body of laborers," "sufficient leisure ... to cultivate freely the graces of life," and concludes that "[t]his condition of society, so greatly preferable to the present, is not only perfectly compatible with the stationary state, but, it would seem, more naturally allied with that state than with any other" (338–339). Sheldon Wolin credits Mill with the "inversion of one of the basic liberal postulates concerning history: instead of the belief that moral and intellectual progress depended upon unceasing material advance, true progress was identified with the stage when material growth had ceased" (1960, 321).

Insisting on the possibility of progress in the economically stationary state, Mill cautioned against conflating one kind of growth with another: "It is scarcely necessary to remark that a steady condition of capital and population implies no stationary state of human improvement" (390–391). But such a conflation is precisely what we find in *John Halifax, Gentleman*, which renders the expansion of capital desirable in part by linking it to other kinds of growth such as familial procreation.

Multiple kinds of growth occurring simultaneously: this phenomenon, according to W. W. Rostow, explains the process of modernization and constitutes one of its key phases. While a society is going through its "take-off" stage toward modernization, "Growth becomes its normal condition. Compound interest becomes built, as it were, into its habits and institutional structure" (1960, 7, qtd. in Daly 1974, 149). If, during modernization, "growthmania" must mark a society's habits, that process is no doubt mediated by ideology of the kind we encounter in *John Halifax, Gentleman*. One of the functions of that ideology is to assure members of society that growth will be fairly distributed if not equitably distributed, that is, that growth will spread wealth but not spread equality. Daly writes,

> We are hooked on the habit of exponential growth. But this is seen as a healthy addiction from the view of social stability. One famous economist [H. C. Wallich] has told us that, "Growth is a substitute for equality of income. As long as there is growth, there is hope, and that makes large income differentials tolerable." (1974, 150)

Long recognized as holding up the myth of the self-made man, *John Halifax, Gentleman* simultaneously presents the expansion of capital as the expansion of wealth in the population, albeit a limited population of bourgeois families and their heirs. Growthmania in the novel, as we have seen, is evident in the alignment of both familial expansion and narrative development with economic growth. Further, the novel presents the accumulation of John's capital as a process that improves the plight of his laborers without their partaking in that wealth in a significant way. The growthmania that shapes the plot and themes of *John Halifax, Gentleman* not only obscured economic inequality but also led to environmental crises, including climate change. The impossibility of divorcing the "self-expansion of capital" from the combustion of ever increasing amounts of fossil fuels in the age of industrial capitalism finds a memorable expression in the protagonist's attachment to the hearth. As the myth of the self-made man meets the dictates of "inheritance society," the hearth, with its dependence on coal and connotation of family, signals the ways in which the burning of fossil fuels is inextricably linked to the concentration and transmission of wealth. The fossil economy enlisted middle-class domestic ideology to create a narrative of boundless expansion, and the sprawling plotlines of *John Halifax, Gentleman* reify such expansion while at the same time signaling its overreaching.

NOTES

1. Jesse Oak Taylor discusses the hearth's connection to extra-domestic economies (2016, 52–53).
2. Patricia Yaeger discusses the ways in which we can temporally categorize literature based on the history of the use of energy resources (2011, 305–310).
3. Benjamin Morgan argues that the era of fossil capital was "also the era that imaginatively grappled with the intersecting planetary scales of ecology and empire" (2016, 609–635). Nathan Hensley and Philip Steer argue that literature formalized "the endlessness of fossil-capitalism's own structure" (2019, 76). Elizabeth Carolyn Miller examines the literary dimension of the fossil economy in George Eliot's *The Mill on the Floss* and William Morris's work, arguing that the fossil economy inspired a "distinct temporality" in the former case and a "surface aesthetic" in the latter (2015, 402; 2019, 86).
4. The intersection of economics and ecology has recently received critical attention. Taylor argues that the materiality of the (coal-induced) London smog contrasted the abstractness of the finance economy in Charles Dickens's *Our Mutual Friend*, and that the global circulation of petroleum found an apt analogy in the fungibility of blood in Bram Stoker's *Dracula* (2016, 122–141). Turning to the ramifications of thermodynamics, Allen MacDuffie argues that in the literary imagination "the dream that unbounded energy … w[ould] provide an escape from an enclosing, limited environment" was prevalent (2014, 192).
5. The ideological work of the novel has attracted critical interest, though not in regard to the fossil economy. Silvana Colella argues that *John Halifax, Gentleman* "contributed to the naturalization of self-interest" (2007, 397 and 410).

6. A brief summary of the novel is in order, since, despite its popularity in the nineteenth century, it is not widely known in our own. John Halifax first drives a cart of skins at a tanyard, where he is employed by the father of the narrator, Phineas. Then he works as an apprentice and a partner at that business, finally becoming a manufacturer of cloth, in which line of work he makes his fortune after replacing water power with a steam engine. A poor man, John falls in love with and marries Ursula March, who becomes estranged from her wealthy and powerful relatives as a result. As John accumulates social and financial power, the two start a family. Phineas lives with them as their friend and confidant, and their happiness is complete, until, that is, their oldest child dies in a melodramatic episode. The family otherwise prospers and grows as John's social and financial influence deepens, so much so that he singlehandedly prevents a bank run in his local community during a national financial crisis. The rest of the novel traces the adult children's lives, reporting their economic and marital triumphs. The novel comes to a close with the deaths of John and Ursula.

7. Rather than self-expansion, Ben Fowkes employs the phrase "the self-valorization of capital" in his translation (Marx 1977, 612).

8. In Marxian economics, accumulation, self-expansive as it may be, is not endless, as capitalism runs into endemic crises. Marx's principle of "the tendency for the general rate of profit to fall" had its roots in the classical economists' work (Marx 1981, 319).

9. Deanna Kreisel explains that the Victorians, following Malthus, feared that "excessive accumulation" would bring capitalism to an end (2012, 20). For the Ricardian position on growth, see Blaug (1958, 6).

10. The desirability of growth depends on whether the nation is already developed. According to the ecological economist Tim Jackson (2017), it is developed nations that can give up growth, not developing ones.

11. Herman Daly's work established the advocacy for steady-state economics. See Daly (1971, 1996). Daly proposes that we "replac[e] the economic norm of quantitative expansion (growth) with that of qualitative improvement (development) as the path of future progress" (1996, 1).

12. Thomas Piketty writes that prior to the Industrial Revolution, the growth rate was "virtually zero" (2017, 93). Geoffrey M. Hodgson makes the same point (2015, 361).

13. Keynes, by contrast, thought that the market was inherently unstable. For the Keynesian position, see Skidelsky (2010, 101–102).

14. Ricardo maintained that "growth will be accompanied by … diminishing returns to labor and capital" (Barnett and Morse 1963, 59).

REFERENCES

Anonymous. 1856. John Halifax, Gentleman. *Saturday Review of Politics, Literature, Science, and Art* 2:30 (May 24): 84–85.

Barbier, Edward B. 2013. *Economics, Natural-Resource Scarcity and Development: Conventional and Alternative Views.* New York: Routledge.

Barnett, Harold J., and Chardler Morse. 1963. *Scarcity and Growth: The Economics of Natural Resource Availability.* Baltimore: The John Hopkins Press.

Barry, John. 2009. 'Choose Life' Not Economic Growth: Critical Social Theory for People, Planet and Flourishing in the 'Age of Nature'. In *Nature, Knowledge, and Narration, Current Perspectives in Social Theory,* ed. Harry F. Dahms, vol. 26, 93–113. Bingley: Emerald Group Publishing.

———. 2016. Green Political Economy: Beyond Orthodox Undifferentiated Economic Growth as a Permanent Feature of the Economy. In *The Oxford Handbook of Environmental Political Theory,* ed. Teena Gabrielson, Cheryl Hall, John M. Meyer, and David Schlosberg, 314–317. Oxford: Oxford University Press.

Blaug, Mark. 1958. *Ricardian Economics: A Historical Study.* New Haven: Yale University Press.

Colella, Silvana. 2007. Gifts and Interests: *John Halifax, Gentleman* and the Purity of Business. *Victorian Literature and Culture* 35: 397–415.

Craik, Dinah Mulock. 2005. *John Halifax, Gentleman,* ed. Lynn M. Alexander. Peterborough: Broadview Press.

Daly, Herman. 1971. *Essays Toward a Steady-State Economy.* Cuernavaca, Mexico: Cidoc Cuaderno.

———. 1974. Steady-State Economics vs. Growthmania: A Critique of the Orthodox Concepts of Growth, Wants, Scarcity, and Efficiency. *Policy Sciences* 5 (2): 149–167.

———. 1996. *Beyond Growth: The Economics of Sustainable Development.* Boston: Beacon Press.

Douthwaite, Richard. 2006. *The Ecology of Money.* Cambridge: Green Books.

Eliot, George. 2015. *The Mill on the Floss.* New York: Oxford University Press.

Hensley, Nathan, and Philip Steer. 2019. Signatures of the Carboniferous: The Literary Forms of Coal. In *Ecological Form: System and Aesthetics in the Age of Empire,* ed. Nathan Hensley and Philip Steer. New York: Fordham University Press.

Hodgson, Geoffrey M. 2015. *Conceptualizing Capitalism: Institutions, Evolution, Future.* Chicago and London: The University of Chicago Press.

Jackson, Tim. 2017. *Prosperity Without Growth: Foundations for the Economy of Tomorrow.* New York: Routledge.

Jevons, William Stanley. 1865. *The Coal Question: An Inquiry Concerning the Progress of the Nation and the Probable Exhaustion of Coal Mines.* London and Cambridge, MA: Macmillan and Co.

———. 1878. Commercial Crises and Sun-Spots. *Nature* 19: 33–37.
Kreisel, Deanna. 2012. *Economic Woman: Demand, Gender, and Narrative Closure in Eliot and Hardy*. Toronto: University of Toronto Press.
MacDuffie, Allen. 2014. *Victorian Literature, Energy, and the Ecological Imagination*. Cambridge: Cambridge University Press.
Malm, Andreas. 2016. *Fossil Capital: The Rise of Steam Power and the Roots of Global Warming*. London and New York: Verso.
Marx, Karl. 1906. *Capital: A Critical Analysis of Capitalist Production*. Vol. 1. Translated by Samuel Moore and Edwards Aveling. London: Swan Sonnenschein.
———. 1977. *Capital: A Critique of Political Economy*. Vol. 1. Translated by Ben Fowkes. New York: Vintage.
———. 1981. *Capital: A Critique of Political Economy*. Vol. 3. Translated by David Fernbach. London: Penguin.
Mill, John Stuart. 1896. *Principles of Political Economy with Some of Their Applications to Social Philosophy*. Vol. 2. New York: D. Appleton and Company.
Miller, Elizabeth Carolyn. 2015. William Morris, Extraction Capitalism, and the Aesthetics of Surface. *Victorian Studies* 57: 395–404.
———. 2019. Fixed Capital and the Flow: Water Power, Steam Power, and *The Mill on the Floss*. In *Ecological Form: System and Aesthetics in the Age of Empire*, ed. Nathan K. Hensley and Philip Steer. New York: Fordham University Press.
Moore, Jason W. 2016. The Rise of Cheap Nature. In *Anthropocene or the Capitalocene: Nature, History, and the Crisis of Capitalism*, ed. Jason W. Moore, 78–115. Oakland, CA: PM Press.
Morgan, Benjamin. 2016. Fin du Globe: On Decadent Planets. *Victorian Studies* 58: 609–635.
Piketty, Thomas. 2017. *Capital in the Twenty-First Century*. Translated by Arthur Goldhammer. Cambridge, MA: Belknap Press.
Ricardo, David. 1819. *On The Principles of Political Economy and Taxation*. London: John Murray.
Rostow, W.W. 1960. *The Stages of Economic Growth*. Cambridge: Cambridge University Press.
Skidelsky, Robert. 2010. *Keynes: The Return of the Master*. New York: Public Affairs.
Smith, Adam. 1843. *An Inquiry into the Nature and Cause of the Wealth of Nations*. Edinburgh: Thomas Nelson.
Taylor, Jesse Oak. 2016. *The Sky of Our Manufacture: The London Fog and British Fiction from Dickens to Woolf*. Charlottesville: University of Virginia Press.
Turner, John. 2014. *Banking in Crisis: The Rise and Fall of British Banking Stability, 1800 to the Present*. Cambridge: Cambridge University Press.
Wolin, Sheldon S. 1960. *Politics and Vision: Continuity and Innovation in Western Political Thought*. Boston: Little, Brown.
Yaeger, Patricia. 2011. Editor's Column: Literature in the Ages of Wood, Tallow, Coal, Whale Oil, Gasoline, Atomic Power, and Other Energy Sources. *PMLA* 126: 305–310.

CHAPTER 6

Sustainability

Sustainability and Its Discontents: The View from the Nineteenth Century

Deanna K. Kreisel

Fear lurks behind the proliferating, sanitized term "sustainability."
—*Alaimo (2012, 559)*

In a recent essay, literary scholar Stacy Alaimo highlights the dangers of the panacea of environmental sustainability and suggests that the concept "may be serving a psychological function in the social consciousness" (559) by allowing the ecologically minded to sidestep difficult questions about economic justice and biodiversity. Alaimo notes that humanities scholars, who "challenge reliance upon the authority of 'nature' or 'science' in order to address problems that in their origin and solution are primarily social and cultural," have a crucial role to play in developing more ethically responsive models of sustainability (Kitch, Adamson, et al.; qtd. in Alaimo, 560).

D. K. Kreisel (✉)
University of Mississippi, Oxford, MS, USA

© The Author(s) 2019
E. Hadley et al. (eds.), *From Political Economy to Economics through Nineteenth-Century Literature*, Palgrave Studies in Literature, Culture and Economics, https://doi.org/10.1007/978-3-030-24158-2_6

129

That is, of course, assuming environmental and economic "sustainability" is a realistic, desirable, or even coherent goal. Even in its most anodyne formulations, sustainability is haunted by unanswerable questions. The seemingly straightforward definition given in the Brundtland Report (officially entitled *Our Common Future*), published by the United Nations World Commission on Environment and Development in 1987, defines sustainability as development which meets "the needs of the present without compromising the ability of future generations to meet their own needs" (1987, n.p.). The new-materialist critic will immediately demand: generations of what? Even if we assume that "future generations" means human beings—already a deeply controversial exclusion—crucial questions still remain. *All* human beings? How many? At what standard of existence? And for how long? (And this is not even considering how such a state of affairs is to be brought about and maintained.)

As the Brundtland definition implies, sustainability and conservation discourse has long been, and continues to be, dominated by the imperative to maintain human life and civilization under conditions similar to those that we now enjoy. This focus on the needs of human beings—rather than the needs of other-than-human creatures, biospheres, or ecosystems—also tends, through its emphasis on maintenance of the status quo, to favor relatively privileged human beings of the global north. As Alaimo notes, sustainability discourse tends to "render the lively world a storehouse of supplies for the elite" (558). When framed in such anthropocentric terms, environmental stewardship comes to resemble simply ideological cover for an instrumentalist orientation toward nature. As Nathaniel Wolloch has pointed out, "the history of economic considerations of nature was one of consistent development of one main theme—the emphasis on the ineluctable need to maximize the use of natural resources and thus further human development.... This is a history of continuity rather than change" (2017, x).

This chapter will proceed with the following two assumptions: (1) In order to take up Alaimo's call for a humanities-driven reassessment of the sustainability idea, we should begin with the origins of the concept in nineteenth-century discourses of population and resource management. (2) Such a history will underscore the inconsistency, untenability, and perhaps even bad faith of our contemporary focus on sustainability. The concept itself is the legacy of nineteenth-century political economy and its uptake in Victorian popular consciousness—for sustainability is essentially an economic concept. The questions of population and resource management, sustainability's central areas of concern, are ones with which political economy (and later, economics) have long wrestled.[1] By tracing the economic roots of sustainability in the nineteenth century this chapter will help reveal its inherent complexities and contradictions.

POPULATION ACCORDING TO MALTHUS

While the word "sustainable" did not come to refer specifically to the reduction of environmental impact until 1976, the concept has a much older history.[2] Proto-sustainability practices in the form of environmental stewardship can be traced to the development of forestry management and other conservationist agricultural practices in the middle ages. According to Paul Warde, the German concept of *Nachhaltigkeit*, or "lasting-ness," is usually dated to Hans Carl von Carlowitz's *Sylvicultura oeconomica* of 1713, yet can be found as early as the 1650s (2011, 153). Ulrich Grober explains that after the Thirty Years' War, "the economists and foresters of the German mini-states developed a vision: the possibility of providing a long-term, secure and steady supply of wood from *der ewige Weld* (the eternal forest). Out of this vision emerged the concept of *Nachhaltigkeit*, sustainability" (2012, 75).[3]

The concept of sustainability as currently understood began to have real traction only after the 1798 publication of The Reverend Thomas Malthus's *Essay on the Principles of Population*. Malthus's argument is simple yet devastating: population increases geometrically (exponentially) yet food supply increases arithmetically (linearly); eventually the sharper upward curve of population growth meets the shallower upward curve of food production at a crisis point, where famine becomes unavoidable and population growth will inevitably be "checked." Malthus's influential thesis on the limits to growth make his work a natural starting point for a history of sustainability—which is one compelling reason to turn to the nineteenth century more generally as the intellectual and economic crucible of the concept. (Other reasons include the increase in carbon production occasioned by the industrial revolution, and the birth of political economy as a professional discipline in the early decades of the century.) As Margaret Schabas notes, "the main contribution of the *Essay* was to bring attention to bear on the problem of scarcity, not only of land, but also of capital" (2005, 105).

For literary critics, particularly of the Victorian period, Catherine Gallagher's reading of Malthus remains most influential. She argues that the paradox at the heart of Malthus's thesis is that the very vitality and fecundity of human bodies become the undoing of the social body:

"Malthus simultaneously sees the unleashed power of population, the reproducing body, as that which will eventually destroy the very prosperity that made it fecund, replacing health and innocence with misery and vice.... Hence, no state of health can be socially reassuring" (2006, 39). What is most important about Gallagher's analysis for a history of sustainability is her insight that the Malthusian thesis refocuses economic discourse on the horizon of *system*: "[Malthus's] essay starts another durable plot line of classical political economy, in which the gross organic entity is less a metaphorical individual, such as 'the nation' or 'the population,' than what we now call an 'ecosystem'" (43). In Malthus we first see, in a theory of political economy, the consistently developed rhetoric of interconnectedness that we now associate with an ecological sensibility.

As John MacNeill Miller argues in a recent discussion of the "ecological plots" of Harriet Martineau and Charles Dickens, which he shows were strongly influenced by Malthus's *Essay*, our "focus on Malthus as a theorist of scarcity has emphasized his contributions to the theory of natural selection ... [but] the *Essay*'s understanding of interconnection made it central not only to Darwin's development of modern biology, but to his ecological insights as well" (forthcoming, n.p.). Both Gallagher and Miller ground their discussions on a famous passage in the *Essay* in which Malthus suggests that cattle may "eat" human beings as much as the reverse:

> When the price of butcher's meat was very low, cattle were reared chiefly upon waste lands ... but the present price will not only pay for fatting cattle on the very best land, but will even allow of the rearing many, on land that would bear good crops of corn. The same number of cattle, or even the same weight of cattle at the different periods when killed, will have consumed (if I may be allowed the expression) very different quantities of human subsistence.... The present system of grazing, undoubtedly tends more than the former system to diminish the quantity of human subsistence in the country, in proportion to the general fertility of the land. (Malthus 2015, 133–134)

As Miller glosses, "all of human society depends on the geographically specific patterns of the apportioning of soil and sunlight among plants. Our material entanglements ensure that the fates of humans and nonhumans are never fully extricable from one another." What is important about Malthus's image is the way it reimagines the food system as an *ecosystem* in which the fates of different species are enmeshed. The coy parenthesis that follows the phrase "will have consumed," "(if I may be allowed the expression)," prepares us to read the clause that follows as a Swiftian "quantities of human *beings.*" Malthus's imaginative (re)configuration—along with, as we shall see shortly, its attendant contradictions—is an important precursor to contemporary discourses of sustainability, particularly in the way it presages recent discourse about the environmental costs and social inequities of meat production and consumption.[4]

While most commentators, both contemporary to Malthus and in our own day, have focused on the relentless pessimism of his thesis, it also depended on the fundamental predictability of natural laws, as Schabas points out: "he maintains that it would be impossible to develop a 'human science' if nature were 'fickle and inconstant'" (2005, 106). In Malthus's own words, "The constancy of the laws of nature, and of effects and causes, is the foundation of all human knowledge" (73). Herein lies another crucial paradox of the Malthusian thesis, one which continues to bedevil contemporary sustainability discourse. Immediately after the passage about cattle eating men quoted by Gallagher, Malthus goes on to blunt the implications of this radical vision of ecological interconnectedness—that is, the implications of the kind that modern-day ecocritics draw about the decentering of the human—by returning the question to one of human agency:

> I would not by any means be understood to say, that the former system either could, or ought, to have continued. The increasing price of butcher's meat, is a natural and inevitable consequence of the general progress of cultivation; but I cannot help thinking, that the present great demand for butcher's meat of the best quality, and the quantity of good land that is in consequence annually employed to produce it, together with the great number of horses at present kept for pleasure, are the chief causes, that have prevented the quantity of human food in the country, from keeping pace with the generally increased fertility of the soil; and *a change of custom in these respects*, would, I have little doubt, have a very sensible effect on the quantity of subsistence in the country, and consequently on its population. (134–135)

For Malthus, at least in the early editions of the *Essay*, the description of the problem is a preamble to a discussion of how it might be addressed through the altering of human behavior. As Gallagher notes, "In two sections of the *Essay*'s first edition that were later heavily revised or altogether scrapped, he shifted his focus from inevitable biological constraints to alterable market forces.... And once reconceived in this way, the problem of population pressure, although always an impediment to perfect happiness, appears at least partially responsive to human will" (2006, 43–44). Malthus's location of the problem—and solution—at the level of "custom" also anticipates the way the majority of popular sustainability discourse is framed: as a question of consumer choice and responsibility.[5] Yet human agency (in the form of foresight and self-control) is a vexed concept. For Malthus, nature is the consistent and predictable expression of divine providence, yet human sexual passions are also part of nature and cannot be circumvented. Indeed, a central motive in Malthus's hasty scribbling of the 1798 pamphlet was his desire to refute William Godwin's utopianist prediction (in *An Enquiry Concerning Political Justice* [1793]) that human sexual passion will eventually be extinguished under a rationalist system of social and economic equality. Malthus objects:

> Mr Godwin considers man too much in the light of a being merely intellectual....
> The voluntary actions of men may originate in their opinions; but these opinions will be very differently modified in creatures compounded of a rational faculty and corporal propensities, from what they would be, in beings wholly intellectual. (108)

Yet it is crucial to note that sexual restraint in the form of abstinence and late marriage were the *only* morally acceptable preventive checks to population that Malthus proposed (as opposed to the "positive" checks of famine, disease, and war). According to Malthus, a "slow progress in population cannot be traced to a decay of the passion between the sexes. We have sufficient reason to think that this natural propensity exists still in undiminished vigour" (35). And here is another central paradox of Malthus's thesis: sexual passion is as vigorous as it has ever been, and surely will continue to be so, and the only acceptable check against the misery of inevitable famine is rational restraint of that passion from creatures "compounded of a rational faculty and corporal propensities" (109).

In this disguised appeal to an attenuated human agency that is feared unequal to the task, surely we recognize from its very beginnings the melancholic resignation that characterizes so much recent sustainability discourse? Even when not explicitly tethered to humanity's inability to curtail its base passions (sexual desire *qua* reproduction for Malthus, selfish consumerism *qua* carbon production for us), most treatments of the sustainability concept are marked by a sense of futility, even impossibility. In a beautifully argued meditation on the conundrum of sustainability, Allan Stoekl characterizes this sense of futility as a problem of representation: "How do we represent this future in order to calculate the appropriate level of our resource consumption?... Should their world resemble ours?" Even on a more practical level, as soon as we attempt to calculate all possible external costs of any environmental impact we are quickly confronted with, in Stoekl's phrase, the "sublime of externalities": "We suspect that the impossibility of calculating externalities [economic costs or benefits accruing to a party who did not choose them] is akin to the withdrawal of God: if we really could calculate externalities all would be possible, foreseeable; without it, we walk through the desert, yearning for the moment of deliverance" (2013, 44).

William Lloyd's Extensions to Malthus

Malthus was not the only population theorist writing in the early decades of the nineteenth century. A central figure in the discussion was William Forster Lloyd, whose *Two Lectures on the Checks to Population* (1833) expanded and developed the implications of Malthus's thesis in important ways. The lectures more fully explore the operational "checks" to population that Malthus had outlined, which he had divided into the "positive," which increase the number of premature deaths, and the "preventive," which curtail the number of births. For Malthus, the latter category is essentially equivalent to checks due to human activity (or lack thereof): what he terms "moral restraint," or abstinence and late marriage. (While Malthus alludes throughout his work to "vice" as a potential preventive check to be avoided, Lloyd instead refers without overt moralism to "promiscuous intercourse" [by which he means all sexual activity without a reproductive aim] that "beyond a certain degree, prevents the birth of children" [1980, 474]). Malthus essentially brackets positive checks due to any causes other than restraint, such as lowered fertility due to malnutrition or disease; his two categories of checks, then, break down into those that are a result of human agency and those that lie (largely) outside its purview.

Lloyd alters Malthus's schema by dividing checks along a different axis:

Suppose that the cases, in which prudential restraint arises from the fear of a want of sustenance, were clearly distinguishable, by some manifest token, from those in which it depends on other motives.... Then the view of the subject would be comparatively simple, and we might draw a hard line of distinction between the different checks, separating them into two classes, and placing on one side of the line all those motives, and all those diseases and other causes, which diminish fecundity or destroy life, and which arise from a scarcity of the means of subsistence; and on the other, all causes productive of the same effect, but originating in moral and physical circumstances totally independent of this scarcity. (476)

In other words, rather than dividing checks into categories based on which end of the population equation they affect (births or deaths), or those due to human agency versus natural forces, Lloyd proposes dividing them according to whether or not they are caused by a shortage of food. He thus reorients Malthus's model by making the central, driving engine of population the quantity of available sustenance. This may indeed be the way most simplistic versions of the model view its operations—food is turned into human bodies, and when the food runs out the bodies will be reduced in number—yet, as we have already seen, Malthus himself does not present the question in such organicist terms.

The reason Lloyd effects this thought experiment is ultimately in order to argue for the natural benefits of private property. He argues that "systems of equality, with a community of labour and of goods, are highly unfavourable" to the preventive check or moral restraint (478). Where property is held in common, the interest in one's own labor becomes "so small as to elude perception" and "the motive for economy entirely vanishes." In this case, Lloyd argues, "the future is struck out of the reckoning" because "the constitution of the society is such as to diffuse the effects of individual acts throughout the community at large, instead of appropriating them to the individuals, by whom they are respectively committed" (479).

Lloyd uses these fairly commonplace Lockean apologetics not for their own sake, but to further an argument about population growth with a particular emphasis on affective relations to futurity. Without regard for the future, men will marry early and have children they cannot support, since

in a community of goods, where the children are maintained at public tables, or where each family takes according to its necessities out of the common stock, these difficulties are removed from the individual. They spread themselves, and overflow the whole surface of society, and press equally on every part. All may determine their conduct by the consideration of the present only. All are at liberty to follow the bent of their inclinations in an early marriage. But, as we have already seen, it is impossible to provide an adequate supply of food for all who can be born.... [T]he shares of subsistence are continually diminishing, until all are reduced to extreme distress. (480)

The organicism of Lloyd's vision of the social field is striking: Society is a "whole" with a "surface," around and against which the importunities of sustenance "press" with greater and greater exigency. Although in Lloyd's metaphor it is the "difficulties" of maintaining children that spread and overflow the surface of society, the reader is invited to imagine the hordes of surplus children themselves "pressing" against the metaphorical breast of the commonwealth.

The scenario Lloyd describes is now referred to as the "tragedy of the commons."[6] Lloyd's illustration of the phenomenon, as in the earlier example from Malthus, also has recourse to the relative health of cows and grazing land: "Why are the cattle on a common so puny and stunted? Why is the common itself so bare-worn, and cropped so indifferently from the adjoining inclosures?" (482). The answer is that each individual herdsman, acting purely from self-interest, will continue to graze more and more heads of cattle as long as he reaps all the benefits of their sale but shares their costs (in the form of the common stock of grass) with the other herdsmen.

Lloyd's cattle thus "eat" men, but in a more indirect manner than Malthus's. Whereas in the earlier example, cattle and human beings were in a sense competing for the same sustenance (land diverted to cattle grazing is land that is not being used to grow food directly for human consumption), in Lloyd's scenario, the intervening structure of a "system of equality" is necessary to draw out the interconnectedness of bovine and human welfare. In the logic of Lloyd's text, the scenario of land held in common is imposed upon an imaginary pre-existing state of "natural" self-interest: "I do not profess to be here considering generally the merits of systems of equality, and, therefore, I shall not stop to inquire, whether any, and what substitute, for the motive of private interest, can be suggested, to stimulate exertion, to prevent waste, and to check the undue increase of population" (480). It is only in the case of a frankly bizarre combination of perfect self-interest and zero regulation with commonly held property that the tragedy of the commons as Lloyd describes it would pertain.[7]

Lloyd ultimately concludes, at the end of his second lecture, that the theory of population thus supports the already established "common reasons" for private land ownership, "since the earth can never maintain all who can offer themselves for maintenance" (495). The institution of private property is thus naturalized in Lloyd's scenario, and consequently, so are the concomitant checks to population.

MALTHUS AND HIS DISCONTENTS

Both Malthus and Lloyd (and other nineteenth-century Malthusians and neo-Malthusians, including evolutionary theorists Charles Darwin and Alfred Russel Wallace) thus directly contravene the older mercantilist claim that growing population is not just a sign, but also a driver, of economic prosperity. While Malthus's thesis largely prevailed in Victorian England (with some important exceptions), elsewhere the iron law of population was challenged, blunted, or outright rejected in political-economic and popular discourse. Possibly the thesis did not have much purchase in areas with large tracts of land perceived to be "waste" and small settler populations. For example, as American writer Charles M. DuPuy argues, "The earth teems with raw material, awaiting the magic of labor and capital to mould and fashion into usefulness.... The world is not over-populated, and certainly its crude products are not all utilized. Properly organized, there should be ample room for the exercise of all grades of faculties" (1875, 1–2). Just as the concept of *terra nullius*—the claim that unimproved land, unmixed with labor, is "waste" and therefore unowned—has underpinned justifications for European colonialism for half a millennium, so settler colonies saw a high birth rate as crucial not only to the "improvement" of such land, but also to the subduing (i.e., genocide) of indigenous populations.[8] The frankly extirpative logic of the *critique* of Malthusianism anticipates, in interesting ways, leftist criticisms levied *against* Malthusianism in recent decades, a question to which I will return.

There were other, more politically palatable, critiques of the Malthusian thesis in the nineteenth century.[9] One of the most important—and scathing—critics of Malthusianism was, of course, Karl Marx. For Marx and Engels, Malthus's thesis was erroneously ahistorical; he ascribed to organic laws of nature a putatively inevitable situation that is instead historically contingent on capitalist means of production. Piers J. Hale describes a significant countertradition to Malthusianism in nineteenth-century evolutionary discourse, complicating received notions of Darwin's indebtedness to Malthus in formulating the concept of natural selection (2016). There was also a rich tradition of socialist anti-Malthusianism extending from Marx through to Morris and Kropotkin. As Hale notes in his analysis, the anti-Malthusianism of the Romantic radicals such as Godwin, Southey, and Coleridge (discussed in detail by Gallagher) did not simply go away, but continued to be an important part of socialist thought throughout the century, "a tradition [of] anti-Malthusian evolutionist politics that ran through into British socialism, [and] was rejuvenated in the London radical clubs in the 1880s" (Hale 2016, 198).

It is, finally, worth mentioning that Malthus himself becomes a critic of reductive Malthusianism, in a sense. While it is a commonplace to note that there are two substantially different versions of the *Essay*—the pamphlet of 1798 and the subsequently expanded and more thoroughly researched editions[10]—few critics outside the discipline of history of economic thought wade deeper into the contradictory morass of theories represented by Malthus's magnum opus, *The Principles of Political Economy* (1820). In this later work, Malthus is much more concerned about insufficient effective demand, the threat of gluts and stagnation, and refuting the reassurances of Say's Law underpinning Ricardian political economy, than worrying about over-population. (On the contrary, population *growth*—along with opening up colonial markets—is one suggested solution to the problem of effective demand.)

Anti-Malthusian arguments thus cluster around three central themes: (1) The population conundrum is a result of capitalism and is thus not inevitable or "natural," (2) the finitude of resources can be addressed through cooperation and regulation, and (3) technological development (usually driven by capitalist speculation) will continue to increase food production and the exploitation of other resources, theoretically forever. Earlier critiques of Malthusianism are the intellectual antecedents of the intensive debate surrounding population growth and control that continues today. While this chapter cannot do full justice to the complexity of these arguments, three key themes are important to note. First, since the late nineteenth century, population control has become associated, particularly amongst leftist and feminist critics, with racist eugenics. Second, most traditional economists, because of their presumptions about continuous economic growth, have concluded that Malthusian anxieties are unwarranted, and that the population problem has been "solved." And third, environmentalists and ecocritics are much less sanguine about population and recently have begun to sound the alarm about the possibility that we might be approaching the carrying capacity of the planet. (Indeed, the morality of childbearing was a topic already explored by Thomas Hardy in *Jude the Obscure* (1895), and less overtly in his earlier novels as well. See Matz 2014.)

In a recent polemic, Donna Haraway tackles head-on the longstanding association of population control with misogynist and racist practices, urging feminists and others concerned with environmental and social justice to revisit the question of human numbers: "The super-peopling of the earth with both humans and industrial and pathogenic nonhumans is a worlding practice premised on the commitment to endless growth and vastly unequal wellbeing" (2018, 71–72); and even more stringently: "anti-racist feminist avoidance of thinking and acting in public about the pressing urgencies of human and nonhuman global populations is akin to the denial of anthropogenic climate change" (87). While Malthusianism might have seemed, for a time, a quaint idea whose applicability had long since expired, environmental crisis has brought Malthus's insights back to the forefront of ecocritical consciousness. As Alan Macfarlane has argued, "as resources reach their limits and the external costs of the massive use of carbon energy become apparent in pollution and global warming, it appears that the ghost of Malthus has arisen again" (2008, 573).

Resource Exhaustion

The second foundational pillar of sustainability is resource management. While Malthus of course dealt with both of these questions in the *Essay*—it is the relationship between numbers of people and resources in the form of human sustenance that is, after all, his central concern—the resources side of proto-sustainability discourse grew more complex later in the century as economic thinkers started worrying about the depletion of wood, coal, and other fossil fuel resources. Both debates concern photosynthesis, energy, feedback loops, and the maintenance of human bodies, but anxieties over coal reserves abstract and complicate the brute energy-life calculus on which Malthus's thesis was focused.

Several decades after Malthus and Lloyd, England was gripped by a sustainability panic due not to fears of over-population, but rather to anxieties over the eventual exhaustion of coal reserves. In a sense, this concern was a continuation of the early-modern discourse of forest management, with the crucial difference that the later theorists were also grappling with a post-Lyellian understanding of the vast time scales involved in the replenishment of fossil fuel resources, as opposed to wood. (Charles Lyell's *Principles of Geology* [1830–1833] was published precisely contemporaneously with the later editions of Malthus's *Essay* and Lloyd's lectures on population). Of course, this is a radically anthropocentric view of the matter—as is conceptualizing parts of nature as "resources" for human use in the first place. In theory, coal is every bit as renewable as Scotch fir, but the time periods involved in its replenishment render it, practically speaking, non-renewable from the perspective of human beings.[11]

There were two distinct waves of anxiety over coal exhaustion, as Nuno Luis Madureira (2012) has helpfully outlined. In the earlier decades of the century, Britons' sense of the size of their coal reserves was characterized by "geological pessimism," due to the fact that surveys had taken place primarily in coalfields that were already undergoing depletion: "Given the lack of up-to-date knowledge on the stock of British solid fossil fuels, isolated cases of depletion which statistically held little current relevance were perceived as on the verge of snowballing into a frightening future" (2012, 400). However, the results of the British Geological Survey in 1861, as reported by its director, geologist Edward Hull, at least temporarily laid those fears to rest: "the above supply of coal will last for about 1000 years…. [F]or many generations to come, the mineral resources of England are capable of bearing any drain to which they can possibly be subjected either for home or foreign consumption" (1861, 139).

Hull's estimate quelled anxieties over coal depletion for a time; however, equanimity on the question lasted only a couple of years. In 1863, William George Armstrong sounded the alarm again:

The phase of the earth's existence suitable for the extensive formation of coal appears to have passed away for ever; but the quantity of that invaluable mineral which has been stored up throughout the globe for our benefit is sufficient (if used discreetly) to serve the purposes of the human race for many thousands of years…. Turning, however, to our own particular country, and contemplating the rate at which we are expending those seams of coal which yield the best quality of fuel, and can be worked at the least expense, we shall find much cause for anxiety. (1864, liii)

The problem, according to Armstrong, is that Hull's report did not take into account increasing demand for coal. Extrapolating from current consumption patterns, Britons could expect their coal reserves to be exhausted in 212 years, and for true abundance (and hence British economic superiority) to last closer to 100 years. As Madureira argues, Armstrong's address represents a shift from a purely geological view of the question to a more properly economic one (2012, 405). It also chimed with a national panic that had only very recently been quieted, and thus readily found a believing public ear.

Shortly after Armstrong revived public anxiety over coal exhaustion, William Stanley Jevons sharpened and developed the economic view in his highly influential study *The Coal Question* (1866). The crucial insight of this work has since been dubbed the "Jevons Paradox" and continues to affect discussions of resource conservation to this day. The paradox essentially states that as technological development increases the efficiency with which a resource is used, prices will be driven down and demand will thus increase, creating a "rebound" effect which ultimately leads to greater overall consumption. Jevons's estimate for the time frame for coal exhaustion was 100 years, as opposed to Armstrong's 212. (Armstrong had predicted the end of *abundance* in 100 years, and *exhaustion* in just over 200.)

It is important to note that by "exhaustion," Jevons meant the point of practical impossibility of extraction, as he clarified in his second edition:

> Many persons perhaps entertain a vague notion that some day our coal seams will be found emptied to the bottom, and swept clean like a coal-cellar. Our fires and furnaces, they think, will then be suddenly extinguished, and cold and darkness will be left to reign over a depopulated country [note that Jevons implies population is not an independent variable!]. It is almost needless to say, however, that our mines are literally inexhaustible. We cannot get to the bottom of them; and though we may some day have to pay dear for fuel, it will never be positively wanting. (1866, v–vi)

Jevons thus refocused the problem of resource depletion away from the abundance of "nature" and toward the human problems of consumption patterns and technology.[12] While he may have drastically underestimated the amount of accessible coal, his emphasis on human behavior and economic laws (rather than divine providence or static natural reserves) as crucial factors determining long-term resource supply turned the debate into something more closely resembling a "sustainability" discussion. In our current moment, when the limited environmental resource of utmost concern is carbon sinks rather than fossil fuel reserves,[13] these are the factors—human behavior and economic laws—around which sustainability discourse again circles, in the form of price caps, carbon offsets, clean(er) energy development, and usage reduction.[14]

Another striking similarity between the Victorians' anxieties over resource depletion and our own is the way a vigorous public discussion marked by pessimism and fear co-exists with a popular discourse of chirpy optimism. That latter discourse, in Victorian-era writings, can be divided into three types: reassurances about the inexhaustibility of coal reserves, justifications for the human use of those reserves, and, as Benjamin Morgan has recently discussed, an attempt to resolve the tension between incommensurable time scales.[15] These imperatives, as one would expect, often co-exist in the same texts.

In "The Coal Question," a short anonymous piece published precisely in the brief period between Armstrong's and Jevons's analyses (Anonymous 1863), the author spends paragraphs rehearsing the various resource catastrophes that possibly await Britain, helpfully reminding the reader that coal is not the only resource that can be depleted: "it is highly curious that the fright about fuel has not been pushed home, beyond the coal question. There is reason to believe that even before coal is exhausted wood will be exhausted" (226). After raising the various dire scenarios that might ensue were wood and coal both to be exhausted, perhaps even simultaneously—"Imagine the British Isles … without fuel, or with only a scanty supply at an enormous price. Before such a consummation, the population would have dwindled in proportion to the decline of fuel"— the author abruptly shifts registers to close on a bizarrely optimistic note. Interestingly, his prediction is the precise *opposite* of the Jevons Paradox, which was to have such an enormous impact two years later: "We do not believe, however, that the calamity we are imagining will ever come to pass, for we have faith in science and invention, and cannot suppose that the present barbarous, wasteful means of obtaining heat will last for another century or two. As soon as the price of fuel rises with diminished supply for an increased population, ingenuity will full surely be at work to meet the deficiency, or furnish a substitute" (227). This belief in the salutary benefit of technological advances in extraction and development are, of course, still with us—and are still subject to the same objection from the point of view of Jevons's Paradox (see, e.g., Alcott 2005). The coexistence of a pervasive anxiety about over-population in the wake of Malthus's

Essay and a vigorous, reassuring discourse about the inexhaustible bounty of nature strike a modern reader as irresponsible or bizarre—or would, anyway, if it were not so familiar to us in our own historical moment.

THE FUTURE

If we take the foundations of sustainability discourse to be population growth and resource allocation, the continuities between the preoccupations of nineteenth-century writers and those of the present day are striking. Both anxieties and assurances continue to take remarkably similar forms—an insight with the potential to be somewhat depressing. (We still haven't figured these things out?) Yet the repetitions and revisitings are also understandable: The problem of sustainability is essentially one of futurity.[16] Sustainability discourse, no matter how it is defined or framed, demands that social and economic structures be organized not only in the most efficient and fair manner for the people, creatures, and earth of today—a difficult enough question to address—but that they also be so organized for *tomorrow*.[17]

For this reason among others, the sustainability concept has been the subject of important recent critiques. Stacy Alaimo, Leerom Medovoi, Allan Stoekl, and Jeremy Davies, for example, have pointed out the deep problems inherent in the concept. As Davies notes, "to talk of sustainability and steady-state economics is to deal in abstractions that would be equally applicable at any time; it is to engage in a romance of stasis" (2016, 199). That is, sustainability discourse attends to spatial constraints (resources, population, the carrying capacity of the planet) while fantasizing that temporal constraints can be overcome—that the current state of affairs can go on nearly forever.

There are also fundamental philosophical premises that sustainability discourse tends simply to take for granted: First and foremost, that those alive today do, or should, care about those alive in the future. What are our bases for this assumption? Are they the same or different than they were for the Victorians? If the latter, what has changed and why? While the technical requirements of true sustainability (however defined) are central to the difficulty of its implementation, we should not discount the possibility that its philosophical muddledness is also a crucial factor. The fact that for the Victorians, as well as us, sustainability discourse tends to swing wildly between extremes of optimism and pessimism—that it mobilizes an affective economy that is also out of scale—seems to indicate a perhaps irresolvable tension inherent in the concept. Before we can determine *how* to go about achieving sustainability, perhaps we first need to figure out *whether* and justify *why*—a task that Victorian sustainability discourse set out for us, and left unanswered.

NOTES

1. Climate change is a more recent addition to this constellation of problems.
2. Recent treatments of sustainability by Allen MacDuffie and Leerom Medovoi have traced tensions in the word's etymological history that imply its inherent incoherence or untenability (MacDuffie 2014; Medovoi 2010).
3. While Grober's aim is to emphasize the ancient roots of the sustainability concept in order to lament our post-lapsarian state, the thesis of Warde's study is the relatively recent *invention* of sustainability (Warde 2018, 4).
4. See Pickles (2017), Greenwood (2018), and Carrington (2018).
5. There has been recent pushback against "consumer responsibility" discourse and an attempt to re-frame the problem of climate change as due largely to corporate greed. See Darby (2018).
6. The term comes from ecologist Garrett Hardin, who coined the phrase after rediscovering Lloyd's pamphlet in 1968 (Hardin 1968).
7. Similar critiques have been levied at Hardin's employment of the concept. See the special issue of Environmental Science & Policy entitled "Interrogating the Commons," particularly Araral (2014).
8. See Bashford and Chaplin (2016). For an indispensable overview of *terra nullius* that traces the concept much farther back than the origin in John Locke that is usually cited, see Pateman (2007).
9. See Wiltgen (1998) and Charbit (2009).
10. Although, as Yves Charbit argues, "there is a strong theoretical and doctrinal continuity between the successive versions" (2009, 10). For an excellent discussion of the tensions and contradictions across Malthus's body of work, and a convincing attempt to reconcile them, see Chap. 2 of his book. See also Chapter One of Kreisel (2012) for discussion and bibliography.
11. For an excellent overview of the Victorian conception of time scales, see Jonsson (2018).
12. *The Coal Question* fanned the flames of coal panic for a time, but over the next two decades, further geological surveys assuaged British anxieties by substantially re-evaluating the size of available coal reserves. See Clapp (1994), Wrigley (2010, 2016).

13. Carbon sinks are reservoirs—either natural (such as trees, oceans, and soil) or human-made—that remove carbon dioxide from the atmosphere and store it for an indefinite period of time.

14. "It is worth noticing that if Jevons is right, then encouraging energy-efficiency as a means of reducing carbon emissions would be a counterproductive policy" (Madureira 2012, 409).

15. Elizabeth Carolyn Miller's recent work has also considered the narrative formations attendant upon these resolutions in the work of William Morris, George Eliot, Joseph Conrad, and others (E. C. Miller 2015, 2017).

16. One of the central concerns of queer ecology, an important new direction in ecocritical thought, is the question of our affective relations to futurity; this work has drawn from foundational queer theory on "the antisocial thesis" by Leo Bersani, Lee Edelman, Jack Halberstam, Elizabeth Freeman, and José Esteban Muñoz, among others. See, for example, Mortimer-Sandilands (2010), Seymour (2013), and Kreisel (2018).

17. The conceptual synthesis of long-term population and resource management is the steady-state economy. Adam Smith and David Ricardo feared the stationary state as the inevitable future of capitalism (Marx referred to it as the "bourgeois 'Twilight-of-the-Gods'"), while later thinkers such as J. S. Mill and John Ruskin welcomed the stationary state (Marx 1952; Mill n.d.; see also Parham 2017). Recent versions of zero- (or even negative-) growth economies in response to ongoing environmental crisis have been championed by ecological economists, most prominently Herman Daly (1991, 1996).

References

Alaimo, Stacy. 2012. Sustainable This, Sustainable That: New Materialisms, Posthumanism, and Unknown Futures. *PMLA* 127 (3): 558–564.

Alcott, Blake. 2005. Jevons' Paradox. *Ecological Economics* 54 (1): 9–21.

Anonymous. 1863. The Coal Question. *Littel's Living Age*, October 31.

Araral, Eduardo. 2014. Ostrom, Hardin and the Commons: A Critical Appreciation and a Revisionist View. *Environmental Science & Policy*, Interrogating The Commons 36 (Feb.): 11–23.

Armstrong, William. 1864. Address of the President. In *Report of the Thirty-Third Meeting of the British Association for the Advancement of Science*. London: John Murray.

Bashford, Alison, and Joyce E. Chaplin. 2016. Malthus and the New World. In *New Perspectives on Malthus*, ed. Robert J. Mayhew, 105–127. Cambridge: Cambridge University Press.

Carrington, Damian. 2018. Beef-Eating 'must Fall Drastically' as World Population Grows. *The Guardian*, December 5, sec. Environment. https://www.

theguardian.com/environment/2018/dec/05/beef-eating-must-fall-drastically-as-world-population-grows-report.

Charbit, Yves. 2009. *Economic, Social and Demographic Thought in the XIXth Century: The Population Debate from Malthus to Marx.* Dordrecht and London: Springer.

Clapp, B.W. 1994. *An Environmental History of Britain since the Industrial Revolution.* London and New York: Longman.

Daly, Herman E. 1991. *Steady-State Economics.* 2nd ed. Washington, DC: Island Press.

———. 1996. *Beyond Growth: The Economics of Sustainable Development.* Boston: Beacon Press.

Darby, Luke. 2018. Billionaires Are the Leading Cause of Climate Change. *GQ*, October 11. https://www.gq.com/story/billionaires-climate-change.

Davies, Jeremy. 2016. *The Birth of the Anthropocene.* Berkeley: University of California Press.

DuPuy, Charles M. 1875. *Wasted Faculties.* Pamphlet Reprint. 1875 Dupuy 53647.O.25. Library Company of Philadelphia.

Gallagher, Catherine. 2006. *The Body Economic: Life, Death, and Sensation in Political Economy and the Victorian Novel.* Princeton: Princeton University Press.

Greenwood, Ariel. 2018. 'Eat Less Meat' Ignores the Role of Animals in the Ecosystem. *Civil Eats*, January 26. https://civileats.com/2018/01/26/eat-less-meat-ignores-the-role-of-animals-in-the-ecosystem/.

Grober, Ulrich. 2012. *Sustainability: A Cultural History.* Translated by Ray Cunningham. Devon, UK: Green Books.

Hale, Piers J. 2016. Finding a Place for the Anti-Malthusian Tradition in the Victorian Evolution Debates. In *New Perspectives on Malthus*, ed. Robert J. Mayhew, 182–207. Cambridge: Cambridge University Press.

Haraway, Donna. 2018. Making Kin in the Chthulucene: Reproducing Multispecies Justice. In *Making Kin Not Population: Reconceiving Generations*, ed. Adele E. Clarke and Donna Haraway, 67–99. Chicago, IL: Prickly Paradigm Press.

Hardin, Garrett. 1968. The Tragedy of the Commons. *Science* 162 (3859): 1243–1248.

Hull, Edward. 1861. *The Coal-Fields of Great-Britain: Their History, Structure and Duration: With Notices of the Coal-Fields of Other Parts of the World. With Illustrations.* 1st ed. Edward Stanford.

Jevons, William Stanley. 1866. *The Coal Question: An Enquiry Concerning the Progress of the Nation, and the Probable Exhaustion of Our Coal-Mines.* 2nd ed. London: Macmillan.

Jonsson, Fredrik Albritton. 2018. Learning to Scale: The Case of Victorian Britain. In *Work in Progress: Economy and Environment in the Hands of Experts*, ed. Frank Trentmann, Anna Barbara Sum, and Manuel Rivera, 35–46. Munich: Oekom Verlag.

Kitch, Sally, Joni Adamson, and Faculty Working Group on Humanities and Sustainability. 2008. *Contributions of the Humanities to Issues of Sustainability.* Arizona State University Press.

Kreisel, Deanna K. 2012. *Economic Woman: Demand, Gender, and Narrative Closure in Eliot and Hardy.* Toronto: University of Toronto Press.

———. 2018. Response: Queering Time. *Victorian Studies* 60 (2): 236–242.

Lloyd, William Foster. 1980. W. F. Lloyd on the Checks to Population. *Population and Development Review* 6 (3): 473.

MacDuffie, Alllen. 2014. *Victorian Literature, Energy, and the Ecological Imagination.* Cambridge: Cambridge University Press.

Macfarlane, Robert. 2008. Malthusian Trap. In *International Encyclopedia of the Social Sciences,* ed. William A. Darity Jr., vol. 4, 2nd ed., 572–574. Detroit, MI: Macmillan Reference USA.

Madureira, Nuno Luis. 2012. The Anxiety of Abundance: William Stanley Jevons and Coal Scarcity in the Nineteenth Century. *Environment & History* 18 (3): 395–421.

Malthus, T.R. 2015. *An Essay on the Principle of Population and Other Writings.* Penguin.

Marx, Karl. 1952. *Theories of Surplus Value.* Translated by Emile Burns and G. A. Bonner. New York: International.

Matz, Aaron. 2014. Hardy and the Vanity of Procreation. *Victorian Studies* 57 (1): 7–32.

Medovoi, Leerom. 2010. A Contribution to the Critique of Political Ecology: Sustainability as Disavowal. *New Formations* 69 (69): 129–143.

Mill, John Stuart. n.d. *Principles of Political Economy with Some of Their Applications to Social Philosophy.* Library of Economics and Liberty. http://www.econlib.org/library/Mill/mlP61.html.

Miller, Elizabeth Carolyn. 2015. William Morris, Extraction Capitalism, and the Aesthetics of Surface. *Victorian Studies* 57 (3): 395–404.

———. 2017. Extraction Ecologies and Victorian Literature. Keynote Address Presented at the North American Victorian Studies Association Conference, Banff, Canada.

Miller, John MacNeill. forthcoming. The Ecological Plot: A Brief History of Multispecies Storytelling, from Malthus to *Middlemarch. Victorian Literature and Culture,* Open Ecologies, 2020.

Mortimer-Sandilands, Catriona. 2010. Melancholy Natures, Queer Ecologies. In *Queer Ecologies: Sex, Nature, Politics, Desire,* ed. Catriona Mortimer-Sandilands and Bruce Erickson, 331–358. Bloomington, IN: Indiana University Press.

Parham, John. 2017. A Not So 'Stationary State': John Stuart Mill's Sustainable Imagination. In *Victorian Sustainability in Literature and Culture,* ed. Wendy Parkins, 14–31. London: Routledge.

Pateman, Carole. 2007. The Settler Contract. In *Contract and Domination*, ed. Carole Pateman and Charles W. Mills, 35–78. Cambridge: Polity Press.

Pickles, Matt. 2017. The Ethical Arguments Against Eating Meat, April 28. http://www.ox.ac.uk/news/arts-blog/ethical-arguments-against-eating-meat.

Schabas, Margaret. 2005. *The Natural Origins of Economics*. Chicago: University of Chicago Press.

Seymour, Nicole. 2013. *Strange Natures: Futurity, Empathy, and the Queer Ecological Imagination*. Urbana: University of Illinois Press.

Stoekl, Allan. 2013. 'After the Sublime,' After the Apocalypse: Two Versions of Sustainability in Light of Climate Change. *Diacritics* 41 (3): 40–57.

Warde, Paul. 2011. The Invention of Sustainability. *Modern Intellectual History* 8 (1): 153–170.

———. 2018. *The Invention of Sustainability: Nature and Destiny, c. 1500–1870*. New York: Cambridge University Press.

Wiltgen, Richard J. 1998. Marx's and Engels's Conception of Malthus: The Heritage of a Critique. *Organization & Environment* 11 (4): 451–460.

Wolloch, Nathaniel. 2017. *Nature in the History of Economic Thought: How Natural Resources Became an Economic Concept*. London; New York: Routledge; Taylor & Francis Group.

World Commission on Environment and Development. 1987. *Our Common Future*. United Nations. http://www.un-documents.net/our-common-future.pdf.

Wrigley, E. A. (Tony). 2010. *Energy and the English Industrial Revolution*. Cambridge: Cambridge University Press.

Wrigley, E.A. 2016. *The Path to Sustained Growth: England's Transition from an Organic Economy to an Industrial Revolution*. Cambridge: Cambridge University Press.

PART III

Property

CHAPTER 7

Rent

"When a House Is So Much More": Character, Tenancy, and Property in Victorian Fiction

Audrey Jaffe

In *Evicted: Poverty and Profit in the American City* (2016), Matthew Desmond describes a landlord, "Sherrena," as she surveys Milwaukee's North Side. She sees, he writes, what other people see: "street after street of saggy duplexes, fading murals, twenty-four hour day cares, and corner stores with "WIC accepted here" signs. But she also sees something more. In terms that blur the difference between places and the people who use or inhabit them, "she knew … the vicissitudes of life, by shades and moods … which multifamily, which church, which bar … She knew the ghetto's value and how money could be made from a property that looked worthless to people who didn't know any better" (10). The "saggy duplexes" and "fading murals" are the signs of renters in distress. What Sherrena sees, and by seeing knows, is the "look" of a cityscape when it comes to the business of owning, renting, and, in this particular context,

---

The quotation headlines a 2018 *New York Times* article by Jen A. Miller.

A. Jaffe (✉)
University of Toronto, Toronto, ON, Canada

© The Author(s) 2019   153
E. Hadley et al. (eds.), *From Political Economy to Economics through Nineteenth-Century Literature*, Palgrave Studies in Literature, Culture and Economics, https://doi.org/10.1007/978-3-030-24158-2_7

evicting, and how that look enables some to profit from the impermanence and decay etched on the landscape of modern urban life.

She is, in other words, a speculative pedestrian—the moniker Charles Dickens gave his persona "Boz," the narrator of the short sketches known collectively as *Sketches by Boz* (1836–1837). (Based on the urban sketch-writing genre practiced by Addison and Steele in the 1700s, and others such as George Sala, John Thompson and Adophe Smith, and Blanche Jerrold and Gurtave Doré in the nineteenth, these are the earliest pieces for which Dickens is known. Published as "ephemera" in newspapers and magazines in the early 1830s, they were collected in one and two-volume editions in 1836–1837).[1] Boz is the wanderer or flâneur who surveys the city, scanning the urban landscape for signs of economic activity with a special interest in the decline and decay of persons and structures. These observations of London life in the 1830s, especially the pieces collected as "Scenes," focus on lower-class activity in the city: on modes of transportation, such as hackney coaches and omnibuses; on entertainments, such as Vauxhall Gardens; on markets, especially secondary or "fringe" vendors such as second-hand clothes and pawnbrokers' shops. In these pieces, Dickens comes up with a form that captures the 1830s London version of what Desmond's Sherrena sees in twenty-first century Milwaukee: the way structures and population display to the eye alert for its signs what, borrowing and adapting from what the geographer David Harvey has called the "relative permanence" of certain features of urban life, I would like to call the "relative impermanence" of the urban landscape.

Harvey's term refers to the way elements of the built environment come to seem natural over time while the labor that built them is forgotten (1974, 240). An individual's relation to property in modern capitalist society in general, and in Dickens's work in particular, defines a contrast between permanence and mobility that itself characterizes the entrenchment of income inequality that has remained in place from the nineteenth century to the twenty-first.[2] Home ownership during this period becomes part of an ideological claim to the stability of character and to longevity— the longevity if not of an individual life, than of a family's name and wealth. Renting or lodging, by contrast, become signs of economic insecurity and the tenuous identity or character traits (unreliability; unwillingness to work hard, etc.) that tend to be linked to it.[3] Speculative pedestrians (which, I would argue, many urban dwellers have of necessity become) see spaces and structures not only as opportunities for profit or signs of economic status, but also, crucially, as indications of the relation between housing and life: the assumed connections, characterological and financial, between individuals and the spaces they inhabit in the modern urban community.

I wish to explore the degrees of permanence and impermanence that connect specific forms of property with particular kinds of characters and identities in Dickens's work, Victorian ideology, and contemporary US culture. Both Victorian ideology and contemporary US culture reinforce a narrative that links property ownership with maturity, adulthood, and financial success. But both cultures, too, are full of reminders of the impermanence of the seemingly settled or permanent: in the mortgages or taxes that remind "owners" of the incompleteness of their purchase; in the ever-present possibility that property may have to be given up in the face of health care or other costs; in the increasingly frequent disasters such as earthquakes and hurricanes that destroy homes thought to be permanent. In Dickens's novels too, ownership often fails to bring the idea of "more" it seemed to promise, disrupting the narrative's own apparent trajectory from—as I will argue—transience to permanence. That promise is reinforced, in a parallel movement, by the ties critics have established between Dickens's own career and his movement between literary forms, in which the sketch, an ephemeral form linked to the transience of the renter or lodger, is succeeded in the mature author's work by the solidity and completeness of novels, which often end with a central character's assumption of property. In this context, publication form is explicitly linked to literary value: the *Sketches*, ephemeral or transient in their original form, are later assembled into a whole, transformed from ephemera into an enduring form of Dickensian property.[4]

Dickens's "sketching" of the economic landscape and attention to the status of its inhabitants charts a revision of transience into mobility: in the capitalist city, wandering and noticing activate the desire for social mobility, and for property ownership—including, in Dickens's case, the relentless drive toward the ownership of copyrights to his own works, as well as the more obvious symbol of property in Gadshill.[5] The shift from transience to mobility to permanence or ownership became a part of the authorial narrative that defined him—part, again, of that same middle-class ideology that positions house and home as fulfillment. And not only does he begin his writing career with a form called "sketches," but he also produces, during the course of that career, a series of plots in which—and a cast of characters for whom—a certain sketchiness of character and identity is associated with being a renter, while solidity arrives (or seems to) with the conclusiveness of ownership. (In an apt [and Dickensian] detail, early sketches for which Dickens was not paid were called "idlers" [Chittick 43]).

The Speculator as Young Boy

The anecdote with which John Forster begins his biography of his close friend Charles Dickens—a story of the young author-to-be as speculative pedestrian—encapsulates the shift from transience to mobility:

> The house called Gadshill-place stands on the strip of highest ground in the main road between Rochester and Gravesend. Very often had we travelled past it together, many years before it became his home; and never without some allusion to what he told me when first I saw it in his company, that amid the recollections connected with his childhood it held always a prominent place, for, upon first seeing it as he came from Chatham with his father, and looking up at it with much admiration, he had been promised that he might himself live in it or in some such house when he came to be a man, if he would only work hard enough. Which for a long time was his ambition. The story is a pleasant one, and receives authentication at the opening of one of his essays on travelling abroad, when as he passes along the road to Canterbury there crosses it a vision of his former self.
>
> So smooth was the old high road, and so fresh were the horses, and so fast went I, that it was midway between Gravesend and Rochester, and the widening river was bearing the ships, white-sailed or black-smoked, out to sea, when I noticed by the wayside a very queer small boy.
>
> "Holloa!" said I, to the very queer small boy, "where do you live?"
> "At Chatham," says he.
> "What do you do there?" says I.
> "I go to school," says he.
>
> I took him up in a moment, and we went on. Presently, the very queer small boy says, "This is Gadshill we are coming to, where Falstaff went out to rob those travellers, and ran away."
> "You know something about Falstaff, eh?" said I.
> "All about him," said the very queer small boy. "I am old (I am nine), and I read all sorts of books. But *do* let us stop at the top of the hill, and look at the house there, if you please!"
> "You admire that house?" said I.

"Bless you, sir," said the very queer small boy, "when I was not more than half as old as nine, it used to be a treat for me to be brought to look at it. And now I am nine, I come by myself to look at it. And ever since I can recollect, my father, seeing me so fond of it, has often said to me, *If you were to be very persevering, and were to work hard, you might some day come to live in it.* Though that's impossible!" said the very queer small boy, drawing a low breath, and now staring at the house out of window with all his might.

I was rather amazed to be told this by the very queer small boy; for that house happens to be *my* house, and I have reason to believe that what he said was true.

The queer small boy was indeed himself. (4–5)

This story is so well known that it may not seem worth repeating—but repetition is in many ways its point. When Dickens was young, Forster writes, his father told him that if he worked hard he might someday own Gadshill or a house much like it; this after the boy expressed his admiration for the house (and the admiration of real estate by a such a young person is of course a key detail). Later, again as Forster recounts it, he and Dickens often passed by the house, and Dickens always alluded to the story, which, Forster tells us here, is "validated" by Dickens's repetition of it elsewhere, just as the whole—and the myth it repeats—is itself validated by the fact that the adult author purchased not just any house but that same exact one, as if to affirm for himself and others what he and all the world already knew—that he had indeed worked hard and fulfilled his childhood dream.

Repetition reinforces the anecdote's fairy-tale quality: it is a wish fulfillment, simultaneously miraculous and ordinary, individually tailored but also infinitely generalizable. The imagined encounter suggests that desire for the big house is both universal (there must be many such boys) and unique, and that the wishes of some boys—the "queer," literary ones in particular—are so powerful that these boys are especially likely to succeed. But it also captures a more characteristic nineteenth-century trajectory: one which leads from transience (the walking by, noticing, that characterizes urban life) to mobility (the noticing of property leads to the desire to rise) to ownership (the achievement of a desired social status, signified by owning property).

Another myth on display in this fantasy is, of course, that of the self-made man, a story both British-Victorian and American, enduring from the nineteenth century to the present day. This capitalist success story manifests itself in the form of home ownership for particular historical reasons—so many that I can only describe a few of them here. We may trace it, for instance, to a set of middle-class values that took hold in the early to mid-nineteenth century—part of a constellation of ideas linking housing, identity, and character. It was in its Victorian configuration shaped by the separate-spheres ideology based on two figures: the wife, mother, and household manager (the familiar figure of the "Angel in the House," after Coventry Patmore's poem) who made the middle-class home a refuge where the Victorian husband and father went to replenish his body and spirit so as to return to work the next day, and the breadwinner successful enough to purchase the kind of home his status demanded. Bill Bryson dates the desire for "splendid townhouses" to the invention of the middle class and the rise of the middle-class professional in the mid-nineteenth century. "Suddenly there were swarms of people with splendid townhouses that all needed furnishing, and just as suddenly the world was full of desirable objects with which to fill them. Carpets, mirrors, curtains, upholstered and embroidered furniture and a hundred things more that were rarely found in houses before 1750 now became commonplace" (2010, 229).

But the desire for "splendid townhouses" (a specifically urban formulation, though I am speaking of the country house as well) also derives from, and bears traces of, an older if equally fantasmatic "Lord of the Manor" scenario involving nostalgia for that extended (and therefore even more imaginatively permanent) period during which societies were structured around those who owned the land, those who worked the land, and those who supplied the capital that enabled this process to exist, as Ricardo articulated in his *Principles of Economy* (1817). Indeed, the ideas of land and landedness, wealth and indestructibility that prop up the feudalist fantasy in general and little Charles Dickens's desire for Gadshill in particular are essential to Ricardo's definition of rent as "that portion of the produce of the earth which is paid to the landlord for the use of the original and indestructible powers of the soil" (Hunt and Lautzenheiser 2011, 92). The "dream" of property projected in this fantasy is consistent with a lord-of-the-manor image more attuned to the age Dickens was leaving behind than the one he was entering; the Gadshill house suggests the landed gentry, the estate worked by peasants in fealty to their master. But if the idea of rent has its origins in agriculture and the working of the land in fealty to its owner, in the urban context the imagery of earthiness and the land gives way to that of urban decay with which lodgers, renters, and those without any sort of home are often associated. More generally, the representation of owner and renter in Dickens's work and elsewhere in Victorian culture is marked as an opposition between permanence and impermanence, with the renter represented as a fleeting, partial, and not wholly proper subject—a transient on the way to ownership, if not stuck in a renterly midpoint.

AWAY FROM THE DIRT

We know that Charles's father, John Dickens, was a poor manager of money, and we know too that what his son represents as his own childhood trauma, in the "Autobiographical Fragment" (Forster 1872, 30–50), is an episode directly caused by his family's own housing crisis: as a small boy he was sent to work at Warren's Blacking, a shoe polish factory, because of his father's improvidence and the family's removal to debtors' prison. The imagery of working alongside dirty boys, and being himself literally and symbolically besmirched by this labor, appears throughout the "Fragment." Anthony Trollope, in his autobiography, writes of a similarly traumatic upbringing caused by his father's financial bungling—at the heart of which, too, is a story about a house and the inability to pay for it. Trollope writes of his father:

> In his early days he was a man of some small fortune and of higher hopes. They stood so high at the time of my birth, that he was felt to be entitled to a country house, as well as that in Keppel Street; and in order that he might build such a residence, he took the farm. (1999, 3)

That farm proves to be, as Trollope writes, "ruinous." Eventually, in an attempt to avert financial disaster (after the purchase of several other properties) Trollope's father bought a second farm, which fared no better than the first. With no capital and no particular skill at farming, the son writes, "[T]his was the last step preparatory to his final ruin" (7). Trollope emphasizes the "wretchedness" that followed, with the young Trollope living in the "wretched tumble-down farmhouse" and being tormented at school because of his lower-class appearance and status—"a wretched farmer's boy, reeking from a dunghill," who found himself sitting next to "the sons of big tradesmen who had made their ten thousand a-year" (12). Needless to say, in both cases, the narratives of the sons' successes serve as a counterpoints to and corrections of their tales of fatherly failure and filial shame; the story of rising from the dirt is a story of coming clean and rising into property. Unlike the fathers, the sons gained fame and fortune, provided for their families, and purchased the houses and homes they desired.

To be "a man of some small fortune and of higher hopes," feeling "entitled" to a fine piece of property, as Anthony Trollope describes his father, is to be a middle-class man of the nineteenth century. The small fortune, if used wisely, provides a window onto—and potentially opens a path toward—a larger one, while the "hopes," like the desire to purchase Gadshill, become a kind of pyramid, fueling the dream of the next financial venture, as in the buying of a farm so as to eventually buy the country house. That this sequence of events has the structure of, and sometimes results in, a "bubble"—a structure not supported by any firm ground (like the disastrous farmhouse, "always … in danger of falling into the neighbouring horse-pond")—is hardly undermined by the fact that some people, like Dickens, managed to achieve it; as in twentieth- and twenty-first-century America, the success of some individuals fuels—and fails to serve as a reality-check for—the desires and fantasies of others.

As industrialism transformed the ownership of agricultural land into the ownership of urban space and structures, it transformed the producer into a different kind of renter: one who did not produce wealth from land but rather earned wages. That the societal structure changed radically with the onset of the Industrial Revolution—that urban land was no longer "worked" but rather occupied by workers whose labor continued to feed a system of owners and landlords—did nothing to diminish the glory of the idea of becoming one of those owners. In fact, it arguably increased that desire, since the display of status became, as Bryson and others have pointed out, one of the middle class's chief concerns.

RENT

"What is rent a payment for?" Harvey asks provocatively, in an essay not on Victorian England but on 1970's Baltimore. Ricardo's theory of rent relied on the idea of scarcity: that land is not uniformly productive, and rates of rent will depend on the relative productivity of separately owned plots. Harvey's focus is not agriculture, but rather the way capitalism structures space itself as scarcity: rent is "a payment made by a user for the privilege of using a scarce productive resource which is owned by somebody else." Neoclassical economics, he points out, has taken the person out of the rent concept: "rent is regarded as a payment to a scarce 'factor' (which is a 'thing' concept) rather than as an actual payment to people." Divorced from the persons who actually pay and receive it, rent "appears ... innocently in the neoclassical doctrine of social harmony through competition" (240).

The term "relative impermanence" links the ephemerality, transience, and unkempt-ness that come to be attached, to varying degrees, to Victorian London as well as twentieth- and twenty-first century Baltimore and Milwaukee; it relies on the metonymic structure J. Hillis Miller defined as the *Sketches'* key method, tying the identities of persons or characters to the spaces they occupy and the clothing and objects they possess (1971). The speculative pedestrian arguably puts the person back in these depersonalized structures, but both he and the figures he depicts are defined chiefly by their relation to property. Dickens's later novels, I will suggest below, show that despite his early writings depicting the tenuous nature of lodging and renting, and a career trajectory that took him from renter to owner and from sketch-writer to novelist, he never ceased seeing property as a matter of relative impermanence.

Stratification

If the modern, urban renter is detached from the earth and produces only wages, the new and more severe stratification of persons into representatives of economic classes, along with the ideology of the home as static, peaceful, and orderly might be said to have reattached him to the earth: not as source of indestructible wealth, but rather as dirt, or what Mary Douglas has famously called "matter out of place" (1966, 41). A series of oppositions between transience and permanence, dirt and cleanliness, disorderliness and order helped secure a distinction between the rising middle classes in the nineteenth century and those below them in the social hierarchy: a distinction in need of securing in an age of rapid social mobility. It was a distinction that played out in fictional form as well, to some extent in the difference between major and minor characters detailed by Alex Woloch (2003). If the renter existed at all in mainstream, mid-century Victorian fiction (and I refer here to figures who are "permanent" renters, such as Skimpole, rather than those who rise into property, like John Harmon), he could be said to merely rent out space in the narrative, while the property owners, or those centrally involved in dramas about the transmission of property (including the desire for it) take up narrative space as its key protagonists and most fully realized characters. This trajectory from partial to more complete subjectivity plays out in the narrative of Dickens's own career and is reinforced by the literary forms and characters he developed as that career progressed.

If, as Desmond writes, "[l]ife and home are so intertwined that it is almost impossible to think of one without the other" (2016, 300), rent is the structure that most visibly displays the status of persons with only a tenuous hold on both. The Dickens character who is perhaps most aware of this situation is *Bleak House*'s Harold Skimpole ([1853] 2003), who is represented as being childlike because (not being the boy Charles Dickens was) he has no idea of permanent possession, asking nothing of society but to "let him live" (119), and whose relation to money and property is represented as a refusal of attachment—to persons as well as property. "Chairs and tables ... were wearisome objects; they were monotonous ideas, they had no variety of expression, they looked you out of countenance.... How pleasant, then, to be bound to no particular chairs and tables, but to sport like a butterfly among all the furniture on hire, and to flit from rosewood to mahogany, and from mahogany to walnut, and from this shape to that, as the humour took one!" (296). Skimpole's expectation that someone else will always pay is, of course, represented in *Bleak House* as reprehensible; the moral code of finance requires us to pay our own way, whether in cash, in spirit, or in life itself. (But in the context of such payment—as in the examples of Nemo, the novel's copywriter, or Richard Carstone, worn away by the case of Jarndyce and Jarndyce, and *Bleak House*'s overarching critique of a legal system whose participants are buried, like the case itself, in the innumerable costs, psychological as well as financial, of possession—the logic of ignoring cost altogether is, like Skimpole himself, unexpectedly appealing).

And if paying to exist is what capitalism in its various forms requires us to do, rent is a good metaphor for it—maybe in fact its best description. Asking us to pay for occupying space, capitalism requires us to regard that space as impermanent. And indeed, the drama of rent (the fact that it lends itself to drama, as Puccini's *La Bohéme* or the musical based on it, Jonathan Larson's "Rent") lies in its dependence on the movement of impermanent persons through only slightly less impermanent structures: structures whose sheltering nature, however provisional, temporarily offsets but also sharpens our sense of the transient—and therefore theatrically tragic—nature of human existence.

The Sketches

In the portion of Boz's *Sketches* grouped as "Scenes," the landscape and those who populate it are characterized by impermanence and disorder. In "Seven Dials," "The streets and courts plunge in all directions, until they are lost in the unwholesome vapour which hangs over the house-tops, and renders the dirty perspective uncertain and confined" (1995, 92). Characters' status as products of Dickens's imagination attests not, as is the case with major characters in the later work, to an effect of solidity or importance, but rather to one of transience: of identity not fully possessed because there is no space possessed, or even necessary, to house it. The idea that people, places, and possessions move through the city in various stages of moral and economic decline is the "Scenes'" narrative conceit: transience and decay are built into their form as well as their content. Indeed, if the novels repeatedly trace an upward trajectory—that of the *Bildungsroman*, or a more general movement on the part of key characters toward stability and property—the sketches offer little if anything in the way of plot, but rather repeated (and much simpler) trajectories of decline and decay on the part of structures as well as persons. In "Brokers' and Marine-Store Shops,"

> How different, and how strikingly illustrative of the decay of some of the unfortunate residents in this part of the metropolis! Imprisonment and neglect have done their work. There is contamination in the profligate denizens of a debtors' prison; old friends have fallen off; the recollection of former prosperity has passed away.... There they are, thrown carelessly together until a purchaser presents himself—old, patched and repaired, it is true, but the make and materials tell of better days and the older they are, the greater the misery and destitution of those whom they once adorned. (213)[6]

And in "The Pawnbrokers' Shop," a comparison of female customers in increasing levels of despair and degradation ends with the following summary:

> Who shall say how soon these women may change places? The last has but two more stages—the hospital and the grave. How many females situated as her two companions are, and as she may have been once, have terminated the same wretched course, in the same wretched manner. One is already tracing her footsteps with frightful rapidity. How soon may the other follow her example! How many have done the same! (229).

Decline is not only a human condition: the pawnbrokers,' like the gin shop, is both instrument of and witness to the disrepair of the people who make use of it—a "receptacle" for misery and distress. "Shops and Their Tenants" ends by focusing on the "innumerable changes" in the shop's ownership, as the tobacconist gives way to a theatrical hair-dresser, a bonnet-shape maker, a greengrocer, and then a tailor—figures whose identities merge with the nature of material they sell or the service they perform. There is no ownership of identity, here, only borrowing, with elements or names drawn from what one temporarily wears or does; identities lie on a trajectory people share by virtue of briefly occupying the same borrowed space, bearing as their only names the names of their trades. Identity is both borrowed from and projected onto a series of temporary surroundings, and is fungible, as are the places it occupies. Inquire for a "Thompson" at a lodging house, "and you will find several" (92); of the wards in Newgate prison, Boz writes, "a description of one is a description of the whole" (239).

The clothing in "Meditations on Monmouth Street" becomes an overarching metaphor for the idea of a structure that people do not own but merely move through. Indeed, Dickens highlights the sketch's subjects as structures defined by their permanent impermanence, so that even clothing, itself subject to inevitable decline and transformation, becomes, in "Monmouth Street," temporary housing for persons with only temporary identities—identities that, like the clothing that represents them, are soiled and ill-fitting:

> The first was a patched and much-soiled skeleton suit; one of those straight blue cloth cases in which small boys used to be confined.... It had belonged to a town boy, we could see; there was a shortness about the legs and arms of the suit; and a bagging of the knees, peculiar to the rising youth of London streets.

The passage notes as well the whiteness of the knees, where their owner had rubbed them on the ground; the "numerous smears of some sticky substance about the pockets," and the "ink of pretty tolerable blackness" where the previous owner (or inhabitant) had evidently wiped his pen (99). In a world in which clothing provides temporary housing, the life of these clothes lies in the story they tell of their previous owner—a story, in this case, told in dirt.[7]

The street itself is a relatively permanent structure: "A Monmouth Street laced coat was a by-word a century ago, and still we find Monmouth Street the same…. Through every alteration and every change, Monmouth Street has still remained the burial place of the fashions, and to judge from all present appearances, it will remain until there are no more fashions to bury" (98). The narrator's "speculation" consists of populating the second-hand clothing on display with creatures from his own imagination, the "imaginary wearers" who might be envisioned occupying the waist-coats, shoes, and other garments available for sale to new owners. Indeed, the sketch supports the kind of metonymic reading J. Hillis Miller defines as tying realism to a narrative of decline: "A prison, and the sentence—banishment or the gallows…. We had no clue to the end of the tale, but it was easy to guess its termination" (1971, 101). But a revised account might see nineteenth-century realism as organized around an opposition between rising and falling not because of an inevitability built into realism's generic structure, but rather because Victorian economic ideology tied life to an opposition between self-making on the one hand, and decay and decline on the other—and both established and reified, through repetition, the connection between habitation and identity.

The abbreviated stories Dickens tells about these persons and places subordinate anything else that might be told about them to their economic status, in the form of the mechanisms that house them and move them around, and the decaying sites they and their decaying possessions occupy. As "signs of the times," part of the infrastructure of 1830s London, all of these things represent an urban life in flux, an impermanence that may remind readers of the desirability of permanence: of owning rather than renting. Here structures, buildings, or new tenants have only a temporary purchase, as we say, on life, before they are replaced by others who are interchangeable with them because of the economic status they share. This, Harvey notes, is the "urban landscape," in which "there may be considerable individual mobility," while the "social relations of labour under capitalism" remain stable and are reproduced (254).

Much of the criticism of the *Sketches*, and indeed of Victorian periodical literature in general, relies on a basic idea of the suitability of the ephemeral form of the sketch to its ephemeral subject matter; it also tends to insist, as Miller did, on a career trajectory in which Dickens's editors group the sketches in a narrative arc, forming a trajectory from scene to character to story.[8] In doing so, they bestowed something like permanence on the impermanence of the sketch form, transforming the sketches into another monumental Dickensian achievement, deserving to be possessed rather than borrowed or rented, with a key position in a career narrative about the development of an author training himself via observations of city life. This transmutation suggests the mobility of the sketch form itself within the context of Dickens's career.[9]

PROPERTY AND PERSONS

The identification of characters with the kind of housing they occupy persists throughout Dickens's work; indeed, the major novels are stories of property: of structures, like Chancery in *Bleak House* ([1853] 2003), that are concerned with inherited property and resemble it in their intractability, or *Little Dorrit* ([1848] 1998), with its emphasis on Casby, the property owner, and the rent he extracts from his tenants via the ambivalent figure of Pancks, and, finally, the drama of the fall of the Clennam house itself. *Our Mutual Friend* ([1865] 1997) gives us the story of the Dust-Heaps and the attempt to will them away, but it also includes Silas Wegg's fantastical appropriation of "Our House," a scenario in which—in another movement from transience to mobility—Wegg imagines himself the owner of the house in front of which he has positioned his stall, his own precarious livelihood positioned adjacent to and subsumed in his fantasy of ownership. The account of what he sells and where he sells it forms in large part his introduction as a character, just as that of Noddy Boffin, which follows closely upon it, rests on his status as resident of Boffin's Bower; its premium on "comfort," and the arrangement the couple have agreed upon to divide the property, or the "part of the room" allotted to each to arrange as he or she sees fit. "In consequence we have at once Sociability … Fashion, and Comfort" (Dickens 1997, 63). And on, and on; including the links established between the stinginess and resentfulness of Mrs. Wilfer (again in *Our Mutual Friend*) stemming from her lower-middle class status, which requires the family to take in a lodger—John Rokesmith—whose tangential identity can be resolved only when, in the novel's final chapters, he marries the daughter, receives his inheritance, and moves himself and his new family into a permanent home. Along the way, we meet such characters as the orphan Sloppy, homeless until adopted by Betty Higden, who is herself a subject of high pathos because, like *Bleak House*'s Jo, she must always move on—eventually dying outdoors as she flees to avoid the workhouse.

The most prominent role given to the idea of rent in the later novels appears in *Little Dorrit*, which features a representation of poverty in the inhabitants of Bleeding Heart Yard, and their persecutor in the form of the ambivalent rent-collector Pancks. Harvey discusses the idea that renters, despite their transitory status, may develop a sense of community, and that idea appears here. For if *Little Dorrit*'s major characters, including a few of the Yard's inhabitants, are distinguished by name, for the most part the inhabitants of Bleeding Heart Yard appear as a collective, as in their response to a new "foreigner" in their midst:

> [T]he Bleeding Hearts were kind Hearts, and when they saw the little fellow cheerily limping about with a good-humoured face, doing no harm … they began to think that although he could never hope to be an Englishman, still it would be hard to visit that affliction on his head.… They began to accommodate themselves to his level, calling him 'Mr. Baptist," but treating him like a baby. (323)

They are also spoken for as a collective by Plornish, in whose words the poor in the Yard "was always at it," "it" being the business of being poor:

> What was they a doing in the Yard? … There was the girls and their mothers a working at their sewing … day and night and night and day, and not more than able to keep body and soul together after all.… There was people of pretty well all sorts of trades you could name, all wanting to work, and yet not able to get it. (157)

Plornish's summary of the relation between the poor man and the rent he is asked to pay is perhaps one of the novel's most acute articulations: "his illogical opinion was, that if you couldn't do nothing for him, you had better take nothing from him" (157–158). It also articulates the demand, cited repeatedly in Desmond (2016), that renters with no source of income "must" find some way to pay if they wish to keep their housing—a strategy employed frequently by those seeking their eviction.

The sketch-to-novel trajectory of Dickens's career is often represented apologetically, as if reluctantly acknowledging the *Sketches* as "poor" in relation to Dickens's greater glory as novelist; it is not my desire to do any more apologizing here. In fact, I want to suggest that the renters' ethos reappears in the later novels in ways that suggest Dickens's own awareness of the relative impermanence of all property. For property in Dickens is never as solidly possessed as the idea of home—the feeling of "more"—it promises. The transience (or sketchiness) of rent and the "look" of human capital that accompanies it is visible in Bleeding Heart Yard; in the Cratchits of "A Christmas Carol" (1848) and the Coavinses of *Bleak House*; in the figure of Nemo, also in *Bleak House*, whose own transient life is matched by a gaunt and haggard look suggesting the interiorization of the property ethos I have been outlining. There is also the case of the brief-lived boy Dick, befriended by Oliver in *Oliver Twist* (1839); Betty Higden; Gridley, Carstone, and Jo. These characters, some of whom die in the street, exist largely to illustrate the evils of poverty, the neglect of persons by the larger system and its institutions. Such itinerant characters disrupt the narratives and lives of the more solid and ostensibly permanent ones, fracturing the centrality of figures whose economic and narrative situations are more fully developed and ostensibly more secure. Rather than positioning the *Sketches* as an apprentice form of writing, repurposed and strengthened by an ever-increasing closeness to narrative on the part of author, editors, and critics, in fact, we might see them—along with the transience they suggest—as something like a political unconscious, a record of permanent impermanence, as if the *Sketches'* figures-in-decline cling to the later work, unsettling the apparent solidity of the link between character and ownership. This unsettling might suggest, as do the novels themselves (and as does the prominent position Dickens gave the Warren's Blacking episode in his career) that Dickens's own psychological hold on that link remained tenuous. The *Sketches'* chief function has become their contribution to an autobiographical narrative in which they anticipate or foreground that more permanent-seeming form, the novel. But along with the evidence from Dickens's own childhood, they may also serve as reminders of the relative impermanence of the apparently permanent: the ephemeral, contingent status of modern urban life and the forms that distinguish it.

Coda I. The Housing Crisis

Were we not sufficiently aware of the "so much more" that a house is, the early 2000s, in which a crisis in housing set off a worldwide financial crisis, reminded us. In the 2000s, the United States was in the midst of what became known as a housing bubble (a term that suggests that, in addition to the ideological ways in which a house is said to be "overvalued," it also becomes emblematic of the problem of determining value: the thing that is reliably more or less—but never equal to—what it is worth). In the early

2000s, mortgages sold to people who couldn't afford them were "bundled" by brokers who passed them around amongst themselves, selling and reselling them without informing their owners, and in many cases losing track of the owners just as owners inevitably lost track of the institution that held the mortgage. Buyers who had relied on the idea that real estate would never decrease in value (and this is one interpretation of the "more" that housing was always supposed to be) were forced into foreclosure, losing their homes and the money they had put into them as their "overvalued" properties became "undervalued" ones. Many homeowners found themselves "underwater"—owing more on their property than it was worth—and defaulted on their loans, taking down along with them the firms that had loaned them money. The "bubble" that began the financial crisis was the overblown nature of housing prices, based on the outsized valuing of the house/home itself: its status as the goal and nexus of the "American Dream."

Coda II. The Eviction Machine

In 2018, *The New York Times* published a series of articles collectively titled "Unsheltered," about eviction and rent control in New York. The first two parts focus on strategies used by landlords to force tenants out of rent-controlled apartments; others describe a process called "the eviction machine," an elaborate system by means of which the bureaucracy and the courts function together to move vast numbers of New York City renters out of their apartments. What began as a system to "foster the repair and preservation of New York's aging housing stock" became "a business opportunity" (Kleinfeld and Barker 2018), as decrepit conditions were used to force tenants out of their apartments.

Many of Dickens's late novels are organized around eviction machines: a series of seemingly general, impersonal, legal, and bureaucratic structures that maintain a lethal grip on the lives of individual characters. In fact, we could say that the eviction machine is a nineteenth-century invention, reproducing the series of formulations such as "Nobody's Fault" and the Circumlocution Office in *Little Dorrit* and Chancery Court in *Bleak House*: vast, impersonal systems within which individuals are compelled to live and suffer. Dickens represented such systems as elements of modern bureaucratic culture; in Harvey's terms, they shape a landscape in which man-made structures take on an aura of permanence. Chancery Court is depicted as a kind of giant landlord, with "decaying houses and … blighted lands in every shire" (15); Jarndyce and Jarndyce is likened to life itself: "innumerable children have been born into the cause; innumerable young people have married into it; innumerable old people have died out of it" (Dickens 2003a, 16).

Chancery's end in *Bleak House*—the fact that it does end, a bubble burst by the pressure of its own futile energies—points toward Dickens's awareness of the impermanent permanence of the structures he is describing: the unsettledness built into the capitalist dynamic of which they are the machinery. In fact, Dickens perpetuated both ideas: that of the imprisoning, impersonal, machine, and that of the individual, vulnerable persons who, just as they brought these structures into being, inevitably caused their destruction. Returned to the dirt—exploded by their own internal pressure, like the Clennam house at the end of *Little Dorrit* or the Trollopian farmhouse—these machines both reproduce and redefine the bubble: ungrounded, they are propped up only by a set of expectations that, feeding on one another, lead to a desire for more that no built structure can satisfy. *Little Dorrit* ends with its central characters, Amy Dorrit and Arthur Clennam, not in a house rather but walking down the crowded streets; the home shared by John Harmon and his wife Bella at the end of *Our Mutual Friend* is founded on the ephemeral yet also solidly golden dust-mounds, with the bad humor and ill-will of the father who sought to control their destiny as well as his son's ostensibly erased. Such images call into question the idea of ever fully possessing a house that is always so much more, a phrase which itself suggests capitalism's continual dependence on such unsettled desires.

NOTES

1. See Schlicke (1999, 2005), Chittick (1990), and Agathocleous (2011) on Dickens and the urban sketch.
2. See Desmond (2017) for a discussion of the relationship between property ownership and inequality.
3. Tenuous identity can also mean illness and even death, as Desmond (2016) makes clear.
4. Coriale makes this point (2008, 802).
5. Garcha (2009) provides a detailed account of movement and stasis in Dickens's *Sketches*. I thank Elaine Hadley for her help with this formulation.
6. The idea of decay also works metonymically, tying persons to structures.

7. When Oliver arrives at the Maylies', the ragged, dirty clothes he wore as a member of Fagin's establishment are memorably (and repeatedly, since he is rescued several times) swapped for clean, well-fitting ones.
8. Also ephemeral was their initial form of publication: Boz's sketches appeared in newspapers and magazines before being collected in a single volume as *Sketches by Boz*. See Schlicke for a full account of individual pieces.
9. As Danielle Coriale points out, the publication of the *Sketches* in book form "transformed his writing from journalism to literature" (802).

References

Agathocleous, Tanya. 2011. *Urban Realism and the Cosmopolitan Imagination in the Nineteenth Century: Visible City, Invisible World*. Cambridge: Cambridge University Press.

Bryson, Bill. 2010. *At Home: A Short History of Private Life*. London: Doubleday.

Chittick, Kathryn. 1990. *Dickens and the 1830's*. Cambridge: Cambridge University Press.

Coriale, Danielle. 2008. *Sketches by Boz*, 'So Frail a Machine'. *Studies in English Literature, 1500–1900* 48 (4): 801–812.

Desmond, Matthew. 2016. *Evicted: Power and Profit in the American City*. New York: Crown Books.

———. 2017. How Homeownership Became the Engine of American Inequality. *The New York Times Magazine*, May 9, 2017.

Dickens, Charles. (1836–1837) 1995. *Sketches by Boz*. Edited by Dennis Walder. London: Penguin.

———. (1865) 1997. *Our Mutual Friend*. Edited by Adrian Poole. London: Penguin.

———. (1848) 1998. *Little Dorrit*. Edited by Stephen Wall and Helen Small. London: Penguin.

———. (1853) 2003a. *Bleak House*. Edited by Nicola Bradbury. London: Penguin.

———. (1839) 2003b. *Oliver Twist*. Edited by Philip Horne. London: Penguin.

Douglas, Mary. 1966. *Purity and Danger*. New York: Routledge.

Forster, John. 1872–1874. *The Life of Charles Dickens*. London: Cecil Palmer.

Garcha, Amanpal. 2009. *From Sketch to Novel: The Development of Victorian Fiction*. Cambridge: Cambridge University Press.

Harvey, David. 1974. Class-Monopoly Rent, Finance Capital and the Urban Revolution. *Regional Studies* 8 (3): 239–255.

Hunt, E.K., and Mark Lautzenheiser. 2011. *History of Economic Thought: A Critical Perspective*. New York and London: M.E. Sharpe.

Kleinfeld, N.R., and Kim Barker. 2018. Where Brooklyn Tenants Plead the Case for Keeping Their Homes. "Unsheltered". *The New York Times*, May 20.

Miller, Jen A. 2018. When a House Is So Much More. *The New York Times*, August 5.

Miller, J. Hillis. 1971. The Fiction of Realism: *Sketches by Boz, Oliver Twist*, and Cruikshank's Illustrations. In *Dickens Centennial Essays*, ed. Ada Nisbet and Blake Nevius, 85–153. Berkeley and Los Angeles: University of California Press.

Schlicke, Paul. 1999. *Oxford Reader's Companion to Charles Dickens*. Oxford and New York: Oxford University Press.

———. 2005. Risen Like a Rocket': The Impact of *Sketches by Boz*. *Dickens Quarterly* 22 (1): 3–18.

Trollope, Anthony. (1883) 1999. *An Autobiography*. Edited by Michael Sadleir and Frederick Page. Oxford: Oxford University Press.

Woloch, Alex. 2003. *The One vs. The Many: Minor Characters and the Space of the Protagonist in the Novel*. Princeton, NJ: Princeton University Press.

CHAPTER 8

Corporation

The Zero-Sum Game of Corporate Personhood

Clare V. Eby

The corporation has been the privileged form of business organization for well over a century. It allows for the separation of those who run a firm (management) from those who own it (stockholders); for the supplanting of individual entrepreneurship with organizational hierarchy; and for the enjoyment of privileges like limited liability. Corporations have become so ubiquitous that they may seem quite unremarkable. They can easily be rationalized by what James Kwak calls *economism*, or "the basic idea that markets must know best"; by that rosy light, corporations appear to be a natural, even inevitable, means for ensuring economies of scale, producing goods and services at the lowest cost (2017, 127). But just as Kwak shows that the win-win assumptions of economism obscure how the so-called "free" market does not in fact provide equal access to everyone, so corporate ascendancy is neither inevitable nor benign. Because corporations represent intense concentrations of wealth, their very existence promotes economic inequality—and because they are recognized as persons, the privileges they enjoy, many of them unavailable to human persons, threaten our own.

C. V. Eby (✉)
University of Connecticut, Storrs, CT, USA

© The Author(s) 2019   173
E. Hadley et al. (eds.), *From Political Economy to Economics through Nineteenth-Century Literature*, Palgrave Studies in Literature, Culture and Economics, https://doi.org/10.1007/978-3-030-24158-2_8

Corporate personhood is a legal invention. Lawyers acknowledge its counterfactual nature by calling corporate personhood a "legal fiction," a made-up construct intended to achieve particular goals set by human actors. While disputing that legal fictions are distinct from other equally artificial components of the law, Simon Stern admits that "doctrines like corporate personhood show us how law takes seemingly ordinary terms and attaches them to a system where they take on a different meaning, yielding new and often unforeseen results as they interact with the rest of the system" (2017, 323). As we shall see, as the corporation becomes a formidable economic power, the abstract formulation of its legal personhood has been exploited to fill the corporation with very real privileges that allow it to seize political power as well. Simply put, the legal fiction of corporate personhood has enabled a zero-sum game that permits the systematic transfer of economic resources as well as rights associated with citizenship. This zero-sum game fosters at once economic and political inequality by extracting rights from natural persons in order to amplify the rights of corporations. This development has been widely scrutinized following the US Supreme Court decisions in *Citizens United* (2010) and *Burwell v. Hobby Lobby* (2014), which I examine briefly in closing, but the legal precedents stretch back for centuries.

The Progressive era marks the "corporate reconstruction of American capitalism" (Sklar 1988), and so is particularly critical for understanding the origins of the zero-sum game. After a brief glance at legal history, I turn to literary fictions that respond to this new phase of capitalism, contesting and counter-theorizing corporate personhood when it was not yet taken for granted. Specifically, *The Squatter and the Don* (1885) by María Amaparo Ruiz de Burton and *The Octopus* (1901) by Frank Norris insist on the difference between metaphorical personification and human embodiment, developing a critical analysis of corporations. Then I examine how Progressive era claims for corporate property rights under the guise of the Fourteenth Amendment of the US Constitution introduce a racial dimension to the zero-sum game by covertly codifying a white privilege that cannot be located in a human body even while displacing the legitimate claims of freedmen and women. Finally, I will glance at how a postmodern riff on the nineteenth-century novel, Richard Powers's *Gain* (1998), responds to the legal history of corporate personal unaccountability, as well as to its own literary predecessors.

THE CORPORATION AND LEGAL THEORY

Corporations were created as a vehicle for holding assets collectively and in perpetuity. The origins stretch back to ancient Rome. Circa the third century B.C.E., the *societas publicoranum* was invented to permit a group of persons to hold property collectively while allowing the organization itself to survive the death or bankruptcy of a member. Notably, from the outset the corporate form was understood as constituting "special privileges," in the words of Adam Winkler, and as such could be created only "by a decree of the Senate or the emperor" (2018, 44). Corporations are also deeply entwined with canon law; in the fourth century, the Catholic Church itself claimed corporate status to ensure the continuity of its assets beyond the lives of individual members. During the Middle Ages, secular iterations multiplied: boroughs, municipalities, guilds, and universities assumed corporate status in order to retain property in perpetuity. In the early seventeenth century, European nations began issuing charters to trading companies, granting these public-and-private corporations longevity not enjoyed by business partnerships, which were dissolved after the completion of a targeted endeavor (Winkler 2018, 45; Blair 2013, 789). In the late eighteenth century, corporations were chartered to finance quasi-public works such as bridges (Blair and Pollman 2017, 256). There are substantial differences between these early corporate forms and today's for-profit behemoths, to be sure, but the original legal intent of allowing continuous ownership of property beyond the human lifespan remains foundational.

One of Sir William Blackstone's most consequential decisions in his *Commentaries on the Laws of England* (1765–1769) was to position the corporation not in the section dealing with "things" but rather under the category of "persons." While that placement does not grant full personhood to corporations, it does mystify their fundamental purpose (to organize assets) by implying an equivalence to humans. We might think of Blackstone as positing the quasi-personhood of corporations. Yet this logic immediately becomes strained due to his emphasis on a trait that decidedly eludes human persons: immortality. Reasoning that "all personal rights die with the [natural] person," Blackstone explains that the law recognizes corporations as "artificial persons, who may maintain perpetual succession, and enjoy a kind of legal immortality" (1753, 293). While his notion of corporate immortality derives from the "perpetuity" of the *societas publicoranum* and the church, if we follow Blackstone's reasoning, we can also see that he theorized corporations as a hedge against the fundamental nature of embodied human beings: mortality.

Blackstone sidesteps the difficulties of postulating an immortal quasi-person by introducing another simile, although this rhetorical move creates further conundrums. While a corporation is like "a person that never dies," it also resembles how "the river Thames is the same river, though the parts which compose it are changing every instant" (293). This comparison registers the corporation's ability to change constituent parts even while existing in perpetuity but it conflicts with the notion of it as quasi-person. In addition, the river metaphor captures the corporation's paradoxically intangible form; it has volume and magnitude while being impossible for human hands to physically grasp. But while other metaphorical bodies (such as a writer's body of work) also lack materiality, the notion of a quasi-person who is immaterial as well as immortal defies comprehension. Blackstone's watery metaphor participates in a long and consequential tradition of conceptualizing corporations as having quasi-physical bodies that they actually lack. The word *corporation*, indeed, derives from the Latin *corporatus*, meaning *form into a body* (Newfield 2014, 63).

Corporations do not actually have bodies as natural persons do, however. To be fair, Blackstone does note some characteristics distinguishing the corporation's "invisible body" from its human counterpart. Drawing from that very fact, he makes a crucial observation: the corporation cannot be found "guilty of battery," is "not liable to corporeal penalties," and can neither be imprisoned nor outlawed (297). The disembodied corporation's ability to elude punishment will become crucial to the zero-sum game by facilitating its unaccountability to humans. Blackstone could not have anticipated this problem because he understood the quasi-person as necessarily serving the needs of human masters. As he says, a corporation is created only "when it is for the advantage of the public" (293). The idea dates back to the *societas publicoranum*: because the corporate form was a special privilege conferred by the state, it would be granted to serve only a demonstrable public need.

The American counterpart to Blackstone, James Kent, introduces a different metaphor. He inverts the actual disembodiedness to imagine the corporation as constructed "chiefly for the purpose of clothing bodies of men" (1882, 307). This vestment is something of a magic cloak, transforming those who wear it into "one single, artificial, and fictitious being" (309–310). Extending Blackstone's recognition of the difficulties of punishing corporations for wrongdoing, Kent describes the corporate garment as granting its wearers the extraordinary ability to dodge "any personal hazard or responsibility" (330). The impunity does not seem to worry him, perhaps because he observes the proliferation of corporations through the lens of American exceptionalism. "We are multiplying, in this country," he says, "to an unparalleled extent, the institution of corporations, and giving them a flexibility and variety of purpose unknown to the Roman or English law" (271). Had Kent penned the *Commentaries* in the latter part of the nineteenth century rather than in the 1820s, his triumphalism might have been modulated into a more cautionary tone, for he otherwise well understood the tendency of corporations to become monopolies and in fact cites Adam Smith's view that monopolies are "generally injurious to the freedom of trade" (271).

Building on the common law, US case law has theorized the corporation in various ways to account for its consolidation of economic resources. Legal nomenclature can be maddeningly inconsistent but three important models for the corporation are termed "concession," "aggregate," and "real entity" theories. The first two, based on premises that sit together uneasily, informed most nineteenth-century decisions.

The concession theory follows from the precedent established by Rome and reiterated by Blackstone: because corporations were created by special charter, the state *conceded* their existence. *Trustees of Dartmouth College v. Woodward* (1819) exemplifies this idea. As Chief Justice John Marshall put it, "A corporation is an artificial being, ... existing only in contemplation of law." Like Blackstone, Marshall takes for granted that a corporation would be "beneficial to the country" (*Trustees* 1819, 636, 638). As an influential text from 1900 remarks, "the corporation is, and must be, the creature of the state" (Maitland 1900, xxx).

The corporation's evolution from public servant to its master began as states passed laws to make the process of incorporation more routine. Ironically, the roots of this movement lay in attacks on special privilege. In the Jacksonian era, reformers distrusted special charters as opportunities for politicians to play favorites. Their concerns sparked, in the words of Morton Horwitz, a movement between 1850 and 1870 for "'free incorporation' laws that would break the connection between the act of incorporation and political favoritism and corruption" (1992, 73). As such laws made incorporation pro forma, it ceased to seem a special privilege conceded by the government. But this shift opened a Pandora's box in also allowing firms to incorporate without regard to—and even in defiance of—public welfare. And due to the law's having recognized corporations for centuries as necessarily serving a public function, to this day, private, for-profit corporations benefit from precedents based on assumptions that no longer prevail (O'Melinn 2006, 201).

A second theory of the corporation was crucial to this shift. Under this second theory, the legal fiction evolves from metaphorical personhood to situate the corporation as a person who can claim rights, specifically property rights, to protect the economic interests for which it was formed. The "aggregate" or "association" theory posits the corporation as the sum total of the individuals who comprise it. Reasoning that the rights of those natural persons deserved protection, proponents of this theory extended derivative rights to corporations, and as legal ethicist Tenielle R. Brown puts it, "blurred the previously clear-cut lines between artificial and natural persons" (2013, 29). However, corporate rights were still understood as quite restricted. Margaret M. Blair and Elizabeth Pollman note that through most of the nineteenth century, corporate personhood was merely a "shorthand expression for a legal entity that represents an association of individuals, rather than an ontological assertion about the nature of corporations" (2017, 246). And while numerous cases affirmed corporate property rights, more intangible liberty rights (such as free speech) were reserved for human persons until considerably later (Winkler 2018, xx; Blair and Pollman 2017, 262; Bloch and Lamoreaux 2017).

Whereas the concession and association theories alike posit the corporation as an artificial entity created by the state, a third legal theory of the corporation as a "real entity" grants it independent ontological status. According to this theory, the corporation becomes an autonomous, distinct entity with an existence apart from its owners. Horwitz traces the idea back to an 1881 treatise about the history of German associations, a portion of which was translated into English in 1900 under the title *Political Theories of the Middle Ages* (1992, 71). This theory paved the way for claiming autonomous rather than derivative rights for corporations. As Attiba R. Ellis explains, under the real entity theory, "the corporation is entitled to political personhood as a right intrinsic to the corporation itself" (2011, 740).

RAILROADING CORPORATE RIGHTS: *THE SQUATTER*
AND THE DON AND *THE OCTOPUS*

The Squatter and the Don and *The Octopus* set their sights on the same corporate target around the time it was claiming full personhood. As the first industry to develop into a "huge, professionally-managed corporation" (Blair and Pollman 2017, 263), the railroad was an obvious focus. Railroad companies invented corporate organizational structures that persist to this day (Chandler 1977). Of particular concern to both Ruiz de Burton and Norris was railroad activity in California. In 1869, the California-based Central Pacific had joined with the eastern-based Union Pacific to complete the first transcontinental railroad, thus providing a transportation system enabling the first national market in the US. The railroad, of course, charged a fare for each economic transaction it facilitated. This immensely profitable system was not financed by private funds alone; it depended also on the transfer of vast public wealth to corporate coffers. The Central Pacific received nine million acres of land and millions of dollars of bonds and construction costs from the US government. This scheme was rationalized according to the familiar economistic logic that what's good for corporations is necessarily good for America: by "developing" far-flung territories, the railroad was increasing land values for western citizens.[1]

Ruiz de Burton disputes that rosy interpretation. Part historical novel, part romance, *Squatter* is unified by its condemnation of what Ruiz de Burton terms in her concluding chapter "the invader," though the disruptive aggressor actually takes two forms (1992, 365). The first involves national and racial borders; the second, corporate bodies. Set during 1872–1876, the novel centers on the Alameres, an aristocratic Mexican family living in San Diego. Their substantial acreage had been located within Mexico prior to the 1848 Treaty of Guadelupe-Hidalgo, which ended the Mexican-American War and transferred considerable Mexican land to the US. In exchange, the treaty promised that Mexican landowners would retain property titles (now within US borders) and be recognized as US citizens. But many Californios (to use Ruiz de Burton's favored term) found their ownership legally challenged. As this racially motivated dispossession was unfolding, the first group that Ruiz de Burton calls "invaders" further defied Mexican land ownership: Yankee "squatters" staked out homesteading claims on ranch land owned by Californio "dons."

Ruiz de Burton sets this dispute, in turn, within a larger plot featuring a corporate "invader." In *Squatter*, the Alamares and their friends have been eagerly awaiting the completion of a second railroad, the Texas and Pacific. Intended to terminate in San Diego, this line promised to link the fledgling city into a second massive transportation network, which its proponents believed would ensure economic prosperity for the region. But since this project would have challenged the northern railroad's monopoly, the Central Pacific bribed Congress to sink it.

Ruiz de Burton identified that conspiracy between corporate railroad and Congress as a challenge to free trade. Her economic views can be difficult for modern readers to track as she was in equal measure pro-capitalism and anti-monopoly. The distinction was becoming anachronistic when she published the novel in 1885 because the entrepreneurial capitalism she celebrates was giving way to corporate capitalism. Moreover, as Brook Thomas shows, Ruiz de Burton's endorsement of entrepreneurial capitalism ignores systemic problems that led to crises like the Panic of 1873 (2013, 889). Still, her views remain instructive because they assume a mythic ideal of competitive capitalism that rationalizes economic inequality—and that persists even to this day. One of *Squatter's* Yankee good guys makes millions speculating on stocks and mining; he also plans to start a bank in San Diego. Ruiz de Burton has no objection to speculation or finance; rather, it's the "Central Pacific monopolists" that she considers diabolical (297). Throughout *Squatter* she attacks the infamous "Big Four"—Collis P. Huntington, Charles Crocker, Mark Hopkins, and ex-California governor and first president of Stanford University, Leland Stanford—who controlled the Central Pacific.

Challenging monopoly by going after actual persons, Ruiz de Burton subverts the theory of the corporation as an aggregate of individuals discussed above. Calling out the individuals hiding behind the corporate form, she shows how the legal fiction of corporate personhood fosters what amounts to a zero-sum game, allowing special privilege for a few at the expense of the many. While she names each of the Big Four, Ruiz de Burton has Stanford actually interact with her fictional characters. Presenting Stanford's identity as doubled—he is at once stand-in for the railroad and a discrete and embodied human—she uses the same logic as the aggregate theory, but does so to discredit Stanford's rationalizations as economic mystification. Two scenes in particular capture Ruiz de Burton's critique.

In a remarkable chapter, Don Mariano Alamar and his Yankee land-owning friends visit Stanford to implore him to stop obstructing the Texas and Pacific railroad that they saw as crucial to the southern Californian economy. Citing Thomas Carlyle and Herbert Spencer, the San Diegans invoke the idea of a higher law to which mortal law should bow. While they do not explicitly mention Blackstone, their appeals resonate with the jurist's assumptions. "No human laws," according to Blackstone, "are of any validity if contrary to" the law of nature, which is "dictated by God himself" (47). Such Enlightenment principles are axiomatic in *Squatter*, but Stanford hides behind economistic rationalizations about the benefits of "competition" (318). It's a laughable excuse, because Stanford is actually protecting monopoly, which forecloses the economic competition to which he appeals. When the Southern Californians persist, Stanford shifts his tune to the crucial admission that "Corporations have no souls, gentlemen, and I am no Carlylean hero-philanthropist" (318).

Ruiz de Burton uses Stanford's chicanery to discredit the corporate position. Having a soul would be, from her vantage point, precisely something signifying personhood. Despite Stanford's being a mortal human, he hides behind corporate soullessness, in doing so confirming his, and the institution's, inhumanity. Developing the point, the Don's friend Mr. Mechlin emphasizes that, besides having "no soul to feel responsibility," the corporation also lacks a physical body to register empathy—it has "no heart for human pity, no face for manly blush." Mechlin indicts all four men hiding behind the corporate form for using their economic clout to destroy southern residents: "'These men—this deadly, soulless corporation,'" he says, "will evermore cast the shadow that will be our funeral pall'" (320). The image of a shroud draws out the sinister implications of Kent's metaphor of a corporation as a garment donned by human beings. Challenging the idea that the corporation gains some sort of derivative humanity because it is comprised of people, Ruiz de Burton devolves the decorporealized railroad back into the actual historical personages who control it, in order to reassert human accountability for corporate malfeasance.

In another scene, Ruiz de Burton identifies Congress with the corporation, thereby critiquing the legalization of corporate depredations. She presents Congress itself as a corporate yet corporeal body, immortal even while being diseased. She chastises legislators for having "the *palsy*, the moral stagnation of the man whose power for good or evil extends to millions of people to unlimited time, whose influence shall be felt, and shall be shaping the destinies of unborn generations, after he shall be only a ghastly skeleton, a bundle of crumbling bones!" (206, Ruiz de Burton's emphasis). In other words, while individual congressmen die, their corporate body—just like the for-profit corporation they serve—persists in perpetuity, sneering at human frailty and mortality. Congressional legislation, she reiterates, impacts "the lives, the destinies, of their fellow-beings *forever*" (207, her emphasis). Ruiz de Burton cites actual documents showing the Central Pacific bribed Congress to block the Texas line. The evidence reveals, in her words, "a shameful exposure of disgraceful acts, any one of which, were it to be perpetrated by a poor man, would send him to the penitentiary" (210). Her exposé unspools the ramifications both of Blackstone's theorizing that the disembodied, immortal corporation can never be punished in the same way as a corporeal mortal, and of Kent's confession that the form allows it to dodge responsibility. Ruiz de Burton's disclosure of the railroad's ability to commit criminal acts, even while eluding the punishment awaiting a "poor man" who did the same, indicts Congress for expanding corporate privilege without responsibility—and at the expense of human beings. Serving the corporate person rather than the citizens who elected them, Congress thus perpetuates the zero-sum game.

In *The Octopus*, Frank Norris lightly fictionalizes the railroad's name, calling it the Pacific and Southwestern (P. and S. W.). While the title *The Octopus* signals one of the most common Progressive era metaphors for describing corporate power, a more unusual image of a body untethered to any particular species surfaces in a description of a railway commissioner's map. The white map of California has small markings in blue, yellow, and green representing minor rail lines, so faint as to disappear when viewed from a distance. Bold red lines representing the P. and S. W. dominate the map and the narrator describes them as arteries controlling the flow of corporate blood throughout the state, a "plexus of red, a veritable system of blood circulation." This metaphor of an embodied corporation allows Norris to show that the "organism" in fact preys upon its host, the entire state of California:

> The map was white, and it seemed as if all the colour which should have gone to vivify the various counties… had been absorbed by that huge, sprawling organism, with its ruddy arteries… It was as though the State had been sucked white and colourless, and against this pallid background the red arteries of the monster stood out, swollen with life-blood, reaching out to

infinity, gorged to bursting; an excrescence, a gigantic parasite fattening upon the life-blood of an entire commonwealth. (1986, 289)

This passage registers a fundamental change in the relationship of the corporation and the social body. Norris depicts corporate blood as feeding only itself, exposing the demise of the long-established understanding that corporations were invented to serve humans (whether circulating through "the counties" or the "entire commonwealth"). Even "the State" that once created the railroad has been reduced to its prey. This grotesque image suggests that the increasingly empowered corporation will use its economic might to destroy anything that stands in its way.

One of the novel's most famous passages literalizes that point while also showing how corporate capitalism destroys traditional methods of earning a living. When a train charges through a pastoral landscape, "vomiting smoke and sparks" and sporting an "enormous eye, cyclopean, red," the monstrous organism annihilates a flock of sheep crossing the tracks. In his signature purple prose, Norris describes the "prolonged cries of agony, sobbing wails of infinite pain" as metal meets flesh: "It was a slaughter, a massacre of innocents ... To the right and left, ... the little bodies had been flung; backs were snapped against the fence posts; brains knocked out" (49, 50). In addition to annihilating harmless living creatures, the railroad wipes out a farmer's livelihood.

The predatory railroad even destroys some of its own workers. The trajectory of a one-time railroad engineer draws out the sinister implications of Blackstone's observation that while human persons have bodies that can be punished, corporate persons do not. After working for the P. and S. W. for ten years, Dyke finds himself unceremoniously fired. He retools himself into a farmer, only to be ruined by the railroad's extortionist rates for moving crops. Knowing he has no legal redress, Dyke attempts to retaliate by holding up the P. and S. W. at gunpoint, stealing five thousand dollars' worth of gold. But the transfer of corporate property to human hands is fleeting. Another character, speaking to a railroad man, sums up the inevitable trajectory: "You and your gang drove Dyke from his job because he wouldn't work for starvation wages. Then you raised freight rates on him and robbed him of all he had ... He's only taken back what you plundered him of, and now you're going to ... hunt him down like a wild animal, and bring him to the gallows at San Quentin" (423–424). The law does not hold corporations accountable either for exploiting workers (through "starvation wages") nor for activities that appear downright criminal (such as "robb[ing] [Dyke] of all he had"). Instead, the human agent in these unfair economic transactions is reduced to a "wild animal" while the corporation recuperates its assets. The prediction of the gallows for the one-time railroad engineer marks another life lost to the zero-sum game.

The main narrative in *The Octopus* fictionalizes an actual incident in 1880 known as the Mussel Slough affair—a showdown between ranchers and the railroad at gunpoint—which Norris presents as corporate crime hidden behind economistic rationalization. Norris grounds the conflict in the transfer of national wealth from citizens to the corporation. The narrator explains the federal government's granting of alternate sections of land, in a checkerboard pattern, to the P. and S. W. as a "bonus" for constructing the line (96). The corporation then invited ranchers to settle, promising to sell them the property for $2.50 per acre after the land was regraded. Consequently the ranchers have been growing wheat and improving land—as well as establishing homes and raising families—on property they don't actually own. When the P. and S. W. is ready to sell, it demands $27 per acre, more than ten times the promised price, and the ranchers are ruined. The ensuing shootout is accompanied by a battle of words. The railroad hides behind the claim that it must earn a "legitimate" profit. But the ranchers want the same, and they identify routine corporate practice as unpunishable and yet criminal activity: "Can we raise wheat at a legitimate profit with a tariff of four dollars a ton for moving it two hundred miles," one asks; "Why not hold us up with a gun in our faces, and say, 'hands up,' and be done with it?" (11). Both parties seek a "legitimate" profit but the railroad unilaterally decides what that means, betraying the mythic ideal of the competitive marketplace in which buyer and seller agree upon fair terms.

Echoing Ruiz de Burton's treatment of Stanford, Norris also includes a human stand-in for the corporate person, but the corporate avatar in *The Octopus* is intensely, even grotesquely, embodied. "A large, fat man, with a great stomach," S. Behrman is a banker, real estate dealer, political boss, and, most importantly, agent of the railroad. As far as the ranchers are concerned, "S. Behrman was the railroad" (67). Several characters fantasize taking revenge against him, one imagining the pleasure of "sink[ing] his fingers deep into [Behrman's] white, fat throat" (543). Another character, a poet-turned-socialist named Presley, seeks collective revenge by bombing the obese glutton as he sits down to dinner. Cloaked in corporate immortality—at least for the day—Behrman emerges without a scratch even though his dining room is destroyed.

This anthropomorphizing of the corporation as the hated and revolting S. Behrman, practiced both by the narrator and by numerous characters, is ultimately an unproductive way to fight back against the zero-sum game. Killing Behrman would not end the evil done by the railroad, which would simply buy another human to do its bidding—the corporation is, after all, immortal. In the novel's most famous scene, Behrman meets his death as he falls into a grain elevator filled with wheat, drowning in the commodity he spent his life manipulating. As a textbook case of poetic justice, the scene is quite gratifying. But if the goal is resisting corporate power, the scene is more important as a reminder that punishing human agents of corporations does nothing to address the unfair longevity of the corporate person itself that undergirds its impunity.

The Octopus also includes a scene that fictionalizes Norris's own two interviews in 1899 with one of the real-life Big Four, Collis P. Huntington, called Shelgrim in the novel. Unlike Ruiz de Burton's portrayal of Stanford as ruthless, Norris emphasizes Shelgrim's magnanimity. The poet Presley, in many respects a stand-in for Norris, visits the magnate expecting to find "an ogre, a brute, a terrible man of iron." Instead he finds a "sentimentalist" who, faced with news that an employee has taken to drink, doubles the man's salary rather than firing him; and an "art critic" who delivers an informed review of Presley's recently published socialist poem (573, 574). Shelgrim's calculatedly human responses to small-scale events baffle the poet's efforts to hold the corporation broadly accountable. Shelgrim also shields the corporation by abstracting exploitation into economic axioms: "*Railroads build themselves,*" he intones. Absolving himself and the railroad of any responsibility for the lives ruined by the P. and S. W., Shelgrim proclaims, "The Wheat is one force, the Railroad, another, and there is the law that governs them—supply and demand. Men have only little to do in the whole business" (576).

WHITEWASHING THE CORPORATION

Ruiz de Burton's and Norris's focus on the railroad is also noteworthy because that industry was the test case for using the corporation to redefine white privilege as economic advantage. While neither writer addressed the racial implications of the corporate form, both were deeply conscious of race, and their politics at first seem diametrically opposed: Ruiz de

Burton advocates for Californios while Norris dismisses "greasers" and touts Anglo-Saxons. Yet *Squatter* is no less invested in racial essentialism than is *The Octopus.* Ruiz de Burton's celebration of Californios is predicated on their being, as she repeatedly insists, *white.* She rhapsodizes over the blue eyes of the Don's youngest and most beautiful daughter and concludes the novel with a call to "emancipate the white slaves of California" (372). While the racial politics of each novel have received considerable attention, I would like to use their shared investment in racialism as an opportunity to consider how case law positioning the railroad as exemplary corporate person established the grounds for understanding that fictive person as implicitly white. The hypothetical person assumed in founding documents such as the Declaration of Independence has always been implicitly white and male (Van Cleve 2010). Cloaking the corporate person in a white gown during the Progressive era furthers this assumption, thereby consolidating economic and racial privilege.

As noted above, the aggregate theory of the corporation established the legal framework for imputing derivative rights to firms under the rationale that constituent human members deserved protection. While the aggregate theory informed earlier decisions, it crystallized in a landmark Progressive era case involving the railroad. In *Santa Clara County v. Southern Pacific Railroad* (1886), the Supreme Court ruled it discriminatory to deny the railroad a mortgage deduction to offset property taxes that individuals were allowed, since doing so would discriminate against the railroad's owners. Many scholars concur that *Santa Clara* marks the point when the corporation attains full personhood status (e.g. Mayer 1990, 581). The actual provenance of that shift is deeply unsettling. A much-discussed headnote to *Santa Clara*—written not by a justice but rather a court reporter—states, "The Court does not wish to hear argument [sic] on the question whether the provision in the Fourteenth Amendment which forbids a state to deny to any person … the equal protection of the laws applies to these corporations. We are of the opinion that it does" (1886, 396). The misleading suggestion is that the Court endorsed using the equal protection clause of one of the Reconstruction Amendments—passed to protect former slaves—to protect corporations, when in fact the chief justice had instructed the court not to focus on corporate rights. But in the two decades following *Santa Clara*, the disingenuous headnote assumed "sweeping importance" and the case was repeatedly cited to claim Fourteenth Amendment protections for corporations, thereby supporting "legal principles never endorsed by the decision itself" (Winkler 2018, 157). Commenting in 1938 on this unconscionable legacy, Justice Hugo Black noted that in the fifty years following *Santa Clara*, when the Supreme Court invoked the Fourteenth Amendment, over half the time it extended the rights of corporate persons and fewer than one half of one percent sought to protect African Americans (dissent to *Connecticut General* 1938, 90).

The "conspiracy theory" advanced by Charles A. and Mary R. Beard in 1927, which posited that the drafters of the Fourteenth Amendment deliberately used language to include corporations under the definition of persons, was discredited many years ago by Howard Jay Graham (Beard and Beard 1927, 111–113; Graham 1938). However, a robust body of recent legal scholarship informed by critical race theory demonstrates that racial discrimination and corporate privilege display, in the words of john a. powell and Caitlin Watt, a "shared constitutional pedigree in the Fourteenth Amendment" (2011, 885). powell and Watt as well as Amanda Werner emphasize the highly selective interpretation of that amendment so as to benefit corporations, not racial minorities. They note as well the historical coincidence of laws advancing corporate privilege and Jim Crow (Werner 2015, 137; powell and Watt 2011, 886–887).[2] As Werner puts it, "When white supremacy was explicit in law, corporate privilege played a supporting role, … allowing whites to maintain economic dominance" (2015, 134). powell and Watt identify the post-Reconstruction Court's fortifying a "new white solidarity" in two ways: by supporting states' rights and by the doctrine of corporate personhood cemented in *Santa Clara* (2011, 896).

Yet while using corporate personhood to support white solidarity, the Court during the Jim Crow era ruled that corporations could not themselves have a race (Brooks 2006, 2024, discussing *People's Pleasure Park* 1908). This inconsistency reveals the Court's ability to speak out of both sides of its mouth—or to put the point more sharply, shows its hypocrisy. Richard R. W. Brooks theorizes what motivated the Court's contradictory stance on race in the Jim Crow era: "Conceding that corporations possessed racial identities would have … threatened the South's segregationist regime" because it would be an admission that race was attributed by persons rather than being an essential, unchangeable quality of them (2006, 2058). Late in the 1980s, however, the Court would begin attributing race to corporations.[3] Brooks explains this reversal as reflecting the Court's belated acknowledgment that race is after all "a social product," not an innate or essential quality (2072). But since white privilege continues to entail "the right to exclude and to dominate," as powell and Watt claim, "it might be that the real whites in our society are corporations" (2011, 901). While the Civil Rights movement has made it untenable to argue in a court of law for racial superiority, corporate personhood provides a way to retain white privilege through a legal back door.

NATURALIZING CORPORATE LIBERTY RIGHTS: SOME RECENT TRENDS

Given the about-face on whether corporations can have a race, it is unsurprising that Court decisions also demonstrate, in the words of Carl J. Mayer, a "schizophrenic view of corporate personality" (1990, 621). One reason for the contradictory position is that the Court backed away from explicitly theorizing corporate personhood by the late 1920s (Horwitz 1992, 67), even while continuing to *assume* it. Two recent decisions that ratchet up the zero-sum game, *Citizens United v. Federal Election Commission* (2010) and *Burwell v. Hobby Lobby* (2014), show how the Court extends corporate liberty rights at the expense of citizens' rights. It also demonstrates how the twenty-first century corporation benefits from precedents reaching back to at least the Progressive era.

Citizens United affirmed the free speech rights of corporations, but it did not originate the idea that they should enjoy liberty as well as property rights. Indeed, the majority opinion lists over twenty precedents, most from the 1970s forward. Justice Kennedy cites *First National Bank of Boston v. Bellotti* (1978) as establishing the principle that "political speech does not lose First Amendment protection 'simply because its source is a corporation'" (*Citizens United* 2010, 26, citing *Bellotti* 1978). Kennedy also extends *Bellotti's* economistic rationale, reducing civil debate conducted by complex human speakers into a series of pecuniary transactions. "Speech is an essential mechanism of democracy," writes Kennedy, but the "speech" he champions simply means allowing unlimited "corporate independent expenditures" to determine election outcomes (*Citizens United* 2010, 23, 25).

In contrast to Kennedy's economistic understanding of speech, Justice Stevens's dissent reminds us of something that Ruiz de Burton and Norris both knew: corporate persons lack the affective body that distinguishes humans. Stevens attacks the majority's "conceit that corporations must be treated identically to natural persons": while corporations "make enormous contributions to our society," they "are not actually members of it." Stevens also calls out a fellow justice for implicitly endorsing, in a concurring opinion, the aggregate theory: "Justice Scalia appears to believe that because corporations are created and utilized by individuals, it follows (as night the day) that their electioneering must be equally protected by the First Amendment." Reaffirming the difference between human and corporate persons, Stevens insists on the metaphor's limits: corporations "have no consciences, no beliefs, no feelings, no thoughts, no desires."[4] While corporate "personhood" can be a "useful legal fiction," he concludes, "they are not themselves members of 'We the People' by whom and for whom our Constitution was established" (*Citizens United* 2010, dissenting opinion of J. Stevens, 2, 40–41, 75, 76).

When the Court extended corporate rights to include religious freedom four years later, it did not reckon the true cost: rights for women workers. In *Hobby Lobby*, the department of Health and Human Services (HHS) filed suit against three corporations owned by evangelical Christians that had refused to provide company health insurance covering "day-after" contraceptives. The owners cited personal religious objections to abortion, but HHS claimed that the corporations themselves violated the Affordable Care Act mandate to provide preventative health care. Yet the Supreme Court decided that this mandate violated, instead, not simply the owners' but also the *corporations' own* religious beliefs.

Hobby Lobby's rationale is, however, incoherent. In extending religious rights to corporations, Samuel Alito, writing for the majority, creates a patchwork out of the three legal theories of the corporation discussed above—only the quilt is fraying at the seams. Since naming all three theories would draw attention to their contradictory premises, Alito explicitly references only one. Relying on aggregate theory, he claims "that the purpose of this fiction [of corporate personhood] is to provide protection for human beings" (*Hobby Lobby* 2014, 18). However, Alito insinuates that a corporation has its own ontological rights independent of the people who comprise it when he says it's "beside the point" that corporations can't pray or worship because they still can have "religious objectives" (18). Humans, of course, are the ones who pray and worship, but if a corporation itself (and not just the people behind it) can pursue religious objectives, that would make it a real entity, independent of its owners—in which case it couldn't be an aggregate being after all. Alito introduces an additional layer of incoherence by stating, "Modern corporate law does not require for-profit corporations to pursue profit at the expense of everything else," and then describing the "charitable" and "humanitarian" causes on which corporations voluntarily spend their profits, thereby masking business expenses as gifts (23). Such comments nod to, without naming, the concession theory, according to which the corporation served vital civic functions. In Alito's account, corporations are certainly marvelous shape-shifters, one moment for-profit and another not-for-profit. As in *Citizens United*, so in *Hobby Lobby*: a quantifiable corporate expense (in the first case, political contributions; in the second, philanthropic donations) is used to extend to corporations an intangible liberty right. *Hobby Lobby* illuminates the unfair rules of the zero-sum game: granting the corporate person's free exercise rights authorizes it to deny female employees their statutory right to health coverage. The decision prioritizes a legal fiction of personhood over the actual bodies of women workers.

Richard Powers's *Gain* (1998), a postmodern faux-nineteenth-century novel, exposes precisely the inequality perpetuated by the zero-sum game. The novel pursues two narrative tracks. The dominant one, a spoof on the *Bildungsroman*, features a corporation as protagonist/antagonist. The Clare Company begins as a humble colonial soap company, growing into a multinational consumer goods conglomerate with customers in eighty-three countries by the twilight of the twentieth century. The novel tracks the company's evolution, hinging on Clare's incorporation in 1867 under the leadership of its second generation of owners. Powers crafts this moment to demonstrate that incorporating is neither a natural, inevitable, nor a benign decision. Confronting their own mortality, the Clare brothers realize that because "business now far outstripped the single life's span … Survival offered Clare no alternative but incorporation." But to the most principled of the owners, Samuel Clare, "the very word [incorporation] smacked of failure." That is because he recognizes how the corporate form permits "special privileges" unavailable to humans, such as limited liability and immortality. In other words, as Samuel sees it, "cheating" (175). Citing the *Dartmouth* decision discussed above, the narrator notes that the newly incorporated business became "one composite body: a single, whole, and statutorily enabled person." Another Clare brother relays an Ambrose Bierce quip from *Devil's Dictionary*: "Corporation: An ingenious device for obtaining individual profit without individual responsibility." (179, *Devil's Dictionary* quoted in Powers, 180).

Gain's second narrative track, set in the far more restricted timeline of the 1990s, details the human costs of that ingenious device. A divorced mother dying of cancer lives in the Illinois town where Clare is headquartered and so is exposed to many environmental contaminants. Moreover, she uses Clare products herself, from personal care to plant fertilizer, some of which may be carcinogens. Like the reader, she assumes—but cannot actually prove—that her cancer was caused by Clare. Appropriately, the dying woman is named Laura Bodey, and the novel does not spare details of Bodey's dying body. Throughout the novel, Powers cuts back and forth between the narratives, contrasting the fleeting human lifespan with the expansive temporality of corporate immortality. In a scene positioned immediately before Clare's incorporation over one hundred years earlier, Bodey learns that the chemo getting pumped into her body includes a compound manufactured by the company. The corporation has sold her things that are (probably) killing her and it alone sells something else that can (probably not) cure her. In both instances, she pays.

Another crucial scene involves a visit that Laura Bodey's ex-husband makes to Clare headquarters. Much as the nineteenth-century characters of Ruiz de Burton and Norris sought to hold the corporation responsible for its crimes, Don Bodey fumes that the ingenious corporation can evade responsibility for Laura's death. He passes Clare's boardroom and realizes, "If there are humans at the helm, this is where they steer. As close as he's going to come to Them" (292). Channeling Norris's poet-turned-socialist character Presley, Don fantasizes throwing a bomb. But almost immediately, he realizes the utter futility of injuring the disembodied corporation; "the board's not even close to ground zero" and he can't hurt it (292). There is nothing his ex-wife can do but die, and there's nothing Don can do to hold corporate leaders accountable.

Gain's two plots demonstrate the nonidentity of human beings and corporations. They dramatize how the mortality of human beings is incommensurate with the theoretically immortal corporate life cycle. Powers shows that while unusual growth patterns in a human body can signify cancer, rapid growth in a corporation leads to unprecedented profits. Such differences are precisely what we must keep in sight to rewrite the rules of the zero-sum game that has allowed the corporate extortion of rights from human citizens. To borrow a line from George Orwell, it is time to stop allowing some persons to be more equal than others.

NOTES

1. Details on railroad history here and in following paragraphs, including information regarding the Big Four, drawn from Rosaura Sánchez and Beatrice Pita, "Introduction" to *The Squatter and the Don* by María Amparo Ruiz de Burton, 5–54.
2. "During the same period that the Supreme Court decimated the promise of equal protection for blacks, it employed the Fourteenth Amendment to proliferate corporate rights." "Between 1890 and 1910, 288 equal protection cases addressed corporations; only 19 involved descendants of slaves" (Werner 2015, 137).
3. For instance, *Richmond v. Croson* (1989) supported the objections of a corporation owned by whites to set-aside programs for minorities, thus implicitly acknowledging corporate racial identity (Werner 2015, 139).
4. While Justice Stevens's concern—like my own—centers on corporations claiming citizens' rights, Anna Grear similarly differentiates the corporate person from the human person in her analysis of how corporations claim Human Rights for themselves. Much as Stevens points out that the corporation has no conscience, beliefs, or feelings, Grear describes it as lacking the "complex interiority" of human beings (Grear 2012, 81).

REFERENCES

Beard, Charles A., and Mary R. Beard. 1927. *The Rise of American Civilization*. Vol. 2. New York: Macmillan.

Blackstone, Sir William. 1753. *Commentaries on the Laws of England*. Vol. 1. of the Online Library of Liberty. http://oll.libertyfund.org/title/2140.

Blair, Margaret. 2013. Corporate Personhood and the Corporate Persona. *University of Illinois Law Review* 2013 (3): 785–820.

Blair, Margaret, and Elizabeth Pollman. 2017. The Supreme Court's View of Corporate Rights: Two Centuries of Evolution and Controversy. In *Corporations and American Democracy*, ed. Naomi R. Lamoreaux and William J. Novak, 245–285. Cambridge, MA: Harvard University Press.

Bloch, Ruth H., and Naomi R. Lamoreaux. 2017. Corporations and the Fourteenth Amendment. In *Corporations and American Democracy*, ed. Naomi R. Lamoreaux and William J. Novak, 286–325. Cambridge, MA: Harvard University Press.

Brooks, Richard R.W. 2006. Incorporating Race. *Columbia Law Review* 106: 2023–2094.

Brown, Tenielle R. 2013. In-Corp-O-Real: A Psychological Critique of Corporate Personhood and *Citizens United*. *Florida State University Business Review* 12 (1): 1–108.

Burwell v. Hobby Lobby Stores, Inc. 2014. 573 U. S.

Chandler, Alfred D., Jr. 1977. *The Visible Hand: The Managerial Revolution in American Business.* Cambridge, MA: Harvard University Press.

Citizens United v. Federal Election Commission. 2010. 558 U.S.

Connecticut General Life Insurance Company v. Johnson. 1938. 303 U. S. 77. Dissenting opinion of J. Black.

Ellis, Atiba R. 2011. *Citizens United* and Tiered Personhood. *John Marshall Law Review* 44 (3): 717–749.

First National Bank of Boston v. Bellotti. 1978. 435 U.S. 765.

Graham, Howard Jay. 1938. The Conspiracy Theory of the Fourteenth Amendment. *Yale Law Journal* 47: 371–403.

Grear, Anna. 2012. *Redirecting Human Rights: Facing the Challenge of Corporate Legal Humanity.* New York: Palgrave Macmillan.

Horwitz, Morton. 1992. *The Transformation of American Law, 1870–1960: The Crisis of Legal Orthodoxy.* Oxford: Oxford University Press.

Kent, James. 1882. *Commentaries on American Law.* Vol. 2. Google Books. https://books.google.com/books/about/Commentaries_on_American_law_2.html?id=_PFBAAAAYAAJ.

Kwak, James. 2017. *Economism: Bad Economics and the Rise of Inequality.* New York: Vintage.

Maitland, Frederic William. 1900. Introduction. In *Political Theories of the Middle Ages*, by Otto Giercke, trans. F. W. Maitland. Cambridge: Cambridge University Press.

Mayer, Carl J. 1990. Personalizing the Impersonal: Corporations and the Bill of Rights. *Hastings Law Journal* 41 (3): 577–668.

O'Melinn, Liam Séamus. 2006. Neither Contract nor Concession: The Public Personality of the Corporation. *George Washington Law Review* 74 (2): 201–259.

Newfield, Christopher. 2014. Corporation. In *Keywords for American Cultural Studies*, ed. Bruce Burgett and Glenn Hendler, 2nd ed., 63–68. New York: New York University Press.

Norris, Frank. 1986. *The Octopus.* New York: Penguin Classics.

People's Pleasure Park Co. v. Rohleder. 1908. 61 S. E. 794.

powell, john a., and Caitlin Watt. 2011. Corporate Prerogative, Race, and Identity under the Fourteenth Amendment. *Cardozo Law Review* 32 (3): 885–904.

Powers, Richard. 1998. *Gain.* New York: Farrar, Straus, and Giroux.

Ruiz de Burton, María Amparo. 1992. *The Squatter and the Don.* Houston: Arte Público Press.

Sánchez, Rosaura, and Beatrice Pita. 1992. Introduction. In *The Squatter and the Don*, by María Amparo Ruiz de Burton, 5–54. Houston: Arte Público Press.

Sklar, Martin J. 1988. *The Corporate Reconstruction of American Capitalism, 1890–1916.* Cambridge: Cambridge University Press.

Stern, Simon. 2017. Legal and Legal Fictions. In *New Directions in Law and Literature*, ed. Elizabeth S. Anker and Bernadette Meyler, 313–326. Oxford: Oxford University Press.

Thomas, Brook. 2013. Ruiz de Burton, Railroads, Reconstruction. *ELH* 80 (3, Fall): 871–895.

Trustees of Dartmouth College v. Woodward. 1819. 17 U.S. 518.

Van Cleve, George William. 2010. *A Slaveholder's Union: Slavery, Politics, and the Constitution in the Early American Republic*. Chicago: University of Chicago Press.

Werner, Amanda. 2015. Corporations are (White) People Too: How Corporate Privilege Reifies Whiteness as Property. *Harvard Journal of Racial and Ethnic Justice* 31: 129–147.

Winkler, Adam. 2018. *We the Corporations: How American Businesses Won Their Civil Rights*. New York: Liveright.

PART IV

Value

CHAPTER 9

Choice

Narrating Choice in Later Nineteenth-Century Novels and Neoclassical Economics

Amanpal Garcha

"Only after one of the options has been chosen can we see that the unchosen option is not preserved there in its possibility but entirely dissolves, becoming simply a reminiscence or projection" (Grosz 2010, 149). As Elizabeth Grosz observes in putting forth her revisionary account of agency, modern political theory has conceived of freedom as "fundamentally linked to the question of choice, to the operations of alternatives, to the selection of options outside the subject" (149). As she also suggests, while the freedom to choose may appear to be a purely political concept, it inevitably calls to mind the economic operations of capitalism—the "freedom of selection, of consumption, a freedom linked to the acquisition of objects" (149). Like Grosz's argument but proceeding in a different register, this chapter argues that our commonplace association of subjectivity with decision-making is historically contingent and is in part derived from modern economic processes and theories.

A. Garcha (✉)
Ohio State University, Columbus, OH, USA

© The Author(s) 2019
E. Hadley et al. (eds.), *From Political Economy to Economics through Nineteenth-Century Literature*, Palgrave Studies in Literature, Culture and Economics, https://doi.org/10.1007/978-3-030-24158-2_9

First, the chapter will examine nineteenth-century literary depictions of individuals choosing, or trying to choose, and will show that these depictions undergo a pronounced change between the early and later parts of the century. Where earlier novelists generally depict characters who face a series of binary, or "yes or no," decisions, later ones increasingly show choice as far more expansive and thus at times bewildering, as characters contemplate many, simultaneously available options at once. The chapter next suggests that this shift in literary representations of decision-making relates to the historical transformation of Great Britain into a consumer society. This transformation resulted in a shift in economic theory and practice in the later part of the century—in particular, it helped produce "marginalist" or neoclassical economic theories that posited consumption rather than production as the primary creator of economic value. While both literary authors and political economists worked to make the choosing individual central to the British cultural imagination, they represent choice in distinct ways, with political economists imagining that subjects habitually order their preferences to maximize their satisfaction and literary authors showing how subjects try to prioritize their preferences but often fail to do so. I will conclude by asserting that despite these differences, both political economy's simplified, mechanistic view of human choice and later nineteenth-century literature's more fraught depictions have ended up working together to further modernity's identification of subjectivity with capitalist consumption. Such an identification produces a kind of social inertia, wherein individuals become so preoccupied with attempting to discern and rank their desires, they end up not acting at all.

NARRATIVES OF CHOICE IN AND OUT OF THE MARKETPLACE

While indecisive characters have a long history in English literature—Shakespeare's Hamlet exhibits one of the most famous cases of vacillation—Victorian writers begin to portray a particularly modern version of indecision. An illustrative example appears in Anthony Trollope's *Can You Forgive Her?* ([1864–1865] 2004). The entire narrative of *Can You Forgive Her?* centers on Alice Vavasor's attempt to decide between marrying George Vavasor or John Grey, with a secondary plot dedicated to Mrs. Greenow's decision between Cheesacre and Bellfield. Trollope provides a glimpse of the mental state Alice experiences as she tries, and often fails, to decide between her two suitors: "As the mental photographs of the two men forced themselves upon her, she could not force herself to forget those words—'Look here, upon this picture—and upon this'" (386). Alice proceeds through her narrative with the possibility of marrying each man always open to her; she has to decide between two simultaneously available options. In presenting these two mental pictures simultaneously, Trollope's novel marks a kind of break in novelistic representations of choice: few if any novelists had previously depicted a protagonist as possessing an opportunity to consider two romantic rivals at the same time. Instead, as in the cases of Jane Austen's *Emma*, Charles Dickens's *David Copperfield*, and Charlotte Brontë's *Jane Eyre*, novelistic characters in previous decades choose serially: Emma considers Elton, then after declining his offer, considers Frank Churchill and then Mr. Knightley; David Copperfield first falls in love with Dora and only after she dies considers the attractions of Agnes; a similar structure holds for Jane Eyre, Rochester, and St. John Rivers. Though it often goes unnoticed by critics who see in these relationships romantic triangles, novelists writing before the latter half of the century almost always represent choice as a series of "yes or no" decisions that do not involve the consideration of commensurate options, each of which possesses qualities that can be weighed simultaneously against those of the other.

In fact, late nineteenth-century literature is populated by representations of individual minds in a state of wondering indecision as they contemplate not so much whether or not to make a binary choice but how to evaluate a number of often disparate options as to careers, convictions, and objects of desire. These characters try, often unsuccessfully, to evaluate their options with respect to how each might accord with some set of personal preferences or values that they have difficulty defining. Sir James Chettam in the early part of George Eliot's *Middlemarch* ([1871–1872] 1994) reveals to Dorothea, "I have often a difficulty in deciding" because "one hears very sensible things said on opposite sides" (31). Mr. Arabin in Trollope's *Barchester Towers* ([1857] 2014) declares, "It is the bane of my life that on important subjects I acquire no fixed opinion." "I think, and think, and go on thinking," he concludes (394). Tennyson's *Idylls of the King* ([1859–1885] Tennyson 1983) depicts many characters whose principal mental activity is attempting to weigh options against each other. King Leodogran views his own comprehension of Arthur's lineage as a matter to be "debated with himself / If Arthur were the child of shamefulness, / Or born the son of Gorlois, after death, / Or Uther's son, and born before his time, / Or whether there were truth in anything / Said by these three" (27). As Matthew Campbell argues, such indecision is so common in *Idylls* that the epic itself becomes an example of "procrastinating verse" that "hovers over the tragic actions it describes, wary of allying itself with the ethical imperatives that it perceives" (1996, 58). Upon arriving in London and observing the variety of work in the city, Arthur Clennam in Dickens's *Little Dorrit* ([1855–1857] 2003) is paralyzed when it comes to choosing his own job: "the question," Dickens writes, of "what he was to do henceforth in life; to what occupation he should devote himself, and in what direction he had best seek it" is foremost in his mind (125).

Psychologist Barry Schwartz might diagnose the experience portrayed in these texts by pointing to their market origins, as he explains in his influential account of the difficulties of choice in modern societies. For Schwartz, the enormous expansion of goods in the consumer marketplace, the greater options for careers and life-paths, and the overall logic of capitalism have made individuals think of themselves as "people [who] go through life with all their options arrayed before them, as if on a buffet table," with choosing among those options perceived as their primary mode of self-identification (2000, 81). The opportunity to choose among similar, simultaneously available possibilities may seem liberating, but as Schwartz argues (and as my examples from Eliot, Tennyson, and Dickens indicate) its attendant cognitive and emotional demands can be paralyzing, baffling, and thus anything but liberatory.

Trollope's particular embrace of this newer, more open model of choosing also entails an opening up of new and often fraught psychological terrain, as he creates selves out of characters' difficult attempts at comparing several options at once. Trollope constructs individual characters' psychologies by narrating their sometimes-difficult processes of choosing; indeed, for Trollope, subjectivity itself becomes an effect of complex decision-making or indecision. *The Warden* (1855) focuses on Septimus Harding's long process of deciding to abandon his post at Hiram's Hospital. It represents what Elaine Hadley calls Harding's "mental substantiation of devil's advocacy," as Trollope shows Harding "rehearsing opposing positions" and evaluating the moral, ethical, and legal reasons why he might go or stay (2010, 79). Or: much of the pathos in *Phineas Redux* (1873) comes from Finn's uncertainties as to whether or not he desires the political life he lives in London. Finn often wonders at his decision to reenter Parliament, as at the beginning of the novel when he finds himself remembering how parties, power, and Countesses' "drawing rooms" had (as shown in the novel's prequel, *Phineas Finn* [1867–1868]) been open to him, before he abandoned them for a relatively secluded domestic existence with his Irish wife. "He had left all those things [of Parliamentary privilege] of his own free will, as though telling himself that there was a better life than they offered to him. But was he sure that he found it to be better?" (Trollope 2000, 54) In *Can You Forgive Her?*, Alice Greenow often finds herself ruminating on some form of the question, "should she marry for love and if so, should Captain Bellfield be the man?" (Trollope 2004, 499), implying two interlocking choices. And of course, through that novel's title, Trollope calls upon the reader to engage in a lengthy process of deliberation as to whether or not Alice should be forgiven.

Even if Alice's marriage plot is, of course, a financial plot, too, Alice's decision is not immediately recognizable as one that would concern economists—she is not choosing among commodities to buy. Still, its open, expansive structure calls to mind marketplaces that, by the end of the nineteenth century, were characterized by the breadth and variety of products they offered. Schwartz argues that it is precisely the industrial revolution's "development of markets in which practically anything can be exchanged" that helped give rise to individuals' sense that choosing is less a matter of saying "yes" or "no" to any given option than of comparing multiple options to one another. In other words, in the overflowing marketplace subjectivity becomes a matter of expressing a preference for one good over others (2000, 84). The perhaps outsize importance we place on choice is a direct result of modern capitalism: it is "because we fit everything into a market framework that we expect to have choice … in all domains of life" (85).

A number of twentieth-century theorists—including Herbert Marcuse, Jean Baudrillard, and Guy Debord—have argued that capitalism constructs individuals in terms of their desire for, and acquisition of, commodities. According to Marcuse, people now "recognize themselves in their commodities; they find their soul in their automobile, hi-fi set, split-level home, kitchen equipment"; modern capitalism has the ability to "turn [the]waste" of overproduced goods "into need" (1964, 11). In his theory of the "ideological production of needs," Baudrillard similarly asserts that the logic of capitalism produces in subjects "a compulsion to need and a compulsion to consume" (1981, 82). Schwartz's insight about the difficulties faced by consumers as they attempt to choose among the market's many items suggests a more elaborated view of the relationship between capitalism and subjectivity than these theorists provide. In order for a consumer to purchase a commodity, that consumer must not only have a general desire for goods but also be able to choose *one* commodity from the large number on offer. This often difficult, sometimes overwhelming labor of choosing can, in fact, prevent consumption. As recent work in the field of marketing and business psychology suggests, choice among too many options can be "demotivating" (Iyengar and Lepper 2000), causing individuals to turn away from a retailer empty-handed. Late-nineteenth-century writers recognize this labor. Yet their interest in it is not in the service of a thoroughgoing critique of the marketplace's cognitive pressures. Indeed, like today's business psychologists, these writers assume—and narrate the assumption—that the activity of ranking one's desires and choosing among many simultaneous options is a vital expression of a subject's individuality, even if this activity results in frustration and paralysis. To the extent that such paralysis keeps subjects gazing inwardly as they attempt to prioritize their desires for various goods, it does little to counteract the capitalist phenomenon of people "recogniz[ing] themselves ... in commodities"; as long as individuals define their desires as desires for marketable goods and their agency in terms of consumption, they remain consumers even when they are unable to decide which goods to consume.

As historians and literary critics alike have noted, by the 1860s, British culture had come to identify itself with consumerism: it was "a nation of shopkeepers" (Whitlock 2005, 3). Thus, Trollope, Eliot, Dickens, and Tennyson were representing a new form of decision-making at the same moment as Britain experienced a number of changes that signaled its emergence as a consumer society. These include, as historian John Benson states, "a 50 per cent increase in average per capita spending which took place" in the last decades of the nineteenth century; "the establishment of new leisure industries; and the emergence for the first time of large-scale demand from the working class for better food, more fashionable clothes, new forms of entertainment and a growing range of consumer goods" (1996, 7). Markets were full of new goods as industrial capitalism moved from emphasizing production to focusing on selling and, as Rachel Bowlby puts it, from "the satisfaction of stable needs to the invention of new desires" (1985, 1). Literary writers were, of course, not the only ones who registered this shift. The field of political economy moved away from examining large-scale principles of supply and demand and toward focusing on the consumer during "the marginalist revolution" of the mid- to late nineteenth century. As Gordon Bigelow and Regenia Gagnier have shown, moreover, Victorian literature's representations of individuality and consumption dovetail with concepts put forth by marginalism and neoclassical economics.[1]

The act of choosing among many, simultaneously available options is a key one in the consumer-oriented marketplace newly flooded with commodities, and it becomes important to literary representations of individuals' mental activity. *Can You Forgive Her?* begins with an early and emblematic representation of choice-making by Mr. Vavasor, Alice's father, who is deciding among a variety of dishes. Because this instance of indecision prefigures the main characters' vacillations, it illustrates how a particular form of consumer decision-making becomes a model for decision-making generally in Trollope's novel. Mr. Vavasor has as his most consistent, distinctive trait a desire to eat at his club each night rather than at home with Alice. "After his wife's death he dined at his club every day," the narrator writes, and he "was rarely happy except when so dining." Mr. Vavasor's delight in his daily dinners proceeds from his experience of choosing among the various dishes on the menu.

> They who have seen him scanning the steward's list of dishes, and giving the necessary orders for his own and his friend's dinner, at about half past four in the afternoon, have seen John Vavasor at the only moment of the day at which he is ever much in earnest. All other things are light and easy to him— to be taken easily and to be dismissed easily. Even the eating of dinner calls forth from him no special sign of energy. (2004, 41)

In this passage, Trollope sums up the way "freedom of choice" can exert a seductive power over individuals. Anyone who has enjoyed window-shopping or web- or channel-surfing can understand Mr. Vavasor's attraction to the moments when he feels many options open to him and, in quick succession, evaluates those options according to how much he thinks he will enjoy consuming each. This image is a kind of early literalization of Schwartz's metaphor for the individual in the modern marketplace of career, lifestyle, educational, and of course, product options: Mr. Vavasor is one of the "people [who] go through life with all their options arrayed before them, as if on a buffet table." And the driving impulse behind Mr. Vavasor's "happiness" is his ability to consider the prospect of excess consumption that is at once alimentary and economic: it is because he has to settle on a single dish instead of enjoying several that the "eating of dinner calls forth from him no special sign of energy."

Mr. Vavasor's pleasure in being able to choose among a variety of simultaneously available goods—and corollary displeasure in actually making a choice, thereby rejecting a number of possibilities—is linked to Alice's romantic decision-making both narratively (Mr. Vavasor is related to Alice and his scene at the club appears at the beginning of Alice's story) and formally (his options appear before him in a way that is structurally similar to Alice's). Thomas Hardy draws a tighter connection between a character's choices in a crowded marketplace and marital decision-making. In Hardy's *A Pair of Blue Eyes* ([1871–1872] 1998), which also narrates a love triangle, Henry Knight's effort to woo Elfride through the purchase of some jewelry prompts Hardy to dramatize how a subject's efforts to compare commodities in an expansive retail environment calls forth new cognitive and emotional phenomena. Before he leaves Dublin to see Elfride, Knight finds a "a high-class jewellery establishment, in which he purchased what he considered would suit her best." After buying the item, Knight

> opened the morocco case, and held up each of the fragile bits of gold-work before his eyes. Many things had become old to the solitary man of letters, but these were new, and he handled like a child an outcome of civilization which had never before been touched by his fingers. A sudden fastidious decision that the pattern chosen would not suit her after all caused him to … tear down the street to change them for others. After a great deal of trouble in reselecting, during which his mind became so bewildered that the critical faculty on objects of art seemed to have vacated his person altogether, Knight carried off another pair of ear-rings… [A]fter contemplating them fifty times with a growing misgiving that the last choice was worse than the first, he felt that no sleep would visit his pillow till he had improved upon his previous purchases yet again. In a perfect heat of vexation with himself for such tergiversation, he went anew to the shop-door, was absolutely ashamed to enter and give further trouble, went to another shop, bought a pair at an enormously increased price, … asked the goldsmiths if they would take the other pair in exchange, was told that they could not exchange articles bought of another maker, paid down the money, and went off with the two pairs in his possession, wondering what on earth to do with the superfluous pair. He … was burdened with an interposing sense that, as a capable man, with true ideas of economy, he must necessarily sell them somewhere, which he did at last for a mere song. (191)[2]

Knight's tortured self-doubt, indecision, and drive toward making multiple purchases and exchanges seem to express an interior psychological weakness. Yet Hardy makes clear how a retail environment characterized by the presence of a large number of similar items for sale can give rise to behavior that might otherwise appear as a function of innate personality. The urban presence of a multitude of establishments each selling similar goods is a feature of the modern marketplace, and the subject's experience of this market is the opportunity, or pressure, to decide among many versions of the same thing, each of which is immediately available for purchase. It is, after all, the basic similarity between each item Knight buys that gives rise to his self-questioning. He is not looking so much for a wholly different piece of jewelry than the one he buys but rather one that might be somehow "better" in an incremental, difficult-to-discern way. A sign of these items' similarity is not only the fact that he assumes he can take one pair "in exchange" for "the other pair" but also the fact that he can conclude that "the last choice was worse than the first." The differentiations are subtle enough, and the criteria for judgment unstable enough, that each item can seem either readily exchangeable for the other, or better or worse than the other, within the mere difference of a few hours.

It is hard, in other words, to imagine that this particular type of frenetic indecision, involving weighing one option against many similar ones, was common in an older, preindustrial market that offered fewer, more highly differentiated goods. Hardy gestures toward the historical novelty of this type of cognitive effort in his emphasis on how unprecedented it seems to Knight. The jewelry itself presents a fascinating contrast to his habituation to what is "old" because it is "new"; he handles the first item "like a child," as it is "an outcome of civilization which had never before been touched by his fingers." When he attempts to use his "faculty on objects of art" to help him compare the various items and shops, he finds it has "vacated his person altogether": whereas his status as an intellectual has trained him in the capacity to discern between singular objects that as Walter Benjamin might say possess an aura of their "unique existence," he is baffled by the new multiplicity he faces in his shopping trips (1968, 78). He thus behaves with uncharacteristic, uncontrolled anxiety: his frustrating, and seemingly fruitless, repeated visits make his experience resemble the threateningly meaningless repetition characterizing the objects on sale.

In the end, Knight's intolerance for modern forms of decision-making in the market foreshadows his much more narratively consequential intolerance for Elfride's inability to choose between Stephen Smith and himself. As in the case of Trollope's depiction of Alice, Hardy presents a romantic structure that allows for consideration of multiple available potential spouses simultaneously—a structure that is prefigured by a scene of a consumer facing multiple commensurate products. The fact that the products in *A Pair of Blue Eyes* are, in the view of Knight, supposed to secure a stable relationship between him and Elfride but are themselves bafflingly unstable and difficult to distinguish is suggestive of how, as Schwartz indicates, a "market framework" in modern life can extend to other domains of existence.

The Processes and Results of Subjective Decision-Making in Neoclassical Economics

While Trollope and Hardy draw connections between changes in the marketplace and changes in how decision-making might be conceived and represented, Victorian political economy of the period draws similar connections in theoretical discourses about consumption and economic value. The general shift in economic theory away from focusing on the production and distribution of goods and toward theorizing about individuals' consumption of them is well known. The dominant model of economics prior to the latter half of the nineteenth century was the classical model. Adam Smith and David Ricardo conceived of economic systems as primarily driven by systems of production—the labor of workmen, of the produce of the land, and the output of factories—not the desires of individual consumers. In his *Wealth of Nations* ([1776] 1986), Smith connects the expansion of modern economies and the consequent distribution of wealth to innovations such as the division of labor, which "great[ly] increases the quantity of work … the same number of people are capable of performing" and thus increases the overall value of the economies in which the division of labor dominates (112). Holding to the Labor Theory of Value, Smith argued that: "Labour is the real measure of the exchangeable value of all commodities" (136). For Ricardo, "the value of a commodity, or the quantity of any other commodity for which it will exchange, depends on the relative quantity of labour which is necessary for its production" (1817, 11).

In the last half of the nineteenth century, during the same decades that Great Britain moved toward a consumerist society, Carl Menger, W. S. Jevons, F. Y. Edgeworth, Alfred Marshall, and Leon Walras, who are known now as part of, variously, the "marginalist," "neoclassical," and "microeconomic" schools, put forth a revisionary account of economic value. The simplest way of describing their revision is to say that they placed consumption rather than production at the center of economic analysis; economic value (price) became tied to individual preferences rather than, say, manufacturing and labor costs. As Menger put it in his *Principles of Economics* ([1871] 2007), "not only the nature but also the measure of value is subjective"; thus, "a good can have great value to one economizing individual, little value to another, and no value at all to a third" (147). A major aspect of this revision was their focus on consumer choice: for marginalist and neoclassical economists, commodities' value depended not on the labor expended to create them but rather on consumers' expressed desire for some commodities over others.

This shift toward consumer preference solved some problems that had dogged the classical political economists. The most famous of these was the "diamond-water paradox," which Smith himself identified and found himself unable to solve. One part of this paradox that clarifies neoclassical economics' departure from, and explanatory superiority to, the classical school might be articulated as follows. In an everyday scenario, where water is easily procured, the price of water is far below that of diamonds, but under different conditions—say, when a consumer is dying of thirst—that consumer would pay far more for a glass of water than for a diamond. Smith's and Ricardo's proposition that labor is the basis of value cannot explain the differing prices of water and diamonds in these two scenarios; presumably, the labor that goes into producing a diamond is the same in both, but the prices are very different. Neoclassical and marginal economists can easily explain this differential: value derives from the "marginal" utility that consumers believe they will gain from the item to be purchased, not the labor expended in creating the item. For a person dying of thirst, the water's utility is high, but for someone who has plenty of water, the diamond's utility—in showing status or providing some other kind of pleasure—is higher. Moreover, the price of water will diminish as thirst is quenched: a fifth glass of water will provide less utility than the first, so consumers will pay less for it. Changes in price are thus tied to changes in subjective preference, which alters depending on how much of an item a consumer desires.

These later economists at least putatively imagined that they were moving the focus of economics away from abstract reasoning and toward a description of real-world phenomena: the behavior of individuals within an economy. The most important consumer behavior, for them, was the exercise of choice. Over the more than a century since the emergence of neoclassical economics, however, a multitude of criticisms have been lodged against these thinkers' analysis and understanding of how consumers choose. Within economics itself, the field of behavioral economics arose in the 1970s as a corrective to the neoclassical notion that individuals guide their decisions according to estimations of utility that they expect each option to offer them. Daniel Kahneman and Amos Tversky, two leading behavioralist thinkers, laid the groundwork for the field through their research on decision-making; they were able to "demonstrate experimentally that people systematically deviate from the predictions of expected utility-theory and some of the axioms upon which it is based" when their options were framed in different ways or when they were deciding between long-term versus short-term gains (Levy 2002, 271). Owing to the research of Kahneman, Tversky, and many other scholars working in a number of fields, "it has become abundantly evident," neuroscientists Jonathan Cohen and Kenneth Blum insist, "that the pristine assumptions of the 'standard economic model'—that individuals operate as optimal decision makers in maximizing utility—are in direct violation of even the most basic facts about human behavior" (2002, 194; quoted in Schüll and Zaloom 2011, 518).

Such criticisms about how the neoclassical school envisioned decision-making underlie far more damning visions of neoclassical economics, such as that of André Orléan. For Orléan, the preferences posited by neoclassicism do not

> have anything in common with the way in which human beings in any age or in any place have actually behaved. It is as though the neoclassical consumer, insofar as he could ever have really existed, were the result of a prolonged modification of human subjectivity, carried out by society for the express purpose of adapting it to the demands of commerce ... The neoclassical view of the consumer is emblematic of a more general way of looking at the world. It asks us to imagine that individual agents know exactly what they want under all circumstances. (2014, 41)

It might seem as if the "neoclassical view" that Orléan cites shares little in terms of its understanding of decision-making with Trollope or Hardy. In certain uncommon situations—as with a consumer in a desert confronted with a choice between water or diamonds—neoclassicism makes plausible assumptions about how subjects would rank-order their preferences according to expected utility. But, as Hardy suggests in his depiction of Knight's behavior, individuals more often have great difficulty knowing their desires or evaluating options, becoming distracted by the sheer variety of them or the minute differentiations between them.

Still, the differences between the late-century economic writing by Jevons, Marshall, and Menger and the literary representations of decision-making in Trollope and Hardy are often less significant than their commonalities. Each sees the individual's capacity to decide between a number of available, commensurable options as central to humans' mental activity; and each associates (the economists much more directly) this capacity with consumption in the marketplace. Moreover, in looking not at subsequent, more mathematical and formalized articulations of neoclassicism in the twentieth century but at the nineteenth-century economists' contemporaneous writings, the approaches of authors and economists appear even closer to one another. Despite the eventual trend of neoclassical economists to see the actual minds of consumers as "black boxes" that hide whatever biological or emotional dynamics result in the expression of ordered preferences, mid- to late-nineteenth-century founders of the school had a more nuanced sense than later theorists of what economists can and cannot account for in human decision-making. Alfred Marshall, who is often credited with synthesizing various microeconomic insights into a neoclassical system, describes the economists' procedure as "measuring a mental state" of consumers when faced by various possible items to buy (1898, 71). According to Marshall, who is clearly still influenced by utilitarian consequentialist presumptions concerning the calculus of utility, economists measure this "mental state as men do in ordinary life, by its motor-force or the incentive which it affords to action." "For suppose," Marshall continues,

> that the person, whom we saw doubting between several little gratifications for himself, had thought after a while of a poor invalid whom he would pass on his way home; and had spent some time in making up his mind whether he would choose a physical gratification for himself, or would do a kindly act and rejoice in another's joy. As his desires turned now towards the one, now the other, there would be change in the quality of his mental states; and the philosopher is bound to study the nature of the change.
>
> But the economist studies mental states rather through their manifestations than in themselves; and if he finds they afford evenly balanced incentives to action, he treats them primâ facie as for his purpose equal. He does not attempt to weigh the real value of the higher affections of our nature against those of our lower: he does not balance the love for virtue against the desire for agreeable food... He reaches his provisional conclusions by

observations of men in general under given conditions without attempting
to fathom the mental and spiritual characteristics of individuals. (74)

While Marshall declines to look at the "mental and spiritual characteristics
of individuals," he nonetheless views individuals in some of the same ways
as Trollope does in *Can You Forgive Her?*: as subjects whose capacity to
choose, and whose operations of ordering their desires for multiple objects
on the way to making a choice, are important to their selves, even if
Marshall cannot "fathom them." Marshall's imagined person with fluctuating desires that "turned now towards the one, now the other" is a version of Alice Vavasor's condition "as the mental photographs of the two
men forced themselves upon her," and her mind commands her "Look
here, upon this picture—and upon this" as she attempts subjectively to
decide which she prefers.

The outsize importance Marshall places on decision-making processes
that involve the ordering of preferences—they are central to Marshall's
account of human behavior, even if the economist only perceives their
results—has an analog in Trollope's depiction of Mr. Vavasor as well.
Vavasor is regularly drawn to his club because it offers him the chance to
choose among items to consume on the menu; he values the *process* of
decision-making: the subjective contemplation of internal desires that it
involves. The only time in his life when he is "very much in earnest" is
when he is "scanning the steward's list of dishes" and engaged in ordering
them. In Marshall's account of choice, individuals choose options that
maximize utility, and this maximization can only occur after a product has
been bought, an investment has been made, or a life-path followed.
Whereas Marshall thus concerns himself about the results of a decision and
not the internal processes leading up to it, Trollope is more fascinated by
individuals' long processes of making up their minds and less so by the
results. For many of Trollope's characters, whatever utility might be gained
from making a decision is less captivating than, as Arabin puts it, to "go on
thinking" (2014, 394) about all the possibilities that the modern market
of options has opened. The fact that Mr. Vavasor enjoys scanning the
menu but actually eating the dishes "calls forth from him no special sign
of energy" is an indication of Trollope's own relative indifference to the
utility of choice and greater interest in potential pleasures of contemplative choice-making. Still, this opposition between economist and author is
not as stark as it might first appear: both Marshall and Trollope discuss
extended processes of choosing and the resulting choices; they differ in

the significance they place on processes and results. For both writers, an individual's mental activity is intimately tied to choosing and, in particular, to the subject's effort of organizing his desires into ranked preferences for objects in the world. One discounts the effort and the other discounts the ranking as expressed in an actual choice.

More so than those of Marshall, the theories of William Stanley Jevons would seem to match subsequent characterizations of neoclassical economics as obsessed with abstract, wholly unreal conceptualizations of human subjects who "know exactly what they want in all circumstances" and are able to act according to a rational assessment of the relative strengths of their desires and preferences. In his *Theory of Political Economy* ([1871] 2013), Jevons, after all, advocated for economics to take on a "mathematical character" by the application of calculations based on "the laws of human want" so that an economist could graph the diminishing utility of water to illustrate how a subject's desire for it decreases according to the following pattern: "water, up to a certain quantity, is indispensable; … further quantities will have various degrees of utility; but … beyond a certain quantity the utility sinks gradually to zero" (39). Yet as Robert Sugden has argued, while Jevons has retrospectively been closely associated with a non-empirical, non-psychological strain of economic thinking that treats individuals' minds mechanistically, his writing displays a much stronger interest in how minds actually work. As Sugden puts it, Jevons, like other "important pioneers of neoclassical theory," belongs to a "tradition of psychologically-based theorizing" that led him to publish results of his psychological experiments in *Nature* (2009, 860). As with Marshall, Jevons exhibits an interest in and sensitivity to the sometimes difficult processes of recognizing one's preference. Perhaps precisely because of these difficulties, the only relevant phenomena that he believes can be measured and rendered axiomatic for economic science is the consequential choice.[3] In attempting to describe how economists account for what occurs in the mind of a consumer choosing between two options, he cites the idea that actions provide an accurate measure of "pleasure": "the greatest of two pleasures, or what appears such, sways the resulting action; for it is this resulting action that alone determines which is the greater." "Pleasures," Jevons goes on to say, are "as the mind estimates them; so that we cannot make a choice, or manifest the will in any way, without indicating thereby an excess of pleasure in some direction" (2013, 36).

Yet just as Jevons posits a subject whose most significant psychological characteristic is the accurate estimation of what option might produce the most expected "pleasure," he recognizes the possibility for vacillation in the manner of Knight in Hardy's novel: "it is true that the mind often hesitates and is perplexed in making a choice of great importance: this indicates either varying estimates of the motives, or a feeling of incapacity to grasp the quantities concerned" (2013, 39). Again, the difference between economist and author is one of emphasis: like Marshall, Jevons finally finds most significant the "resulting action," not the process of sorting through "varying estimates" of "motives" and of recognizing the "excess pleasure" that might derive from a certain choice. Hardy, like Trollope, finds most significant precisely the difficult process of grasping one's preference; for Hardy, the end result—in Knight's case, the selection of a piece of jewelry for a woman Knight will never marry—is somewhat absurd. Knight's tragic self-absorption as he tries to match his varying desires for, and different images of, Elfride to his choice of a commodity to purchase is Hardy's main focus; as in his other works, Hardy negates the notion that one can intentionally fulfill one's desires. In this instance, moreover, it is as if Hardy comments on the potential illogic of the marginalists' focus on the results of a decision. The marginalists assume that, in the abstract, choice is the only thing that matters: it is the "motor-force" an individual exercises in making a decision that expresses the greater utility of one option compared to others. Thus, paradoxically, the actual, particular outcome of a choice—the item purchased, the option committed to—is insignificant in terms of its particularity. Under the analytic gaze of the economist, it only matters that a choice has been made. Hardy narrates the maddening consequences of this empty imperative to choose, as Knight's compulsive decision-making proceeds in the absence of an ability to attach meaning to the actual objects he buys.

In sum, even if economists and novelists differ in their representations of decision-making and their estimations of its most significant aspects, they share a sense that selfhood's most important aspects are those that make us aware of the different options we have in front of us and help us evaluate our expected satisfaction with the consumption or adoption of those options. For both, decision-making is an inward-looking process; it does not proceed by looking outwardly to extra-subjective systems of ethics, morality, or justice. George Eliot, in *Middlemarch* for instance, presents just such an alternative, distinct logic of decision-making—one that does not depend on the individualistic, consumerist principles of the marginalists but rather on a regard for a broader system of evaluation.

Eliot shows that indecision resulting from a difficult process of inward evaluation of one's own preference might be contrasted to a different kind of indecision—one that is not so much occupied with comparing objects and the subjective feelings they create as with contemplating larger claims based on rationality, religion, or ethics. After Sir James Chettam's gift of a puppy provokes Dorothea's scorn, the couple engage in a conversation about decisiveness, part of which is cited above. Chettam states that he "env[ies]" Dorothea's "power of forming an opinion" since he sees himself, by contrast, as exhibiting Arabin-like indecision when it comes to significant topics of debate. "I know when I like people," Chettam states,

> "But about other matters, do you know, I have often a difficulty in deciding. One hears very sensible things said on opposite sides."
> "Or that seem sensible. Perhaps we don't always discriminate between sense and nonsense."
> Dorothea felt that she was rather rude.
> "Exactly," said Sir James. "But you seem to have the power of discrimination."
> "On the contrary, I am often unable to decide. But that is from ignorance. The right conclusion is there all the same, though I am unable to see it. (1994, 41)

For Dorothea, the project of decision-making is not personal. There is an abstract framework she believes she can consult to "discriminate between sense and nonsense," or between good and bad. It is a matter of knowing that framework, just as, according to John Stuart Mill, the promotion of "General Happiness" is a matter of knowing the already established determinations of right and wrong. According to Dorothea, "the right conclusion is there"—it does not derive from her sense of her own potential feelings but from outside of her mind and her knowledge. Dorothea is a kind of anti-consumer: the novel begins with her refusing the same type of jewels that so captivate Knight in Hardy's novel. She thus stands as an exception that proves the rule: because she seeks principles of decision-making not via subjective utilities but objective disinterested principles and at the same time rejects the consumerist impulse, her example illustrates the consumerist logic underlying Trollope's and Hardy's representations of subjective decision-making.

In other words, Trollope's and Hardy's representations of characters for whom the ranking of their preferences is an inexact, difficult, or futile process are not so much subversions of the rational choosers put forth by neoclassical thinkers as a different view of them. Unlike Eliot, neither these literary authors nor the economists imagine subjects relying on non-subjective systems of value or behavior in making their choices. In fact, for authors and economists alike, individuals' thinking and feelings are self-contained and structured along the lines of a marketplace, where buyers attempt to discern their relative preferences for the objects on sale. In the broadest sense, the emergence of this fascination with subjective decision-making might be understood as a result of circumstantial and ideological forces: circumstantial in that these novelists and economic theorists wrote when markets became flooded with new items that new modes of production made possible, and ideological in that Western culture was well on its way to creating individualized subjects who understood their subjectivity in terms of the freedom of ownership and consumption. Thus, as Gagnier argues in *The Insatiability of Human Wants: Economics and Aesthetics in Market Society*, the idea that individuals reveal themselves through purchases and through "choice, preference, and leisure or idleness" is a hallmark of literature during the *fin de siècle*—especially in the works of Oscar Wilde—and of neoclassical theories of economics, which together helped construct individual freedom in terms of capitalist consumption (2000, 110).

Twenty-first century audiences easily identify with characters who lose themselves in the contemplation of their options—the popular comedy *The Good Place* prominently features a character, Chidi, who has doomed himself in the afterlife because he cannot commit himself to any of the options modern life puts before him. And one of the major topics addressed by today's psychologists and social scientists is the consequences of expansive numbers of possibilities. So, Sheena Iyengar and Mark Lepper have studied ways in which the expansion of choice has become "demotivating"; and Schwartz has argued that the vast number of options we encounter today has brought with it paralysis and torturous indecision as often as liberation and satisfaction (2000). The idea that the "self-determining self" can and should "mak[e] choices in the world to maximize his or her preferences" leads to what Schwartz calls a "tyranny of choice," where a desire to make the optimal, right choice among a bewildering array of options leads to alienated inaction (80). These social scientists recognize what Trollope, Hardy, and other literary writers of the late nineteenth century show readers: that when choosing becomes an individual matter, requiring introspection about how to rank a large number of options according to desires one may or may not be able to discern, it can result not in a clear expression of individuals' desires, as neoclassical economics supposes, but in political, social, and ethical inertia of the kind that Mr. Vavasor and Knight embody.

Grosz's theoretical project argues that choice does not have to have the supreme value that Western liberalism and capitalism attach to it. We have come to think not just of novelistic characters but of novels themselves as indebted to the idea that multiple options are simultaneously available for the choosing. "Narration," according to Roland Barthes in "The Reality Effect," has "the appearance of a huge traffic-control center" that guides the text through a "trajectory of choices and alternatives," some of which are realized, while others are not (1989, 147). Despite their differences in how they see the processes and possible results of decision-making, both novelists and economic theorists assent to the idea that subjects are decision-makers and that their signal cognitive, mental activity is the discernment and expression of preferences for "choices and alternatives" that might be barely differentiated or even completely illusory: the "alternatives" that a text does not choose to follow is like the "unchosen option[s]" that in Grosz's formulation is a projection or an illusion—perhaps a phantasm created by a market society that asks its subjects constantly to think about their desires for objects they do not or cannot have. Novels as much as neoclassical economics have moved us toward a notion of ourselves as defined by interiorized contemplation of imagined options. These are selves who, as today's psychologists suggest, tend toward an Arabin-like condition in which "on important subjects"—and trivial ones, too—we "acquire no fixed opinion" and instead "think, and think, and go on thinking" with thoughts running in "different directions." (The constant barrage of instant judgments and apparently clear-cut conclusions put forth by media pundits and modern political actors attract audiences precisely because they promise an end to indecision even as overproduction and contradictions prolong it.) Political economy's movement away from general, socially produced ideas of value toward individually centered ones stands as one way its supposed emphasis on, and embrace of, individual freedom has worked to produce a cultural moment in which subjectivity, so defined, is at odds with efficacious action.

NOTES

1. Bigelow (2003, 2) discusses how Victorian culture registered the emergence of neoclassical economics and its focus on "the figure of the consumer" in the latter half of the nineteenth century. See also Bigelow's "The Cost of Everything in *Middlemarch*" (2013) for his analysis of the way the narratives and characters of Eliot's *Middlemarch* stand as critiques of neoclassical economists' "radically subjective theory of economic life" (102). Regenia Gagnier (2000) discusses at length the cultural causes and effects of political economy's emphasis on individual consumers' desire as a central economic force.
2. I am indebted to Chip Mitchell (2014) for calling my attention to this scene from Hardy's fiction.
3. As several scholars have noted, even though Jevons advocated for an economic science based on mathematics, he also believed in inductive data-gathering and scientific observation. For relevant discussions of Jevons' methods, see Sugden (2009), Peart (1993), and Caplin and Glimcher (2014).

REFERENCES

Barthes, Roland. 1989. The Reality Effect. In *The Rustle of Language*. Translated by Richard Howard, 141–149. Berkeley: University of California Press.

Baudrillard, Jean. 1981. *For a Critique of the Political Economy of the Sign.* Translated by Charles Levin. Candor, NY: Telos Press.

Benjamin, Walter. 1968. *Illuminations.* Translated by Harry Zohn. New York: Schocken Books.

Benson, John. 1996. Consumption and the Consumer Revolution. *Recent Findings of Research in Economic and Social History* 23: 2–8.

Bigelow, Gordon. 2003. *Fiction, Famine and the Rise of Economics in Victorian England and Ireland.* Cambridge: Cambridge University Press.

———. 2013. The Cost of Everything in *Middlemarch.* In *Economic Women: Essays on Desire and Dispossession in Nineteenth-Century British Culture*, ed. Lana L. Dalley and Jill Rappaport, 97–109. Columbus: Ohio State University Press.

Bowlby, Rachel. 1985. *Just Looking: Consumer Culture in Dreiser, Gissing and Zola.* London: Routledge.

Campbell, Matthew. 1996. Tennyson's Epic Procrastination. *English: The Journal of the English Association* 45: 44–61.

Caplin, Andrew, and Paul Glimcher. 2014. Basic Methods from Neoclassical Economics. In *Neuroeconomics: Decision Making and the Brain*, ed. Paul Glimcher and Ernst Fehr, 3–17. London: Elsevier.

Cohen, Jonathan D., and Kenneth Blum. 2002. Reward and Decision. *Neuron* 36: 191–198.

Dickens, Charles. (1855–1857) 2003. *Little Dorrit*. London: Penguin.

Eliot, George. (1871–1872) 1994. *Middlemarch*. London: Penguin.

Gagnier, Regina. 2000. *The Insatiability of Human Wants: Economics and Aesthetics in Market Society*. Chicago: University of Chicago Press.

Grosz, Elizabeth. 2010. Feminism, Materialism, and Freedom. In *New Materialisms: Ontology, Agency, and Politics*, ed. Diana H. Coole and Samantha Frost, 139–157. Durham, NC: Duke University Press.

Hadley, Elaine. 2010. *Living Liberalism: Practical Citizenship in Mid-Victorian Britain*. Chicago: University of Chicago Press.

Hardy, Thomas. (1871–1872) 1998. *A Pair of Blue Eyes*. London: Penguin.

Iyengar, Sheena, and Mark Lepper. 2000. When Choice is Demotivating: Can One Desire Too Much of a Good Thing? *Journal of Personality and Social Psychology* 79 (6): 995–1006.

Jevons, William Stanley. (1871) 2013. The Theory of Political Economy. In *Palgrave Classics in Economics*. London: Palgrave Macmillan.

Levy, Jack S. 2002. Daniel Kahneman: Judgment, Decision, and Rationality. *PS: Political Science & Politics* 35: 271–273.

Marcuse, Herbert. 1964. *One-Dimensional Man: Studies in the Ideology of Advanced Industrial Society*. London: Routledge, Kegan & Paul.

Marshall, Alfred. 1898. *Principles of Economics, Volume I*. London: Macmillan.

Menger, Carl. (1871) 2007. *Principles of Economics*. Auburn, AL: The Ludwig von Mises Institute.

Mitchell, Chip. 2014. Blue Eyes, Red Backpacks: Paranoia and the Semiotics of Primary Colors from Hardy to Murakami. Unpublished essay.

Orléan, André. 2014. *The Empire of Value: A New Foundation for Economics*. Translated by M.B. DeBevoise. Cambridge, MA: MIT Press.

Peart, Sandra J. 1993. W. S. Jevons's Methodology of Economics: Some Implications of the Procedures for 'Inductive Quantification'. *History of Political Economy* 25 (3): 435–460.

Ricardo, David. 1817. *On the Principles of Political Economy and Taxation*. London: John Murray.

Schüll, Natasha Dow, and Caitlin Zaloom. 2011. The Shortsighted Brain: Neuroeconomics and the Governance of Choice in Time. *Social Studies of Science* 41 (4): 515–538.

Schwartz, Barry. 2000. Self-Determination: The Tyranny of Freedom. *American Psychologist* 55 (1): 79–88.

Smith, Adam. (1776) 1986. *The Wealth of Nations, Books I–III*. Edited by Andrew Skinner. London: Penguin.

Sugden, Robert. 2009. Can Economics Be Founded on 'Indisputable Facts of Experience'? Lionel Robbins and the Pioneers of Neoclassical Economics. *Economica* 76: 857–872.

Tennyson, Alfred. (1859–1885) 1983. *The Idylls of the King*. London: Penguin.

Trollope, Anthony. (1873) 2000. *Phineas Redux*. Oxford: Oxford University Press.

———. (1864–1865) 2004. *Can You Forgive Her?* London: Penguin.

———. (1857) 2014. *Barchester Towers*. Oxford: Oxford University Press.

Whitlock, Tammy. 2005. *Crime, Gender and Consumer Culture in Nineteenth-Century England*. Aldershot and Burlington: Ashgate.

CHAPTER 10

Global Inequality

Documenting Globalization in Rural India: The Conflation of the "Freedom of the Market" with The "Freedom of the Person" in *The New York Times*

Mukti Lakhi Mangharam

On a summer's day in late May 2016, two "pretty sisters" from a far-off village, "fizzing with laughter," walked down a lane that led to the Bangalore factory in which they would work. Prabhati was 21 and Shashi, 18. When they got to the factory, the laughter was replaced with a language they did not understand—with words like "work" and "faster." Ellen Barry, who tells us the story of these girls, proclaims that these were words "of capitalism, of men and of a bit of freedom" (2016).[1] Barry's fairy tale of freedom, published in September 2016 in *The New York Times*, is titled "Young Rural Women in India Chase Big-City Dreams." The article covers the journey of two sisters from Ishwarpur, Orissa to the

M. L. Mangharam (✉)
Rutgers University, New Brunswick, NJ, USA

© The Author(s) 2019
E. Hadley et al. (eds.), *From Political Economy to Economics through Nineteenth-Century Literature*, Palgrave Studies in Literature, Culture and Economics, https://doi.org/10.1007/978-3-030-24158-2_10

urban environment of Bangalore. There, they serve as piece-rate garment workers in a factory that makes clothes sold in European and American department store retail chains, such as Marks and Spencer and H&M. The article uses a seemingly objective, fact-based, third-person journalistic voice to narrate the journey of these two exotic rural Indians, with Shashi serving as the protagonist and Prabhati as her foil. Within the article's story arc, as the quotation above suggests, the introduction of Shashi to globalized capitalism ends in freedom.

This chapter argues that such an interpretation of the lives of these girls is marked by two pervasive liberal discourses of economic globalization: that of laissez-faire capitalism and that of the "end of history" narrative. The first expresses a belief in a natural order under which unconstrained individuals follow their selfish interests within a marketplace and in doing so contribute to the general good. Within this paradigm of unrestrained individual agency, free markets become a reflection of the natural system of liberty. The second narrative refers to the idea, derived from Hegel, that the historical development of humanity in the West culminates in the universal recognition of human freedom, which is in turn associated with the successful spread of capitalism to all areas of the world (Fukuyama 1992). I argue that Barry embeds these liberal principles into her story using a literary form indebted to the Bildungsroman. In doing so, I build on Joseph R. Slaughter's argument that this form often naturalizes and legitimizes the human person's embodiment of the dominant social premises of the era (2009). By analyzing Barry's adoption of the Bildungsroman genre's embedding of the human person within the prevailing social orders of liberal capitalism, I hope to demonstrate that Barry's account replaces a more expansive notion of the human with an empty subjectivity within which the binaristic and Orientalist categories of Western capitalist freedom versus backward non-Western traditions can wage war with each other. In light of these co-optations, I consider how one may reclaim the "human" from Orientalist discourses of globalization.

In what follows, I first historicize and theorize the laissez-faire principles and "end of history" narrative that inform Barry's "documentation" of Shashi and Prabhati's lives. Then I situate these capitalist discourses within the colonial and postcolonial history of Orissa, the Indian state to which Shashi and Prabhati belong. I juxtapose these histories of colonial exploitation with Barry's *New York Times* piece, which conflates capitalist waged labor with individual freedom, presenting the hardships the girls face as plot obstacles to be overcome in their coming-of-age stories as members of a global workforce. A close reading of Barry's narrative reveals the conceptual impoverishment of the human subject that results from not taking the historical and present limitations of liberal capitalist discourses of freedom into account. At the end of the chapter, I suggest that because Barry's representation is based on an occlusion of the systematic violence of global capitalism in both the West and the Global South, it testifies to a need for new kinds of narratives that can encompass and register the workings of capitalist unfreedoms on a global scale, thereby reinstating a fuller humanity that is not Orientalist, and not simply synonymous with the triumph of global capital. We need narrative forms that do not insist on describing the human person, and the choices she makes, in circumscribed ways determined by capitalist ideologies of globalization.

Laissez-Faire and "The End of History"

Barry's representation of Shashi and Prabhati is continuous with prior colonial and postcolonial characterizations of rural Indian lives within a larger history of laissez-faire capitalism from the colonial era to the present. The concept of laissez-faire arose in eighteenth-century France in reaction to the excessive mercantilist regulations of the day. The concept expressed a belief in a natural order under which individuals followed their selfish interests within a marketplace, and in doing so were said to contribute to the general good. In this sense, laissez-faire was conceptualized as an extension of the idea of natural law, a philosophy asserting that certain rights are endowed by nature, and that these can be understood universally through human reason. Because this supposedly natural system was understood to be the best way to unleash innate human potential, philosophers like Adam Smith also characterized it as a moral program that would deliver the rights of natural law through the market (1995, 507). By extension, free markets became a reflection of the natural system of liberty. Since this "natural" order functioned successfully without the aid of government, the state needed to restrict itself to upholding the rights of private property and individual liberty, to removing all artificial barriers to trade, and to abolishing all seemingly useless laws (510). For Smith, laissez-faire was "a program for the abolition of laws constraining the market, a program for the restoration of order and for the activation of potential growth" (Gaspard 2004).

Broadly, laissez-faire relied on a number of important axioms. The first was that the individual is the basic unit of society. A second claimed that the individual has a natural right to freedom. Another was that the individual's natural pursuit of freedom occurs in line with their selfish interest which, via the sale of one's labor power or of the fruits of one's labor, is also the best vehicle toward achieving the greater good (Smith 1995, 509–511) Another proclaimed that the physical order of nature is a harmonious and self-regulating system and that society, including the market, must mirror this natural state (509).

Alongside the discourse of laissez-faire capitalism, Ellen Barry's article has the "end of history" narrative as its subtext. This narrative refers to the idea, derived from Hegel, that the historical development of humanity in the West culminates in the universal recognition of human freedom, which is in turn associated with the successful spread of capitalism to all areas of the world (Fukuyama 1992). Uday Mehta usefully theorizes the way that the "end of history" narrative was put to work in colonial India as a justification for colonial domination, showing how the "backwardness [of the colonized] is expressed as a historical fact that can be redressed only through the instrument of political intervention and in the register of future time" (1999, 107). Mehta observes the ways in which the liberal "language of a progressive history, along with a reliance on a singular and continuous conception of time, naturalizes often aggressive and violent efforts to suppress multiple and extant temporalities and corresponding life forms" (109). The result, as Barry's article testifies, is the legitimization of only one way of being human, itself a particular instantiation of dominant colonial liberalism. In the present day of Barry's article, this dominant liberalism circumscribes definitions of the "human" to buttress an exploitative global capitalism.

HISTORICIZING LAISSEZ-FAIRE AND "THE END OF HISTORY" IN ORISSA

Three moments mark the history of equating freedom with free-market capitalism in Orissa. The first was the 1866 famine in rural Orissa, and the millions of deaths that occurred as a result of colonial officers who adopted a strict policy of laissez-faire non-interference in dealing with the food crisis. Laissez-faire here was justified as the method through which the most efficient distribution of food would be achieved (Davis 2002, 30–31). Human life was valued in this schema only as a raw vessel of labor power traded in the marketplace in pursuit of one's natural self-interest, so that relief was only provided to people so that they might be able to labor again. The second was the late nineteenth-century commercialization of agriculture, within which Orissa's peasantry was forced to grow cash crops to correct Britain's balance of trade with the rest of the world. Within this moment, laissez-faire was conceptualized as Britain's expansion of its economic interests so as to remake the whole world into a producer or market for British goods (Bose 1993, 38). The starved Indian peasantry was contradictorily conceptualized as made up of individuals laboring for their own interests, albeit under British coercion. The third moment forms the immediate background for Shashi and Prabhati's journey to Bangalore, for it concerns the 1991 liberalization of the Indian economy, which precipitated a sharp decline in agriculture in villages such as Ishwarpur, the girls' home, as well as a growing urbanization. Economic liberalization in India aimed to complete India's journey to "development" toward the end of history by remaking the economy via an expansion of private and foreign investment. This was carried out through a reduction in import tariffs, the deregulation of markets, and a decrease of taxes (World Bank 1991, 1). Within all three historical moments, human freedom was imagined only as individual freedom to labor—to commodify and sell labor power—within a social arena driven by free-market economics, which would in turn profit the society as a whole.

My reading of liberal discourses and practices such as the "end of history" and laissez-faire in India through these three historical moments may seem questionable. After all, such a reading relies on the premise that the colonial emphasis on defining human worth through the capacity for labor was necessarily motivated by domination and exploitation. This interpretation seems to be contradicted by historians such as Andrew Sartori, who claims instead that "the history of liberalism is much more than the pre-history of neoliberalism" (2014, 3) because the colonized Bengali peasant actually used the liberal emphasis on labor to launch a critique of capitalism and colonialism. Their plebian critique, moreover, was specifically liberal because it relied on Lockean arguments about labor's property-constituting capacity—in laboring, Locke argued, man mixed a part of himself, in which he had an indisputable natural property, with the earth, thereby rendering that element of nature on which his labor had been expended into a compound of nature and himself. This portion of nature was thus effectively removed from the common stock and became the property of the one who had first appropriated it and labored on it (Locke in Sartori 2014, 10). Sartori argues that the fact that labor legitimized peasant claims on land during the colonial period suggests that colonial contexts could, under some circumstances, resonate with projects of radicalizing and extending liberal commitments as easily as with circumscribing them. As such, colonial contexts should be understood as potentially the basis for an account of "the embrace of liberal norms, not only of their strategic deployment, refractions, transformation, displacement, compromises and delimitation" (5).

I suggest that Sartori's account of colonial liberalism here does not undermine this chapter's focus on the way that liberal conceptions of history, and associated concepts of laissez-faire, have circumscribed human freedoms by advancing exploitative forms of global capitalism. Even as he points to emancipatory uses of liberalism, Sartori acknowledges that the specifically anti-capitalist trajectories of Locke's thought are bound to practices constitutive of capitalist society. "To inhabit a capitalist society and to participate in its practices might generate ... norms that were critical of capitalist accumulation while remaining fundamentally premised on capitalist social forms for their normative power" (15). In other words, when located within a hegemonic institution like capitalism, those same liberal principles can be understood as buttressing colonial power as well as undermining it. Such an understanding suggests, as I argue in my book *Literatures of Liberation*, that liberal principles are not in themselves responsible for exploitative practices. Rather, it is the institutions and manner within which these ideas have been instrumentalized that renders them exploitative or liberating (Mangharam 2017, 14–15). When bound to hegemonic forms of capitalism and colonialism, universalisms—liberal or otherwise—can take on oppressive manifestations; and when harnessed by subaltern, plebian subjects, as Sartori and I show in different ways, they can be used for emancipatory ends.

In this sense, with Sartori, I am in disagreement with Uday Mehta's argument in *Liberalism and Empire* that liberal abstraction contains within its basic argumentative structure an immanent propensity for colonial domination. Mehta makes the latter case by arguing that liberal abstraction is by its very nature compromised because it insists on a universalism established through the contingencies of the particular cultural configuration of just one part of the world: "Liberalism ... was self-consciously universal as a political, ethical, and epistemological creed. Yet, it had fashioned this creed from an intellectual tradition and experiences that were substantially European, if not almost exclusively national" (Mehta 1999, 1). Both my *Literatures of Liberation* and Sartori's *Liberalism in Empire* show that universalisms do not necessarily have to be opposed to the particular just because they arise from culturally specific locales. This is because, first, European and non-European universalisms must always arise from, and be marked by, their contextual origins, and second, because their originating contexts do not foreclose their adoption within other particular contexts to suit specific struggles against exploitation. This is why one can hold together colonized peasants who are impoverished, famine-struck, and forced to grow opium in the same frame as Sartori's subversive plebian liberals. In my account of the three historical moments presented in the rest of this section below, I am interested in how universalisms were double-edged swords—hegemonic conceptions of labor and property shaped Indian lives in coercive ways even as these same conceptions have functioned as resistance when redeployed by the colonized.

The famine of 1866 affected an area of 40,240 square miles with an estimated population of 11,855,543. Orissa was the region most severely afflicted; out of a total population of three million, at least one million perished (Mohanty 1993, 55). An important causal factor of the famine was the increased exportation and hoarding of rice in famine-struck regions under a government policy of laissez-faire non-interference (55). The recorded export of food grain increased to an unprecedented level in the year 1864–1865, leaving little for storage for 1865–1866. It was estimated that exports of both paddy (rice before threshing) and rice peaked during 1864–1865 and were substantial during 1865–1866, the famine year. Due to decreasing supplies, the weekly price of rice rose by more than four times in Cuttack and Balasore in October 1866 (56). Despite this shortage, the government advised local officials not to import more rice into the region and stabilize rice prices as, following laissez-faire economic principles, market forces would take care of the situation. Famine Commissioners later blamed the board of revenue and the Lieutenant Governor of Bengal as well as the Commissioner of Orissa for not taking proper action (56).

The high death count was attributed to a lack of relief efforts, caused by an adherence to a combination of complementary laissez-faire and Malthusian principles. The latter predicted inevitable doom unless the growth rate of the population was checked. A colonial official thus pointed out in 1872 that the rural population would enter a famine as a "frigate goes into battle, cleared of all useless and inefficient members" (Hunter 1873, xxxi). In addition, laissez-faire advocates opposed food aid for famines occurring within the British Empire. In 1847, referring to the famine then underway in Ireland, founder of *The Economist* James Wilson wrote: "It is no man's business to provide for another" (O Grada 2000, 6) Following such principles, the colonial administrators decided to administer relief only to those who could earn it. The able-bodied were employed in light labor, from the excavation of canals, to construction of embankments and roads. The relief works turned away anyone who was too starved or fragile to undertake hard coolie labor. The weak, women, and children were not admitted even though they needed relief the most. As a result, the famine affected the aged, sickly, and infirm in particular.

The second moment within this history of laissez-faire economics spans the nineteenth and early twentieth centuries and resulted in the large-scale commercialization of agriculture to serve the needs of an international market. This in turn led to growing poverty for the Orissan peasant and the commodification of his/her labor power throughout the nineteenth and early twentieth centuries. During the late nineteenth century, coinciding with industrialization in Britain, colonial India began to grow certain specialized crops, such as indigo, jute, and opium not for consumption in the village but for sale in a national and international market. Sugata Bose comments that such commercialization of agriculture is "a story of imperatives of states and political cultures which behind the facade of a rhetoric of free trade from the early nineteenth century onwards sought to impose and extend sets of monopolies" (1993, 38).

The best example of the building of monopolies through the imposition of supposedly "free" market principles is the opium trade. The East India Company coerced Bengali peasants (a region that then included Bihar and Orissa) to grow opium so it could export it to China, ironically turning China into a forced "free" market through repeated opium wars. It used the profits from these sales to correct its balance of trade with China, purchasing such Chinese luxury goods as porcelain, silk, and tea, which were in great demand in the West. The opium trade, which created a steady demand among Chinese addicts for opium imported by the West, solved a chronic trade imbalance for Britain. Binay Chaudhuri summarizes the three evils which weighed on the Bengali peasantry as a result of the opium trade: "the lowness of the price paid for crude opium; the increasing rigour of the Government in collecting arrears resulting from crop failures; and the uncontrolled exactions" of rents and interest payments by landlords and moneylenders. (1970, 231).

On the whole, the period from the 1860s to 1914 was marked by the colonial unequal exchange of India's raw agricultural commodities—jute, tea, coffee, wheat, oilseeds, and hides—for British manufactured goods, notably textiles. These commercial crops were exchanged through a policy of one-way free trade. Raw goods were supplied to British manufacturers at throw-away prices while manufactured items from Britain could find free entry into Indian markets to compete unfairly against Indian-made goods. In addition, Britain generated an export surplus through the sale of Indian raw materials to the rest of the world, which through an intricate mechanism of payments offset Britain's trade deficits. Moreover, the policy of laissez-faire capitalism tied peasants' livelihoods increasingly to the world market. Price movements and business fluctuations in the world markets, including that of the First World War and the 1930s economic depression, began to affect the fortunes of the Indian farmer (Bose 1993, 49).

The commercialization of agriculture from which Orissa's peasantry suffered was, then, a forced and artificial process, even though it was undertaken under the banner of a supposedly natural "free trade." The poor peasant was forced to sell his produce just after harvest at whatever prices he could get because he had to obtain money to pay the land revenue due to the British government and local landlords. This placed him at the mercy of the grain merchant, who was in a position to dictate terms and who purchased his produce at much less than the market price. Thus a large share of the benefit of the growing trade in agricultural products was reaped by the merchant, who was very often also the village money-lender. Moneylenders extended cash advances to the farmers to cultivate the commercial crops, and if the peasants failed to pay them back in time their land came under the ownership of moneylenders. The commercialization of agriculture benefited British planters, traders, and manufacturers, who were provided with the opportunity to make huge profits by getting commercialized agricultural products at throw-away prices. The commercialization of Indian agriculture benefited Indian traders and moneylenders as well, who were working as middlemen for the British.

The third moment of laissez-faire economics concerns the significant decline of the agricultural sector post 1991, when the Indian economy was liberalized, and the resulting migration of a significant section of Orissa's rural population to urban areas in search of employment, often as cheap labor in multinational piece-rate companies based in the West. As Banikanta Mishra writes, the liberalization process that started in India in the early 1990s has made Orissa potentially the most attractive destination for large capital-intensive projects by private-sector, often foreign, firms. The result has been a serious decline in the agricultural sector. Even though agriculture is still the most significant source of income in Orissa, the gross cropped area and net irrigated area in the state fell during

1993–1994 to 2003–2004 by an average of 1.20% and 4.45% per year, while they showed an average upward trend in the rest of the country (Mishra 2010, 55). Some authors have, in fact, shown that in Orissa there is "a process of pauperisation of agriculture" (Padhi 2009, 111) through, among other things, the under-utilization or non-utilization of land and agricultural labor, degradation and diversion of cultivable land, and stagnant crop and resource productivity. This system of laissez-faire makes no room for farming communities working in a sustainable manner to feed their own families and villages. As Vandana Shiva has detailed, the World Trade Organization's free-trade policies, which precipitated the "dumping" of cheap agricultural products from abroad, depressed local prices. Additionally, structural adjustment policies from the World Bank required India to accept untested seeds from agribusinesses such as Monsanto, which often required specific pesticides and fertilizers. Farmers thus had to invest greater capital in crops, which were increasingly cultivated as monocultures and thus increasingly at risk of failing. This capital was borrowed from local moneylenders at exorbitant interest rates so that when farmers were unable to repay their loans, they saw suicide as their only viable option (Shiva 2009). Given that farming has become a somewhat unsustainable enterprise in Orissa, it is no wonder that Shashi and Prabhati's father, despite being surrounded by rice fields, worked as a "sinewy day laborer, … he had roamed far from the village in his younger days to work in iron foundries in Chennai and Hyderabad" (Barry 2016). It is against this background of a liberalized economy that Shashi and Prabhati's parents sent them to Bangalore to do piecework for international clothing companies. This, then, is the ideological and material history that underlies the twists and turns of Shashi and Prabhati's lives, but which nevertheless does not make it into the article, "Young Rural Women in India [who] Chase Big-City Dreams." I turn to this article's storytelling to investigate the violence done to more expansive notions of the human—including to the viability of sustenance-based, domestic, and non-capitalized ways of life—by these occlusions.

THE CONFLATION OF CAPITALISM WITH INDIVIDUAL FREEDOM IN *THE NEW YORK TIMES*

Ellen Barry is the South Asia Bureau Chief for *The New York Times* and wrote several articles in 2016 and 2017 that focused on women in rural India. Her journalism is essayistic and investigative, offers cultural critique, and also contains an element of advocacy for the women she covers. For instance, a couple of Barry's articles covered the murder of a rural Indian woman by her husband, and Barry's police complaint ultimately led to judicial action against the perpetrator (2017). Nevertheless, despite her advocacy, I argue that Barry takes a stance driven by capitalist ideology in relation to these women when she describes their lives through the Bildungsroman genre and the "end of history" economic globalization narrative. This narrative shaping testifies, I think, to the power of capitalist ideologies, for even as Barry registers capitalist violence, she seemingly must accept it for the "bit of freedom" it offers to the global poor.

The article accordingly involves a consistent conflation of the spread of capitalism with the spread of freedom, and because this notion of freedom relies on the laissez-faire characterization of the wage-laboring individual as the main unit of society, it is consistently defined through a liberal rhetoric of individualism. The piece begins with the subtitle "Experiments like one in Bangalore, luring migrants to fill factory jobs, collide with an old way of life that keeps women and girls in seclusion until an arranged marriage." Right at the beginning of the piece, then, the "end of history" narrative and laissez-faire discourses result in old Orientalist binaries between oppressed non-Western women subjected to seclusion and arranged marriages, and the forces of capitalist modernization that offer the only way out to freedom. Capitalist versions of freedom have subsumed all others here. By only seeing bondage in the girls' rural life outside the factory, Barry reveals a blind spot, for she seems unaware of the alternative bases that a more expansive notion of freedom might rely on.

These "alternative bases" underlying a more expansive notion of freedom are invoked in the work of Saba Mahmood, who argues that liberal notions of freedom and agency have sharply limited our ability to understand the lives of women whose desire and will have been shaped by nonliberal traditions. This is because the liberal tradition understands agency only as the capacity to realize one's own interests against the weight of custom, tradition, transcendental will, or other obstacles (whether individual or collective). Thus the humanist desire for autonomy and self-expression constitute the substrate, the slumbering ember that can spark to flame in the form of an act of resistance when conditions permit. (2001, 206)

In order for an individual to be free, it is required that her actions be the consequence of her "own will" rather than of custom, tradition, or direct coercion—self-fulfillment is understood only as a realization of this autonomous will.

Mahmood argues that we ought to rethink this liberal definition because it ignores the way that all kinds of "free" action—including liberal forms of agency—are formulated from within, and therefore limited by, the possibilities inherent in their originating contexts. (210). Following Foucault and Butler, Mahmood points out that the very processes and conditions that secure a subject's subordination are also the means by which she becomes a self-conscious identity and agent (210).

Mahmood's re-definition of agency means acknowledging that particular historical instantiations of the liberal "autonomous will" are not in fact autonomous at all, for such a will is always shaped by context. In the case of Barry's account of these girls' choices, their will is a product of discourses such as the "end of history" narrative. These discourses also form globalization's "historically specific relations of subordination"—in Mahmood's words—which in turn constitute the circumscribed basis for action undertaken by Shashi and Prabhati. Thinking toward a more expansive notion of freedom, and by extension toward a more complete idea of the human, thus reveals the ways that the notion of the liberal autonomous will legitimates certain forms of oppression, such as poorly paid exploitative piece-meal factory work, while decrying others as mere markers of tradition, such as farming and domestic chores, including marital duties such as cooking and cleaning for the family. While Barry seems to intuit the flawed nature of the binary she sets up between either "liberal capitalism" or "oppressive tradition," an ambivalence suggested by her phrase a "bit of freedom," she nevertheless remains entrapped by it.

These binaries thus continue to overdetermine the characterization and plot of the article so that despite its Bildungsroman structure, Barry does not spend much time on the complex interiorities of women like Shashi and Prabhati. In the countryside, because they are not yet individuals—synonymous here for waged laborer—the two sisters are presented as personifications of an abstracted collective rural sensibility. They are not yet monetized individuals working to pursue their selfish interests for the good of their wider society, so they are not yet modern subjects possessed of individual freedom. As a result, they can only embody backward, rural tradition: "The new girls smell of the village. They have sprinklings of pimples … Their braids bounce to their hips, tight and glossy … On their ankles are silver chains hung with bells, so when they walk in a group, they jingle. "The imagery of the ankles hung with silver chains not only suggests imprisonment but collective entrapment, for it is when they "walk in a group" that they jingle. Their reaction to the urban environment of Bangalore furthers the impression of backward oppression and entrapment being obliterated by modern, capitalist urban space:

> Bangalore is the first city the 37 trainee tailors have seen. They are dazzled by the different kinds of light. Picking their way through the alleys around the factory, a column of virgins from the countryside, they stare up at an apartment building that towers over the neighborhood and wish their mothers could see it.

When they first arrive to work in the city, the girls are a monolithic group, "a column," that stands in juxtaposition to the other columns of factories and skyscrapers. Significantly, this "column" from the village is constituted by "virgins from the countryside," an Orientalist characterization that highlights their lack of sexual freedom over any other characteristic. The visual imagery of the "different kinds of light" that exist in the urban environment of Bangalore suggests the symbolic enlightenment of freedom, suggestively sexual, that the city represents. The article continues to reinforce this idea of conservative, oppressed female collectivities being central to relatively un-monetized environments such as Ishwarpur: "They have come from a village at the end of a road, a place so conservative that the single time they went to a movie theater, their male cousins and uncles created a human chain around them, their big hands linked, to protect them from any contact with outside men."

The characterization of these girls as pre-capitalist collective blank slates on which urban capitalism can realize its freedoms ends up meaning that the village girls have no inner desires or agency in and of themselves, either before or after they enter the workforce. Beforehand, they are portrayed as simply "waiting to see what will happen to them," continually shielded from any process of self-discovery by "big hands" and "human chains."

The article authoritatively confirms their fate if they had stayed in the village:

> [U]pon reaching adulthood, they would be transferred to the guardianship of another family, along with a huge dowry that serves as an incentive to treat them well. The transfer is final. Once married, the new bride cannot return to visit her parents without permission, which is given sparingly, so that the bonds to her old home will weaken. She must show her submission to the new family: She is not allowed to speak the names of her in-laws, because it is seen as too familiar, and in some places she is not allowed to use words that begin with the same letters as her in-laws' names, requiring the invention of a large parallel vocabulary. Each morning, before she is allowed to eat, the daughter-in-law must wash the feet of her husband's parents and then drink the water she has used to wash them.

The passage begins in an ambiguous future voice in the conditional tense, in subordinate clauses, and refers to times and places that are not represented within the article. Then it shifts to the simple present tense as if to confirm its described reality as an objective and transcendent state of horror that habitually and definitively affects such women. In contrast are the wage-laboring women in Bangalore, well on their way to becoming individuals, whose prospects for oppressive marriages are replaced with love and romance. Once they become waged laborers in the city, these girls

> spend their evenings in quiet conversation with boyfriends, whose existence is unknown to their parents. They examine each other's palms for creases that indicate they will be among the small number of Indians—as low as 5 percent, according to one survey—who marry for love. At the factory, they stitch their boyfriends' names on scrap fabric. Male tailors stroll by as they work, dropping love letters folded into fat wads, and the girls read them aloud, to comic effect, at the hostel. "My dear, my lever," someone writes to Shashi in broken English. "I have tied you up in my heart."

The story, then, continues to confirm that the terrible jingling entrapment these girls endure can only be drowned out, symbolically and literally, by incorporation into the globalized labor force. In other words, while the evils of dowry and arranged marriage represent the oppressive past, the empowered, enlightened end of history is represented by the work of the factory. The girls' determination to make that journey is epitomized through an "anthem about self-sufficiency," sung with such reverence that it is given the sanctity of a spiritual experience:

> This job is the story of our lives
> The job is as important as prayer
> We won't fear, and we will go ahead.

In line with such anthems deifying global capitalism, the article represents the alternative—being back in the village—as a waste of human potential. Barry notes that in "2012, the last time the government surveyed its citizens about their occupation, an astonishing 205 million women between the ages of 15 and 60 responded: 'attending to domestic duties.'" Barry represents this as a matter of "increasing urgency for India will not fulfill its potential if it cannot put them to work in the economy." In other words, the lack of freedom of these women is synonymous with the fact that they are "idle, young women," responsible for holding back as much as 27% of India's GDP. From this perspective, it is good news, then, that these women can be "monetized," as Barry puts it.

The article's evacuation of the subjectivity of rural girls, then, conveniently serves another end, for it calculates the value of these women solely in monetary terms as the fulfilling of a function, as commodified labor that can produce profit. If these objects remain unmonetized, they are regarded as "idle," no matter the work they are actually doing. This is why when Shashi's sister Prabhati is sent back to the village too sick to work at the factory, her vacant sewing machine comes to represent all of her being:

> On the assembly line, someone covers Prabhati's sewing machine with plastic sheeting. Three weeks later, two burly men come to push it to an area marked "idle machines." Just like that, Prabhati is back in her mother's thatch hut, feeding kindling into a clay oven … The neighbors stop by, seeking an outcome to the family's experiment. "So, are your daughters back from their jobs?" asks one, in a voice thick with self-satisfaction.

With Prabhati gone, her sewing machine becomes a metonym for her whole selfhood—she herself is now rendered an "idle machine" pushed into a corner of the globe—the village—to face the scorn of her neighbors and traditional domestic oppression.

THE STRUCTURAL VIOLENCE OF GLOBAL CAPITALISM
AS PLOT OBSTACLE

The conflation of waged labor with individual freedom means that historical and systematic structures of inequality are presented simply as plot
conflicts in the style of a Bildungsroman—in other words they are only
obstacles that main characters need to overcome in order to achieve a
pleasant reconciliation with a dominant globalized social order, thereby
achieving a predetermined narrative conclusion. The adoption of Barry's
Bildungsroman plot structure to tell this story is not surprising in light
of Joseph R. Slaughter's seminal argument, in *Human Rights, Inc.* As
already mentioned, Slaughter argues that literary forms, in particular the
Bildungsroman, legitimize and naturalize dominant definitions of the
"human person" by making its "common sense legible and compelling"
(2009, 3). Marc Redfield elaborates on this idea by arguing that the subject of these novels is "possessed of a coherent identity that unfolds over
the course of an organically unified narrative oriented toward an ending
in which … 'maturity' functions as a metaphor for the protagonist's
accommodation to social norms" (2018, 191). Many postcolonial novels
have critiqued these inclinations of accommodation by way of subver-
sion. For instance, Aravind Adiga's *White Tiger*, a satirical redeployment
of the Bildungsroman form, parodies the entrepreneurial urge through
which the individual acclimatizes to a neoliberal social order in its representation of the violent social climbing of a servant in the Indian capital
of New Delhi. Balram only escapes plot obstacles such as crushing poverty by killing his boss, stealing his money and identity, and becoming a
"self-taught entrepreneur," thus undermining the very possibility of
achieving both ethical self-realization and social acceptance for India's
oppressed majority.

Unlike *White Tiger*, Barry relies on the form of the Bildungsroman to
both individualize the capitalist worker and objectify her in line with the
dominant social order—that of liberal global capitalism. Thus, the girls'
journey to Bangalore to work in the factories, with its potential end in the
realization of individual freedom, is presented as a trial, or plot obstacle,
that only the strongest will survive. The article's focus on two different
sisters as its main protagonists affirms this plot structure, for Prabhati is
sent back to the village after she is unable to overcome an illness caused
by overwork, fatigue, and the lack of health care. Shashi, on the other

hand, survives and stays on. To affirm Shashi's victory over the backward forces in the village that await her should she "fail," as her foil Prabhati does, Barry represents the hardships the girls are subjected to as nothing more than character-building obstacles that Shashi has the strength to overcome. Barry does note the toll the work takes on the girls, for they are not paid on time, have to go without food for days, and then when eventually paid, only receive the equivalent of $28 for two weeks of work "after withholdings for pension, health insurance, lodging, food and kitchen furnishings." In a style befitting journalistic objectivity, Barry does not hold back from commenting on the exploitative elements of this labor:

> Incredibly, garments worn in the West are still made by humans—nearly all of them women, working exhausting hours, with few legal protections and little chance of advancement, for some of the lowest wages in the global supply chain.
>
> Cuddles is among the first in the group to be integrated into an assembly line, bent over, eyes straining. Her task is to stitch together three small tags for the Marks & Spencer stretch corduroy skirt: one that identifies the brand, one that gives washing instructions and one the size, a scrap so tiny that it is nearly impossible to hold straight between finger and thumb. If she allows a tag to slip to the floor, or fly away in the gusts from the ceiling fan, her salary will be docked. She will be under pressure to complete this task 100 times per hour for eight hours, with one half-hour break for lunch, for a base daily wage of around $2.

Barry notes the painstaking, exhausting nature of this work as well as the draconian ways in which it is enforced. The girls are forced to be efficient because profits depend on how much labor can be squeezed out of workers in the least amount of time and for the least amount of money. The lunch break is thus only "one half hour" and the labor is remunerated for a shameful sum. However, Barry's response to these appalling numbers, amounting to less than $2 a day, and leading Prabhati to seek medical care from a roadside quack, is only to stress that this is still "more than most of their fathers make."

In fact, Barry notes that ultimately "the amount of the paycheck is not relevant" because the paycheck itself represents the culmination of individual freedom. "They have never earned money before, only asked their fathers for it. A wave of happiness washes over all of them. They do not feel like girls, they say: They feel like boys." In other words, the structural violence of global capital, which uses these women as nothing more than automatons and exploits their labor in order to realize a profit for the 1% on the other side of the globe, is simply excused, skipped over. The low paycheck is no longer exploitation but simply the result of capitalism's deduction of the price of freedom from their pay. Barry's characterization of Shashi after she receives her paycheck is indicative of this equation between freedom and the exploitations of multinational waged labor: "Shashi dances down the stairs and most of the way home. The money sends a wild thrill through her, so that she wishes she could fast-forward through the next month, and the month after that, and after that. So that life is a long string of paydays." Shashi's joy is characterized as the opposite of exploitation; the "wild thrill" of $2 a day makes her wish for life to be nothing more than paydays. In effect, it is a life narratively reduced to no more than the freedom of waged labor, a product of the "historically specific relations of subordination" enabled and created by liberal capitalism (Mahmood 2001, 210).

Because capitalist freedom subsumes all other kinds of freedom in the narrative framework of the Bildungsroman, the story of Shashi's incorporation into global capitalism is increasingly padded with information that characterizes her as a person, in opposition to Prabhati who largely remains a type. We are told that Shashi likes dirty jokes, calls herself 45 kilograms of hotness, and had a secret boyfriend whose existence Prabhati revealed to their parents in an act of betrayal. In Bangalore, Shashi continues to communicate with this boyfriend by spending most of her factory salary on a new smartphone. Barry notes that

> Shashi finds it interesting that she, the screw-up in the family, is the one becoming a city person. She examines her face in the mirror for signs that she is becoming paler. She tells the family that Prabhati should not return, and that she cannot send money home this month. Instead, Shashi arranges for a meeting with Sunil, a boyfriend.

The message is clear: Shashi deserves to be rescued by capitalism for embodying liberal ideals of freedom, while Prabhati does not. Within Barry's article-Bildungsroman, Shashi the individual has overcome enough plot obstacles to achieve a freedom in line with the dominant social order of liberal capitalism.

RESTORING A FULLER HUMAN TO HISTORY AND TO THE WORLD

How, then, do we produce a story of human potentiality that is truly expansive in its envisioning of human flourishing and that encompasses many ways of being? How can we make this human/e story respectful of both individual and collective freedom, and ensure that it doesn't reduce agency to romantic love, factory labor, or urban life? How can we write this story to include domestic and other sustenance-driven forms of work, while also retaining its ability to critique both patriarchal domesticity, global inequality and exploitation, and the systemic abuses of capitalism? Slaughter's critique of the Bildungsroman, and Barry's exemplification of its limitations, leads us to cast a doubtful eye on the potential of different kinds of narrative forms not only to represent but also critique social orders of any kind. Yet various literary critics have pointed to the potential of other novelistic modes to restore a more expansive story of the human in response to the structural violence of global capitalism. Michael Moses, for instance, has shown how the novel genre can, through the mode of tragedy, dramatize the violent and destructive process by which archaic societies are transformed and incorporated into the modern world, testifying to the havoc wreaked upon individual human lives in the name of progress (1995).

If the issue is not then, intrinsically, the novel genre, perhaps the problem rather is the Bildungsroman's thematic insistence on the agency of the individual over the collective, which simultaneously undoes such agency through its reduction of that individual to reconciliation with the hegemonic structures of her society. In order to achieve its validation of a hegemonic social order, the story's narrative form has to simultaneously elevate and minimize the individual. This feature serves the myths of laissez-faire capitalism particularly well for that institution also both minimizes and elevates the individual in its representation of the individual as central to society, but only as long as the individual's labor allows society to achieve its optimal "natural" state of endless capital growth. This tension is apparent in how Barry's Bildungsroman-article represents the structural violence of capitalism as nothing more than an individual character-building struggle, even as it reduces such an individual to nothing more than an empty vessel for capitalism. The human emerges necessarily impoverished by these contradictions, for such a story leaves no room for forms of love, sociality, collective belonging, or work that do not reproduce global capital.

The simultaneous elevation and reduction of the individual within laissez-faire and the "end of history" narrative is represented by the article's treatment of an occasion when the girls' paycheck is delivered too late, so that they are on the verge of starvation, and thus begin planning a strike action. The factory owner discourages them from associating too much with a strike-inciting girl, Jayasmita, arguing that "if you have a basket of fruits and only one is not good, it will spoil the other fruit." "You have to take one out," he enjoins:

> The girls are promised an advance for rice and are ordered to leave his office. They shuffle out. They had been planning to stop working unless they were paid immediately, but their strike has lasted less than five minutes. Jayasmita slumps against a wall, and vows never to try anything like that again. "When you come to a new city," she says, "you have to learn to care for yourself, and not bother with others."

Significantly, forms of free action aimed at producing collective well-being are liabilities in this setting, for they are antithetical to the profitable consumption of labor power that global capitalism depends on. Jayasmita, the "rotten fruit," is left with no choice but to renounce the threatening kind of individual freedom she wishes to exercise because it is instantiated through membership within a collective humanity that would, if empowered, resist capitalist exploitation. Instead, her individual "freedom" is reduced to a form of individualism that can bolster the hegemonic social structures of free-market capitalism: "you have to learn to care for yourself, and not bother with others."

If what produces an impoverished human, then, is the problematically drawn up relationship between the individual and society, itself continuous with the contradictions of laissez-faire capitalism, how can literary genres and modes register a fuller human being and her experiences under the systemic phenomenon of global inequality? Notably, an "end of history" thesis such as the one I have read in Barry's article produces an impoverished human not just by refusing collective action and other ways of living, being, and working, but by playing up the exoticized differences of particular non-Western societies as indicative of a "wrong" or "backward" kind of humanity. Barry's resulting Orientalism was criticized, but also echoed, by readers of *The New York Times* article. Thus one reader complained about the sexualized exoticization of the "column of virgins from the countryside," asking:

> Would a sentence like this ever have been written about a group of girls from Idaho visiting New York for the first time: "Picking their way through the alleys around the factory, a column of virgins from the countryside, they stare up at an apartment building that towers over the neighborhood and wish their mothers could see it." A common thread to each of the Times' features about India over the past year is pervasive exoticism and orientalism.

Unfortunately, other readers echoed Barry's Orientalism in response, commenting: "What an insult to Idaho. There is a vast difference between being a young woman in Idaho vs. being a young woman from a rural village in India. Young women in Idaho are not treated like chattel, are educated and certainly more worldly than the women described here." The latter responder seems to see eye-to-eye with Barry about the uniform domestic exploitation that these girls face, while also condemning these girls for exemplifying a backward class and culture. The logic underlying such widespread Orientalism is revealed by another commenter in her response to the comment thread:

> No, but it might have been written about country girls arriving in New York at the beginning of the 20th century. Just read Willa Cather. The US is not at the same stage of development as India, hence the difference. Stories like this came out of China 20 years ago. China is now moving out of that developmental phase.

This view of the spread of capitalism around the globe comes from a teleological "end of history" understanding, within which enduring patriarchal oppression in India is a result of incomplete capitalist development in comparison to the developed capitalist contexts of the US or Europe. Drawn from neoclassical economic theory, this assumption holds that a society "catches up" as a result of capital diffusion throughout the open market and that "developing" economies will rise above inequality through capitalist expansion and free-market policies (Rostow 1960). The last commenter above shows how such stadial understandings of history reinforce Orientalism because they take part in a historicist developmental narrative that relegates India to what Dipesh Chakrabarty calls the "waiting room of history" (2009, 8). Corroborating Uday Mehta's historicization of the "end of history" narrative, capitalism here represents the culmination of human development and finds its natural home in the West. This leaves other nations engaged in a perpetual race to catch up with a future stage of capitalist development, doomed to suffer from social and economic inequalities rooted in their traditions and cultural histories.

Such discourses and the narrative trajectory they produce obscure the ways in which the system that oppresses women in India is the same one that has produced misery and impoverishment for women in the "developed" West. The jobs being performed by these Indian teenagers are directly connected to the job losses in small town America. What we need, then, is a multi-perspectival narrative mode that includes the whole globe in its frame—somewhat akin to the combined and uneven development approach advocated by the Warwick Research Collective. This unitary but uneven view of capitalist expansion encourages us to see inequality, poverty, and enduring forms of "tradition" as results of the imperialist expansion of capitalism as it persistently searches for competitive advantage and new spaces from which it can extract greater profit. The result is inequality in different forms in both "developed" Northern and "developing" Southern economies. The latter gain jobs but at a terrible cost. And, in the process, the global spread of capitalism cements and exacerbates supposedly "traditional" oppressions such as the dowry system, which as Uma Narayan shows in a brilliant analysis, have only increased (Narayan 1997, 41–80). In the North, on the other hand, globalization leads to job losses, an increase in precarious labor, often performed by women, and a lack of childcare and health services that goes along with such a rise in precarious short-term employment. The effect of this unitary but uneven system of global capitalism, then, has costs in both the Global North and South, namely increasing inequality and precarity.

To capture the journey of an individual within such a global, collective, and systemic state of affairs, Barry might have done well to develop a parallel narrative about the loss of jobs in the manufacturing towns and wastelands of the American Midwest through interviews and journalistic narrative about the lives of women there. And if the Bildungsroman's narrative arc collapses the individual into society, other kinds of multi-perspectival and multivocal modes of representation may have been better able to portray parallel yet situated individual lives as embodied critiques of dominant social orders. By forging such new, more fully global narrative forms, we may avoid losing a more inclusive story of human potentiality and wellbeing to the voided subjectivities of global capitalism.

Note

1. All unattributed quotes henceforth refer to Ellen Barry, "Young Rural Women in India Chase Big-City Dreams." See second entry in References.

References

Barry, Ellen. 2016. Young Rural Women in India Chase Big-City Dreams. *The New York Times*, September 24. https://www.nytimes.com/2016/09/25/world/asia/bangalore-india-women-factories.html
———. 2017. How to Get Away with Murder in Small-Town India. *The New York Times*, August 19. https://www.nytimes.com/2017/08/19/world/asia/murder-small-town-india.html.
Bose, Sugata. 1993. *Peasant Labour and Colonial Capital: Rural Bengal Since 1770*. Vol. 3. Cambridge: Cambridge University Press.
Chakrabarty, Dipesh. 2009. *Provincializing Europe: Postcolonial Thought and Historical Difference*. Princeton, NJ: Princeton University Press.
Chaudhuri, Binay. 1970. Growth of Commercial Agriculture. *IESHR* 7 (2): 25–60.
Davis, Mike. 2002. *Late Victorian Holocausts: El Nino Famines and the Making of the Third World*. New York: Verso.
Fukuyama, Francis. 1992. *The End of History and the Last Man*. New York: Free Press.
Gaspard, Toufick. 2004. *A Political Economy of Lebanon 1948–2002: The Limits of Laissez-faire*. Boston: Brill.
Hunter, W. 1873. *Famine Aspects of Bengal Districts*. Simla: Government Press.
Mahmood, Saba. 2001. Feminist Theory, Embodiment, and the Docile Agent: Some Reflections on the Egyptian Islamic Revival. *Cultural Anthropology* 16 (2): 202–236.
Mangharam, Mukti Lakhi. 2017. *Literatures of Liberation: Non-European Universalisms and Democratic Progress*. Columbus: Ohio State University Press.
Mehta, Uday Singh. 1999. *Liberalism and Empire: A Study in Nineteenth-Century British Liberal Thought*. Chicago: University of Chicago Press.
Mishra, Banikanta. 2010. Agriculture, Industry and Mining in Orissa in the Post-Liberalisation Era: An Inter-District and Inter-State Panel Analysis. *Economic and Political Weekly* 45 (20, May): 49–68.
Mohanty, Bidyut. 1993. Orissa Famine of 1866: Demographic and Economic Consequences. *Economic and Political Weekly* 28 (1/2, Jan.): 55–66.
Moses, Michael Valdez. 1995. *The Novel and the Globalization of Culture*. Oxford: Oxford University Press.
Narayan, Uma. 1997. *Dislocating Cultures: Identities, Traditions and Third World Feminism*. New York: Routledge.

O Grada, Cormac. 2000. *Black '47 and Beyond: The Great Irish Famine in History, Economy, and Memory*. Princeton, NJ: Princeton University Press.

Padhi, Sakti. 2009. Agricultural Growth, Employment and Poverty in Rural Orissa: Some Observations on Recent Trends. In *Orissa's Economic Development*, ed. Raj Kishore Panda, 96–112. New Delhi: Serials.

Redfield, Marc. 2018. *Phantom Formations: Aesthetic Ideology and the Bildungsroman*. Ithaca: Cornell University Press.

Rostow, W.W. 1960. *The Stages of Economic Growth: A Non-Communist Manifesto*. Cambridge: Cambridge University Press.

Sartori, Andrew. 2014. *Liberalism in Empire: An Alternative History*. Berkeley, CA: University of California Press.

Shiva, Vandana. 2009. From Seeds of Suicide to Seeds of Hope: Why Are Indian Farmers Committing Suicide and How Can We Stop this Tragedy? *Huffington Post*. Accessed February 15, 2019. https://www.huffingtonpost.com/vandana-shiva/from-seeds-of-suicide-to_b_192419.html

Slaughter, Joseph R. 2009. *Human Rights Inc. The World Novel, Narrative Form, and International Law*. Fordham, NY: Fordham University Press.

Smith, Adam. 1995. The Wealth of Nations. In *The Portable Enlightenment Reader*, ed. Isaac Kramnick, 505–514. London: Penguin Classics.

World Bank. 1991. India—Structural Adjustment Credit Project (English)—Presidents Report. *www.documents.worldbank.org*, November 11. World Bank.

CHAPTER 11

Equity

Henry Mayhew and Thomas Piketty on Equity and Inequality

Sarah Winter

"I don't know what is the cause of the reduction of the wages,' said a 'rafter,' 'but the men thinks it is generally owing to the cheapness of provisions. They say what's the use of provisions being cheap if they lowers our wages." From these Victorian dockworkers interviewed by Henry Mayhew (Taithe 1996, 176) to early-twenty-first-century macroeconomists, many have commented on what seems to be a commonsensical intuition that stagnation and depression of wages are linked to poverty and pervasive economic inequality in modern capitalist societies.[1] It may still surprise us, however, to consider the striking similarities between certain formulations of the problem of economic inequality offered in the mid-nineteenth century by Mayhew, a journalist and literary man, and those of the French economist Thomas Piketty in his influential *Capital in the Twenty-First Century* (*C21*). Mayhew's *London Labour and the London Poor* (*LLLP*), a survey of the occupations of the working poor and their "struggle, and …

S. Winter (✉)
University of Connecticut, Storrs, CT, USA

© The Author(s) 2019
E. Hadley et al. (eds.), *From Political Economy to Economics through Nineteenth-Century Literature*, Palgrave Studies in Literature, Culture and Economics, https://doi.org/10.1007/978-3-030-24158-2_11

243

scramble for a living" in Victorian London (Mayhew 1985, 14), began as a series of commissioned articles published from 1849 to 1850 in the *Morning Chronicle*, a London daily newspaper. In his first article (19 October 1849), Mayhew describes his empirical approach in investigating "such occupations in London as yield a bare subsistence to the parties engaged in them," stating that

> it is my intention to visit the dwellings of the unrelieved poor [those who received no assistance under the poor laws] ... to discover, not only on how little they subsist, but how large a rate of profit they have to pay for the little upon which they do subsist—to ascertain what weekly rent they are charged for their waterless, drainless, floorless, and almost roofless tenements; to calculate the interest that the petty capitalist reaps from their necessities. (Yeo and Thompson 1971, 103)

One hundred and sixty years later, Piketty translates Mayhew's concerns with exploitation into the economic problem of income distribution when he comments that "the question of what share of output should go to wages and what share to profits—in other words, how should the income from production be divided between labor and capital?—has always been at the heart of distributional conflict" (2014, 39). Mayhew's project, I show, was not just to document the vast array of occupations and living circumstances of the London poor, but also to demonstrate the falsehood of mid-Victorian political economists' theories of the free market and the law of supply and demand as applied to labor. He also exposed how the division of profits between capital and labor was fundamentally unjust, raising the possibility that the working classes could attain a greater share of the national wealth if profit sharing were applied to wages. In the process, Mayhew devised a new social science of the relations between labor and capital, called "social economy," that could in turn demonstrate "the importance of the poor and the working classes as members of the State" (Taithe 1996, 129, 97).

Both Piketty's and Mayhew's research refocused public attention in compelling ways on extremes of economic inequality that had been apparent for decades—in Piketty's account, inequality has fluctuated, receding and reemerging over the past two centuries—but that required a correction of vision and a broader participation by the public to become newly salient as a widespread injustice demanding redress. I discuss Piketty's proposed solutions for today's global economic inequality in this chapter's final section. The majority of the chapter studies in detail Mayhew's definition of equity as the conceptual basis for his theory of just wage shares—in effect, the redistribution of the profits of manufacturing. The word "equity," is defined as "the quality of being equal or fair; fairness; impartiality" according to the *Oxford English Dictionary* ("equity n."). Mayhew employs equity both as a moral principle of fairness or justice and, epistemologically, as "a perception of equality" that would underpin quantitative economic measures and normative political judgments alike (Taithe 1996, 96, 105). Although equity is not a keyword for Piketty, both his attempt to reorient economics toward questions of wealth distribution in order to advance "the debate about the best way to organize society and the most appropriate institutions and policies to achieve a just social order" (2014, 31), and Mayhew's attempt to reconceive political economy on the basis of equity and the citizenship of the poor. Both develop an enduring project to conceive the modern discipline of economics as a socially accountable human science. Mayhew is forgotten as a political economist, but he shares a common topic with Piketty; in fact, their shared topic shows them also to be critics of the currently existing economics of their day and champions of a more socially grounded version of political economy that enables them to make arguments about equity and inequality that were otherwise harder to make.

When set side by side, Mayhew's and Piketty's projects reveal other significant similarities. As a writer of plays, novels, and satirical articles, Mayhew had diverse literary conventions at his disposal, enabling him to formulate the confrontation between the exploited poor and the petty capitalist as a kind of melodrama, but one in which the morally reprehensible character—the petty capitalist—unjustly prevails. In *C21*, alongside graphs, equations, and a massive database, available online, measuring long-term capital and income distributions, Piketty also derives important conceptions of the historical links between income and social status from the nineteenth-century novels of Jane Austen and Honoré de Balzac (2014, 32–33, 53–54). These novelists, Piketty writes, "depicted the effects of inequality with a verisimilitude and evocative power that no statistical or theoretical analysis can match" (2). In reaching toward familiar and politically potent melodramatic conventions implying that the downtrodden might receive justice in the end (Taithe 1996, 19–21; see also Hadley 1995), or using novels as evidence for historical income distributions, both Mayhew and Piketty seek a means beyond numbers and statistics to illustrate the social implications of economic inequality.

There are also commonalities in Mayhew's and Piketty's data-driven research methods. Mayhew seeks "statistical information," particularly from workers themselves and from directors of trade societies, who are requested to send him detailed information on production and wages from their accounting ledgers (Taithe 1996, 89). He also recruits his readers as his collaborators: "I[f] the working-men will but continue to assist Mr. Mayhew in his undertaking, he hopes before long to collect such an overwhelming mass of facts as *must* cause justice to be done to them" (142). Because of its historical moment before the formation of the modern university disciplines, Mayhew's project can be considered as pre-disciplinary and hybrid. While Piketty identifies himself as an economist, he defines his own approach as historical and therefore interdisciplinary (2014, 33).

Perhaps the most incongruous aspect of this juxtaposition of Mayhew's and Piketty's interventions in the political economy or economics of their day, however, lies in Piketty's fame and influence versus Mayhew's obscurity. Piketty's English translator, Arthur Goldhammer, reports that within a year after *C21* was published in English translation in 2014, 2.1 million copies of the book had sold globally in over thirty countries (2017, 27). In contrast, most of Mayhew's incisive commentaries on political economy and exploitation appear in the serial edition of *LLLP* that he published out of his own office in two-penny weekly numbers from December 1850 through March 1852. This serial reprinted some of the original *Morning Chronicle* articles, but, in addition, printed on the wrappers were selections from Mayhew's correspondence with the serial's readers, published with their permission, in which they commented on his studies and he, in response, defended and elaborated his critiques of political economy (Taithe 1996, 86). If it were not for Bertrand Taithe's scholarly edition (1996) of selections from this correspondence, it would only be available in a few archives, as ephemera.[2]

Mayhew's notion of wage equity was founded on his assertion of shared social values that had been undermined by the embrace of political economy as a political creed. Piketty, at his moment, often rejects neoclassical economics and turns instead to economic history to make a case about inequality, calling for a return to political economy. In both these instances, a turn to narrative, to the human expression of economic living, provides testimony to the human cost that laws of supply and demand on the one hand, and neoclassical equilibrium theory on the other, both obscured (see Hadley's chapter in this volume). Piketty's *C21* was in part a response to the Great Recession of 2007–2009 and the predictive limitations of neoclassical economics.

This chapter introduces Mayhew's notion of equity and tracks its development, showing how it emerges through his engagement in London workers' struggles against the exploitative labor relations and diminution of wages under early industrial capitalism. Identifying three major intellectual resources for and stages of Mayhew's inductive thinking, I begin by showing how, in the course of attempting to theorize the forms of exploitation occurring in London's sweated trades, Mayhew developed equity as a key concept to describe, evaluate, and defend workers' economic rights. In the second stage, once the notion of equity appears in Mayhew's correspondence as a basis for arriving at fair wages and shares of profits between capital and labor, he also defines it epistemologically. This further move seems to enable Mayhew to position equity directly against political economy's dominance as a political doctrine, so that equity can be used to articulate alternative, socially responsive standards of distributional justice as based in a widely shared common sense. Thirdly, I suggest that in thinking of labor and capital as properly engaged in a contractual partnership based in equity, Mayhew seems also to have drawn on common law conceptions of equitable judgments. Through this analysis, I reconstruct how Mayhew's equitable project of "social economy" (Taithe 1996, 129), mentioned as a sort of aside in the context of his discussion of exploitation, emerges as a replacement for political economy. Through analysis of a contemporaneous text criticizing free trade and written by a judge, and a key scene in Charles Dickens's novel *Hard Times* (1854), I also find evidence that Mayhew's understanding of equity was not singular, although his empirical focus on measurable data marks his theorizing as more social scientific than legal or literary. Finally, in returning to the common questions about economic inequality that Mayhew and Piketty share, the chapter's conclusion considers how public conversations and collaborative research on economic inequality could be invigorated by a more historically robust articulation of a distributional concept such as equity.

MAYHEW'S "SOCIAL ECONOMY" AND EXPLOITATION IN LONDON'S SWEATED TRADES

Historians have often found Mayhew's various methods in *LLLP* challenging to categorize in disciplinary terms. E. P. Thompson describes him as a man of "prodigious but undisciplined talents," and notes Mayhew's composite identity as journalist, satirist, "systematic empirical sociologist," and, in his later work, "serious criminologist" (1971, 50, 45, 33). Eileen Yeo calls Mayhew "a sociological economist by instinct" (1971, 95), while

Christopher Herbert considers *LLLP* to be a pioneering work in formulating the modern idea of culture, and as possibly, "the most significant ethnographic text of its age" (1991, 204). In his analysis of the serial edition of *LLLP*, Thompson points out that although there are inaccuracies in some of Mayhew's statistical data, such errors should not invalidate his findings because his evidence and methods were "rigorous" and "meticulous" (1967, 58–59). Thompson continues, "[Mayhew's] main work is to disclose, in enormous detail and with great force of contrast, the character of orthodox political economy as it was seen from the underside" (59).

Also key to understanding the *Morning Chronicle*'s commissioning of an expensive social survey of England, of which Mayhew's study of London was only one component, as well as the intense interest generated among its readers, is its mid-Victorian moment, when multiple crises seemed to call for the production of new knowledge enabling more effective prediction and ameliorative action. These crises included: the Great Famine of 1845–1849 in Ireland; the working-class Chartist movement for universal manhood suffrage and revolutions in continental Europe, both of which climaxed in 1848; and a wave of disease outbreaks in London, including cholera (Taithe 1996, 17). The recent publication of John Stuart Mill's *Principles of Political Economy* (1848) also provided Mayhew with an immediate target for contesting orthodox political economy.

Mayhew's initial role as Special Correspondent for the *Morning Chronicle* only lasted a year, however. He resigned due to a dispute with the Editors in October 1850 over their repeated censorship of his reports when they conflicted with the newspaper's avowed support for free trade. He initiated the serial publication of *LLLP* shortly afterward. The dispute had arisen over the Editors' deletion of certain passages from Mayhew's report condemning the employment practices of the Nicoll Brothers, a tailoring company that also advertised in the *Morning Chronicle*. This intolerable act of censorship had been followed by the publication of an article praising the Nicolls' treatment of their workers. Because it was unsigned and had replaced Mayhew's report, it was received and reviewed as if he had authored it. To repudiate this article and publicize the reasons for his resignation, Mayhew gave a speech at a special public meeting on October 28, convened by the Committee of the Tailors of London at St. Martin's Hall. Reading to his audience a letter that he had sent to the *Morning Chronicle*'s Editors in February, Mayhew explained that their "dishonest tampering" violated the agreement under which he had first undertaken the series of reports as an impartial, nonpartisan investigator

(*Report of the Speech of Henry Mayhew*, 6). This event also became an opportunity for Mayhew to publicize his inquiry into the flaws of political economy.

The majority of Mayhew's long speech reiterates his published attack on the Nicoll brothers and other perpetrators of the "slop, sweating, and middleman system" (*Report*, 9), who, instead of maintaining workshops, employed tailors in their own homes, often under subcontractors, and in deplorable "sweated" conditions of extreme crowding, with very short deadlines for completing work, and for very low wages. Tailoring, along with building, shoemaking, and furniture-manufacture was one of London's dual sector trades, more and more prevalent in the 1840s, made up of established workshops, where trade associations were active, alongside smaller employers or middlemen subcontractors whose wages were lower (Williams 1981, 246–259; Goodway 1982, 154). According to Mayhew's analysis, this "illegitimate mode of cheapening labour" forced these tailors to employ family members and other workers at an even cheaper rate, obliged them to pay for their own tools and "trimmings" (i.e. thread), and to work longer hours through day and night and seven days per week (*Report*, 16).

In exposing the exploitative logic of these pervasive sweating practices among the London trades, Mayhew's speech openly contests political economy's claims to scientific status, based on the deductive methods followed by Ricardo and Mill, by deploying his own inductive method, based on the gathering of employment statistics, interviews with workers, and investigations of their working conditions.[3] Mayhew claims that in his original undertaking of the investigative series for the *Morning Chronicle*, "I made up my mind to deal with human nature as a natural philosopher or a chemist deals with any material object; and, as a man who had devoted some little of his time to physical and metaphysical science, I must say I did most heartily rejoice that it should have been left to me to apply the laws of the inductive philosophy for the first time, I believe, in the world to the abstract questions of political economy" (*Report*, 6). Mayhew specifically targets the ideologically pervasive Malthusianism undergirding the standard account of surplus labor. As he explained to the assembled tailors:

> The country is not suffering … from over-population, or too many labourers, as the economists endeavour to make out, but from the over-work of a portion of those labourers … Let any system of work be introduced that shall either compel or induce the workmen to labour for eighteen hours a

day [instead of the regular twelve as in legitimate and better paying work-shops], ... and immediately there must be again one-third, at the least, too many labourers to do the work required to be done. Hence it is evident that *over-work makes over-population*, and—so long as the wages of the workmen are allowed to be regulated by a scramble among the starving, or "the principle of supply and demand" as it is called, rather than by meting out to the labourer his fair proportion of the produce, which is the principle of common sense and common justice—so long as this is the case, the consequence of over-population will be under-payment. Hence we arrive at a plain unerring law, *over-work in a trade makes under-payment*. But the evil is not finished here—*under-payment in its turn makes over-work*; for immediately a man's wages are reduced he sets to work, striving, by labouring longer hours, or working faster, and so doing more, still to make up his former income. (*Report*, 20–21)

Mayhew attacks the doctrine of political economists such as Ricardo and Mill in which surplus labor drives down wages, or, as he explains in more detail in the correspondence (quoting Mill), that wages "depend upon the demand and supply of labour; or, as is often expressed on the proportion between population and capital" (Taithe 1996, 114). In contrast, Mayhew's focus on exploitation, while it does not theorize the social mutability of time itself in the ways Samalin shows Marx to have done (Chap. 3 of this volume), reveals that so-called surplus labor is the direct result of the extortion of more work in less time. Over-population of the labor force is not a natural result of workers reproducing at too great a rate for the labor market to support, as the political economists' Malthusian logic would have it, because "this form of the economical proposition takes no notice of the quantity of labour to be done, or amount of materials to be operated upon for a given amount of capital" (135).

On the basis of this reasoning, Mayhew concludes his speech to the tailors by proposing a new, inductively derived empirical law, italicized in the text of his speech, that translates the political economists' flawed notion of a free market in labour into the actual economic conditions of the illegitimate exploitation of the sweated laborer by the petty capitalist: "*Over-work, then, we see, makes under-pay, and under-pay makes over-work*" (*Report*, 20–21). In other words, Mayhew's new empirical law reveals that the so-called law of supply and demand as applied to wages and the labor market is simply an ideological justification of the effects of the capitalist's suppression of wages in order to maximize profits by reducing expenditures and shifting the responsibility for unemployment onto the workers. The rate of return on profits is therefore a direct product of exploitation or the concerted "cheapening of labour" (19) by employers such as the Nicoll brothers.

In a short-lived 1851 serial titled *Low Wages, Their Causes, Consequences, and Remedies,* Mayhew developed this new empirical law and sought to publicize it beyond the correspondence to *LLLP.* Mayhew puts forward what he called the theory of nominal and actual wages, with the nominal being the employer's declared wage, "merely a blind to the public and the workman," and the actual being the low wages left after the deductions of "extra charges to the worker for tools and materials," really "a kind of indirect taxation" according to Mayhew. "The correct way to understand wages," Mayhew wrote, is to calculate "the *rate* of remuneration, which is the *ratio between* the amount of pay and the quantity of labour" (Mayhew 1851, 467).

In addition to his efforts to organize workers' associations, an important context for Mayhew's economic thinking lies in the Chartists' agitation during the 1840s for labor and political reform. In newspapers and on public platforms, the London Chartists also castigated those small masters who had risen from the ranks of labor for exploiting their workers and complained of capitalists' inequitably aggrandized shares of profit (Goodway 1982, 7–10). Mayhew's interviews in *LLLP* also provide evidence for the widespread sympathy for Chartism among London's uneducated laboring poor and the open espousing of the Charter among organized artisans (224–225). Mayhew is known to have been in contact with London Chartists during his researches, and reportedly appeared at Chartist meetings (Taithe 1996, 21, 40). In the Preface to their pamphlet publication of Mayhew's speech, the Committee of the Tailors of London called Mayhew "our able and disinterested advocate … and the champion of the working classes" (*Report,* 2). At a subsequent meeting of workers on November 5, Mayhew reportedly made a resolution. Deploying again melodrama's personifications of conflicts between the oppressor and the oppressed, he resolved that because Great Britain possessed sufficient resources of wealth and industry to employ all of its population, "the best remedy" for "the lawless and inhuman competition of the fraudulent and strong against the honest and weak … is an equitable arbitration or mediation between demand and supply by the means of co-operation among the people" thus supporting workers' collectives ("Distressed Populations," 1265).

I study in the rest of this section how Mayhew further elaborated his "social economy" and the concept of equity in the course of his published correspondence with London's workers. As part of this conversation, Mayhew contests the linkage postulated by Ricardo between the price of food and the natural rate of wages, as determined by a customary standard of the amount of food required for subsistence (see Blaug 1958, 22–24). We can clarify what Mayhew meant in his speech referring to "equitable arbitration" by considering its relation to his critique of the subsistence wage in one of his responses to a group of correspondents. Commenting on the receipt of a prospectus for a journal to be published by the London coal-whippers, Mayhew requests that they consider "collecting and making known the statistics of labour" related to their trade, thus "contributing their mite to the general knowledge on this difficult question" of wages and the purported labor surplus. Mayhew counsels that the coal-whippers' journal should supply information leading to peaceable reform, but even so asserts that he "believes that the working men of England are grossly wronged by capitalists" because the relation between labor and capital must be a "partnership" based in a "contract" in which "the monied man agrees to advance to the working man his share of the produce in the form of wages." The fact that "this fundamental contract is violated, and that the labourer does *not get his fair share of the produce at the present day*," Mayhew argues, is made plain in the example of "the padlock, to quote a solitary instance, which is made for a halfpenny, [and] sold for a shilling" (Taithe 1996, 96). Here Mayhew seems to be objecting to what Marx would call the capitalist's extraction of surplus value (see Samalin's account in Chap. 3 of this volume). Mayhew points out that unscrupulous employers now manipulate the dogma of political economy. They claim that the price of "necessities" drives wages but they do so in order to cut wages when food becomes cheaper, thereby deriving greater profits.[4] In addition to such manipulation, the exploitative doctrine that wages fluctuate due to the "free market" in labor has been reinforced by its general political acclamation: "the law of supply and demand has got to be recognised by the rulers of the land, and to be considered almost as a part of the commercial creed of the country—the last 'new commandment,' as it were, against which it is political blasphemy to raise one's voice" (96).

In his attack on the capitalist's leveraging of subsistence as a way to suppress wages, Mayhew's ethnographic methods also contribute a different sort of evidence by focusing on child labor as another aspect of the "overpopulation" of the sweated labor market forced upon working families. In one of his letters, he quotes a conversation he had with a married couple of cabinet makers in the sweated sector of the trade. The husband speaks first:

> The greater part of the cabinet makers of the East End have from five to six in family, and they are generally all at work for them … You see our trade's coming to such a pass, that unless a man has children to help him he can't live at all. '*I've worked more than a month together,*' continued the wife, '*and the longest night's rest I've had has been an hour and a quarter; aye, and I've been up three nights a week besides* … You see we couldn't live if it wasn't for the labour of our children, though it makes 'em—poor little things!—old people long afore they are growed up. (Taithe 1996, 128)

Such personal testimonies, voicing suffering and protest, are positioned to speak directly to Mayhew's correspondents. The interaction takes on the further effect of a theatrical performance of a melodrama, when the wife describes her nonstop work at her bench for fifteen hours straight beside her ten-year-old son, until, Mayhew reports, "*Here she burst into a violent flood of tears, saying, 'Oh, Sir! it is hard to be obliged to labour from morning till night as we do, all of us, little ones and all, and yet not be able to live by it either'*" (128). Such literary and performative effects are an integral part of Mayhew's data, demonstrating once again the multi-generic qualities of his "social economy," a project which was open to many voices (see Taithe 1996, 22–32). Moreover, these working-class parents reveal their understanding, shared with Mayhew's readers, of their economic circumstances and the implications of their plight—that both the prevailing wage system and the theory of political economy that was blind to its cruel social effects have failed because working families cannot subsist under this system, even when every single member is forced to labor.

Piketty's most general thesis in *C21* is that economic inequality since the nineteenth century has accelerated when "the rate of return on capital exceeds the rate of growth of output and income" (2014, 1). Piketty comments here on total economic output, and not simply on production, and he notes throughout his study that capital profits are the key area of growth that produces inequality. While he lacks sufficient data to study economic growth and distribution in depth and over time, as Piketty does, Mayhew still reveals that growth in both production and profits on capital plays a central role in exploitation and economic inequality. For example, in one conversation with readers concerning decreases in average incomes from wages, Mayhew provides a graph with hypothetical aggregate data for grain production over four years; it shows how production increases dramatically, while labor costs are "economized" by the "profit-mongers" (employers) through their forcing of productivity (longer hours), even as the wage fund, or the amount of profit set aside for feeding the laborers under the subsistence model, remains flat, with the result that "the profits of those who hold the capital may be increased at a most enormous rate" (Taithe 1996, 152–153).

Mayhew considers the capitalists' disregard for workers and capture of a disproportionate share of the profits contributed by labor to be "one of the crying iniquities of the present day" (Taithe 1996, 112). Here is another instance showing how, in the process of writing his responses to working-class readers, Mayhew developed his notion of equity into a portmanteau, politico-economic concept with a kind of moral currency. The term equity forms two antitheses: "inequity," meaning lack of fairness or unequal treatment, and "iniquity," defined as "Wrongful or injurious action towards another, infliction of wrong, injury; in modern usage generally connoting gross injustice or public wrong" (see "equity, n." and "iniquity, n."). In responding to a correspondent who sees no problem with capitalists' not considering commodity prices in setting wages, Mayhew explains philologically: "To give an *unjust* price is not *equity*, and therefore in-equity, or *in-iquity*, if there be any meaning in words" (Taithe 1996, 179). Mayhew also seems to be working with the modern connotation by invoking the "iniquitous" public wrong of exploitation in opposition to his proposed "equitable wage principle." In a subsequent letter, he defines this new equitable wage principle, which incorporates fairness for both capitalist and workers as "the capitalist being paid a fair interest for the use of his money, a return for his risk, and a salary for his superintendence; while the workmen (who receive a certain weekly wage) are allowed to participate with himself in the profits" (112–113).[5] This equitable wage principle draws on the idea of "*partnership* in the produce" to demonstrate that the two parties, labor and capital, "*should share in the proportion which they contribute towards the result*" (113). In order to be equitable, wages as a share of increasing profits would also increase, instead of stagnating or even decreasing. Mayhew's notion that equitable wages must represent profit sharing is clear in the example of the padlock, quoted above, where he implies that the worker's share in the profits generated by the price point is minimal, and thus blatantly unjust. An equitable wage would therefore be either an addition of a profit share to weekly wages, or would be taken into account in setting wages, rather than their being set either according to the competitive valuations of the so-called free market in labor, or according to the fluctuating prices of food and other necessities. "A share is a portion regulated by equity, and not by a scramble," Mayhew writes (104).

EQUITY AS JUDGMENT

In addition to its economic, social, moral, and political connotations, Mayhew's notion of equity also acquires epistemological features and uses as well as certain legal registers. We can see Mayhew's epistemological presuppositions for his notion of equity as a shared value made more explicit in a response to another correspondent, F. B. B. He finds Mayhew's "observations on labour and capital … very erroneous and mischievous, and calculated to mislead the working classes" (Taithe 1996, 103). Contesting the terms of Mayhew's attack on the law of supply and demand insofar as the law governs wages, F. B. B. asks,

> If wages are not to be thus regulated, I desire to know by what other standard can they be regulated? To talk of "conscience" and "justice," is to use vague terms of no definite meaning … The fault of low wages is not in the capitalists, but in the labourers, who overcrowd the labour market, and compete with each other. If the working classes have no prudence, no self-denial, they ought surely to bear the consequences of their deficiency in this respect—not the capitalist. (104)

Mayhew replies that "the propounders of such doctrines, being unable to perceive that conscience is the exercise of the judgment on moral propositions, and justice the perception of moral equality or equity, are likewise unable to perceive that to deny the existence of the conscience is to deny that there is any such faculty as judgment in man, while to make equity and other moral truths mere conventions is to reduce the most fundamental truths of all, viz., those which depend on a perception of equality, to matters of pure fashion" (105). Mayhew asserts that the inherent moral and epistemic equipment of all human beings is based in this ability to apply equity, as the perception of equality, to any and all relations; such perceptions are equally sensory, epistemological, and moral. There is no division in Mayhew's inductive method between epistemology and morality. Mayhew therefore explicitly aligns the principle of equality, a fundamental tool of quantitative measurement, with equity, a moral judgment of basic fairness in law and common life. Such subjective equitable judgments, based in the moral and epistemic capacities of all human beings, form the basis of Mayhew's revised "social economy."

Mayhew's thinking seems to draw on Enlightenment-era moral philosophy for its epistemology, perhaps even Adam Smith's *Theory of Moral Sentiments* (1759), although he was no admirer of Smith's political economy. It is crucial to underscore that equity as a "perception of equality" in Mayhew's formulation does not posit equivalence or identity; instead, equality understood epistemologically is a *relation* linked to sensory perception, as Hume had postulated in his discussion of Knowledge and Probability in *A Treatise of Human Nature* (1739–1740, Book I, Part 3, Sect. I): "'Tis from the idea of a triangle, that we discover the relation of equality, which its three angles bear to two right ones; and this relation is invariable, as long as our idea remains the same" (1978, 69). Because he is an epistemological naturalist, however, and not a skeptic like Hume, Mayhew asserts not just the universality but also the consistency of conscience and judgment as moral faculties. Subjective judgments of equity therefore carry a demonstrable validity for Mayhew. It is this kind of commonsensical epistemological certainty that Mayhew has in mind when he indignantly repudiates F. B. B.'s relativistic assertion that, "The dictates of 'conscience' depend upon organization and education; what one man's conscience teaches another man's denies." "Does truth depend on the same circumstances?" Mayhew rebuts, "To what organizations and in what schools does 2 + 2 = 5? So of moral truth" (Taithe 1996, 104). Everyone can see what is fair and just, Mayhew argues, as clearly as they can see that 2 + 2 = 4. Capitalists, who extract surplus profits from workers' contributions to production, are the only ones who assert that 2 + 2 = 5, and political economists have transmuted their false arithmetic into a doctrine. Mayhew also seeks to make use of numbers and statistics in his theory of "social economy" in order to persuade readers to adopt his inductive style of reasoning, rather than the abstract and tendentious deductive laws of the political economists.

By asserting that this equitable standard of validity derives from "a perception of equality" that pertains to all objects requiring judgment, including both those material things that can be quantified and those moral values and social relationships that cannot, Mayhew's thinking undermines the scientific credentials of political economy and its tendency to reduce social values to competitive market valuations. More importantly, by insisting on partnerships and wage equity, Mayhew's theorizing builds an equitable relation between capital and labor in place of the exploitation that political economy naturalizes, and thereby postulates the social equality of the poor and the working classes as "members of the State" or fellow citizens (Taithe 1996, 96–97). While equitable profit sharing would not immediately destabilize hierarchies of social class, as a means of economic redistribution, it could lead to greater social equality by shifting proportions of national wealth conceived of as a public good that must be equitably shared.

In his critique of the "doctrine of free labour," Mayhew also seems to evoke the more ancient legal principle of equity, or a judgment according to fairness rather than strict legal rules. As stated by the eighteenth-century Scottish jurist Henry Home, Lord Kames, "To determine every particular case according to what is just, equal, and salutary, taking in all circumstances, is undoubtedly the idea of a court of equity in its perfection" (1800, 15). The law of equity in Mayhew's day was still associated in England with the High Court of Chancery, which would not be abolished until the Judicature Acts of 1873 and 1875. Equity cases in Chancery were most often concerned with disputes entailing fiduciary relationships established by means of trusts, securities, wills, and estates, as well as bankruptcy. Describing the ideological features of the equity jurisdiction that made it difficult to reform, Getzler (2004, 604) points out that "Chancery interpretation of legal phenomena was expressed through equitable conscience and good faith, and a concomitant obsession with fraud," noting also that its specific remedies directed toward persons gave it "the special sense of jurisdiction over the conscience and the body, not just the purse or possessions, of litigants." Mayhew's recourse to the principle of equity in his attack on both capitalist exploitation and political economy's biased doctrines seems to summon a similarly judicial authority to apportion shares of profit and set wages in socially corrective ways not stipulated by law.

Such an equitable judgment would also penetrate beneath monetary transactions toward the morally corrupt wellsprings and failures of conscience driving them, such as the greed of the petty capitalist. Another instance of such equitable thinking appears in a contemporary work titled *Sophisms of Free Trade* (1849), published by Sir John Byles, a Justice of the Court of Common Pleas. As part of his attack on the sophism "Don't over-govern" (otherwise known as laissez-faire), and in response to the recent famine in Ireland, Byles argues that impoverished Irish tenants, "at the mercy of their landlords," should receive monetary compensation not currently allowed by law for improvements they make to their farms:

"Especially ought this to be done when the public have a vital interest in the contract, which that weaker party makes" (1849, 49; see also Atiyah 1979, 382–383). Embedded here is the notion, similar to Mayhew's, that in the absence of statutory protections and the political will to act, equity, as a legal, ethical, and social principle of justice, can redress relations of exploitation, and that such a counterbalancing, broadly remedial intervention is in the public interest.

Mayhew's attack on exploitation by implying the petty capitalist's violation of contractual obligations also has dimensions related to legal equity's preoccupation with fraud. The creeping of purely economic considerations into all quasi-contractual relations and the evacuation of social ties other than pecuniary ones from the mid-Victorian marketplace appear in Charles Dickens novel *Hard Times* (1854), a biting satire of political economy and industrial conflict in a fictionalized factory town. At the end of the novel, Thomas Gradgrind M. P. reaps the consequences of his strictly utilitarian upbringing of his children according only to factual information and aggregate notions of happiness, when his son, Tom, turns out to be a bank robber. Gradgrind hopes to send Tom to the colonies in order to avoid his arrest, but one of the working-class former pupils at Gradgrind's model school, Bitzer, now a bank employee, manages to capture Tom and plans to return him to his employer, the bank owner and industrialist, Mr. Bounderby, in exchange for a reward and a promotion. Gradgrind pleads with Bitzer to release Tom and enable his escape on the basis of Gradgrind's sponsorship of Bitzer's elementary schooling, but Bitzer has learned too well Gradgrind's central lesson, that "the whole social system is a question of self-interest" (Dickens 1996, 306):

> "I really wonder, sir" rejoined the old pupil in an argumentative manner, "to find you taking a position so untenable. My schooling was paid for; it was a bargain; and when I came away, the bargain ended."
>
> It was a fundamental principle of the Gradgrind philosophy that everything was to be paid for. Nobody was ever on any account to give anybody anything, or to render anybody help without purchase. Gratitude was to be abolished, and the virtues springing from it were not to be. Every inch of the existence of mankind, from birth to death, was to be a bargain across a counter. And if we didn't get to Heaven that way, it was not a politico-economical place, and we had no business there. (306)

The fraud to be perpetrated here is Gradgrind's on his son's behalf against the law, but the passage manages to represent Gradgrind's now-rejected politico-economical philosophy as the more fundamental source of the defrauding of the social contract itself. Dickens's lament for the lapse of the deferential relationships of gratitude characteristic of a status-based society enables a critique of economic contracts as having been reduced to merely transactional bargains, void of any value other than monetary, and incapacitated from establishing enduring social relationships based in trust or friendship.[6] According to the novel's satire, much like Mayhew's attacks on the greed of the petty capitalist, in a society where "business" considerations and self-interest determine all human interactions as effectively taking place "across a counter," social relations based more directly in reciprocity and equity have to rely, paradoxically, on the mediated platforms of literature and their fostering of the virtual social relations enabled by the circulation of print.

In their objections to the political creed of political economy, however, Dickens and Mayhew both show in varied ways that social relations based in reciprocity have not expired, but can persist within the mid-Victorian marketplace. What has been eroded are people's confidence in and understanding of the fundamental sociability of the economy, even though its modes of mutual dependence and cooperation are being rerouted through transactional values of competitiveness. Mayhew's ethnographic methods demonstrate this sociality, and the potential for solidarity, as clearly as the popularity of Dickens's unforgettable characters does. The role of both Dickens's popular literature (see also Jaffe's chapter in this volume) and Mayhew's social economy would therefore be, in reaching out to a broadly based reading audience, to reclaim the social by subordinating both political economy and economic interests to the well-being of individuals and society.

Conclusion: Equity, Economic Inequality, and Interdisciplinary Collaboration

Mayhew's collaborative account of commensuration in social and economic life—how values can be estimated and assessed consistently, and thus equitably, across multiple social domains—combines statistical data with a moral and ethical standard of justice understood as equal and fair treatment. Victorian political economy, Mayhew seeks to prove, is a political doctrine that masks itself as a natural science, and it should therefore be corrected and reformed in such a way that it becomes what he calls an inductive science of "social economy" (Taithe 1996, 129), based in data about actual social and economic relationships that could form a legitimate basis for economic policy. Mayhew's suggested remedies for the economic inequality, poverty, and exploitation of his day also included his proposal that workers "should demand from the employers a fair living price for the[ir] work" (93), and that small employers in dual sector trades should form "joint stock" companies through the aggregation of their smaller capitals, so that they could compete with large employers in such a way that wages would not be suppressed across the sector (93, 161).

Unlike Mayhew, who concentrated on business profits and wages, Piketty's study of economic inequality focuses on income from capital or ownership of assets. Piketty locates several recurring trends that are apparent today, including a dramatic concentration of wealth among economic elites internationally. A disproportionate share of aggregate wealth is therefore passed on to heirs, leading to the greater social dominance of inherited wealth, particularly in Europe, while the extremely high income tiers in the United States are often tied to the outsized salaries of corporate directors (see also Krugman 2017). Piketty's proposed remedies for the new "global patrimonial capitalism" (2014, 471) include confiscatory domestic tax rates on top incomes and a progressive global tax on capital, with rates to be set by "collective deliberation and democratic experimentation" (512–513). In his discussion of the twenty-first century "social state," Piketty comes within the orbit of Mayhew's notion of a "social economy" built on equity when he proposes, toward the conclusion of *C21*, that modern redistribution does not imply income transfer from the rich to the poor, but rather it is "built around a logic of rights and a principle of equal access to a certain number of goods [including education, health, and a pension] deemed to be fundamental" (479).[7] In one of his most incisive interventions, Piketty observes, along the lines of Mayhew's ambitions in his social survey and Dickens's vision for a socially inclusive popular literature, that "real democracy and social justice require specific institutions of their own, not just those of the market, and not just parliaments and other formal democratic institutions" (2014, 424). What would such equitable institutions look like? Have any such existed in mid-Victorian Britain or today?

My goal in this chapter has been to think about how Mayhew's dilemmas and ideas, including his serial publication's modeling of open access to readers, may enter into conversation with current interdisciplinary research on economic inequality. In addition to seeing it as a hybrid social scientific and literary project, we could view Mayhew's "social economy" as constituting a socio-political theory rather than simply the objective, impartial project that he claimed it to be. As a normative political principle grounded in workers' struggles and experiences, Mayhew's notion of equity could therefore be valuable today as a component of an interdisciplinary and public dialogue about the shared values that can support greater economic and social justice. Echoing Mayhew's thinking in certain ways, Piketty warns: "There is no fundamental reason why we should believe that growth is automatically balanced" (2014, 16).

Defined as a "perception of equality" that implies a conscientious judgment concerning social justice, equity could be articulated more fully today as a key principle to be used in guiding rebalancing efforts in relation to distribution. Equity may have become a keyword for the moment in politically progressive economic analysis.[8] Reflecting back on the institutionalization of economics among academic disciplines that has given us the current divide between the humanities and the social and natural sciences, Piketty writes: "The truth is that economics should never have sought to divorce itself from the other social sciences and can only advance in conjunction with them" (2014, 32–33). In a recent reconsideration of his methods in *C21*, Piketty recommends that in understanding economic inequality today and in the future, "[mathematical] models should be used with parsimony" and cautions that "they cannot replace the historical narrative, which in my view must be the real core of the analysis" (2017, 554). For Piketty, economics, devoid of such a historical narrative, has clearly played a role in producing today's widespread phenomenon of the invisibility of the vast accumulations of wealth in private hands:

> For millions of people, "wealth" amounts to little more than a few weeks' wages in a checking account or low-interest savings account, a car, and a few pieces of furniture. The inescapable reality is this: wealth is so concentrated that a large segment of society is virtually unaware of its existence, so that some people imagine that it belongs to surreal or mysterious entities. That is why it is so essential to study capital and its distribution in a methodical, systematic way. (2014, 259)

This diagnosis of the public mystification about wealth not only captures another impetus behind Piketty's project, but also clarifies why he turns to novels by Balzac and Austen to illustrate his assertion that "at the beginning of the nineteenth century, the nature of wealth was relatively clear to all readers" (113).[9] Piketty's elaborate historical narrative based in massive collections of tax records and other long-term economic data illustrates the burden on today's disciplines to illuminate the sources of global inequality in the absence of a widely familiar popular narrative capable of defining who is responsible and why this imbalance must be redressed. The melodramatic conventions of Mayhew's study of exploitation almost wrote themselves into his analysis, since the confrontation between workers and "property-mongers" was already understood by many at the time to be an iniquitous wrong. Even for Mayhew, however, a moral appeal was inadequate to settle the political issues at stake, or to dislodge political economy from its doctrinal role in propping up laissez-faire capitalism and all the disasters it incurred across the British Empire (see the chapters in this volume by Bigelow and Mangharam).

As I have begun to show in this chapter, economic inequality could be usefully examined from the perspective of a multivalent concept such as Mayhew's notion of equity, which, instead of pitting quantitative and qualitative methods against one another, retains certain quantitative connotations, but also raises questions about equality and social justice that may not be quantifiable because they imply causes and remedies that are equally moral, social, legal, and political. Equity could provide a multidisciplinary conceptual currency to enable researchers across disciplines and contributors to public debates about social justice and economic inequality to forge a common language to contest the orthodoxies of political economy and its successor, economics.

What possible roles remain for the humanities in such discussions? On behalf of the Editors and contributors to this volume, I would suggest that we consider Piketty's assertion that "real democracy and social justice require specific institutions of their own," as a call for practitioners of literature, the arts, and the humanities to reassert the public value of their varied insights into the lived dimensions of our global "social economy." We can also uphold the democratic values of institutions of higher education—as long as they remain mostly untethered to reductionist market incentives and private political and economic interests—so that they maintain an institutional power and independence to pursue equity and equality as fundamental social and political goals.

Notes

1. All emphases appear in original unless otherwise noted.
2. I have consulted the copy of Mayhew's serial publication of *London Labour and the London Poor* held at the British Library. In his edition of selections from Mayhew's correspondence, Taithe (1996) mentions having visited the

Birmingham University Library, the British Library, the Bibliothèque Nationale, and the Guildhall archives.

3. There is an extensive literature on deductive versus inductive methods in classical political economy; for two useful accounts, see Henderson (1990) and Snyder (2006).

4. In his influential 1944 history of the emergence of the self-regulating market, *The Great Transformation*, Karl Polanyi (2001, 172) describes in ways similar to Mayhew's account how classical economics incentivized labor according to the ineluctable pressures of hunger and mere subsistence.

5. Noel W. Thompson (1984, 39, 220) has shown that early nineteenth-century working-class political economists also criticized classical political economists for promulgating theories of "iniquity" and "inequity." Their proposed "equitable" remedies were different from Mayhew's recommendation of profit sharing because they advocated "refurbished exchange relations" (1984, 222–223) between capitalists and workers that would be derived from wages corresponding to natural values rather than market values.

6. For a more extensive analysis of equity and friendship in law and nineteenth-century novels, see Winter (2016).

7. Such rights are set out in the United Nations Covenant on Economic, Social, and Cultural Rights (1966) and many other similar national and international legal instruments. See https://ijrcenter.org/thematic-research-guides/economic-social-and-cultural-rights-2/.

8. The adoption of equity as a principle for research is evident in the recently founded, non-profit Washington Center for Equitable Growth, which defines its mission as supporting "evidence-backed ideas and policies that promote strong, stable and broad-based economic growth," including research on the detrimental impacts of economic inequality on growth, https://equitablegrowth.org/.

9. Another goal of Piketty's proposed global tax on capital is to "promote democratic and financial transparency" by "generat[ing] information about the distribution of wealth" (2014, 518).

REFERENCES

Atiyah, P. S. 1979. *The Rise and Fall of Freedom of Contract*. Oxford: Oxford University Press.

Blaug, Mark. 1958. *Ricardian Economics: A Historical Study*. New Haven, CT: Yale University Press.

Byles, John Barnard, Sir. 1849. *Sophisms of Free Trade and Political Economy Examined. By a Barrister*. London: Seeleys.

Dickens, Charles. 1996. *Hard Times*. Edited by Graham Law. Peterborough, ON, Canada: Broadview Press.

"Distressed Populations: A Warning and a Doubt." 1850. *The Economist*, 1264–1265, November 16.

"equity, n.". *OED Online*, January 2019. Oxford University Press. Accessed January 19, 2019. http://www.oed.com.ezproxy.lib.uconn.edu/view/Entry/63838?redirectedFrom=equity.

Getzler, Joshua. 2004. Chancery Reform and Law Reform. *Law and History Review* 22 (3): 601–608.

Goldhammer, Arthur. 2017. The Piketty Phenomenon. In *After Piketty*, ed. H. Boushey, J. Bradford De Long, and M. Steinbaum, 27–47. Cambridge, MA: Harvard University Press.

Goodway, David. 1982. *London Chartism: 1838–1848*. Cambridge: Cambridge University Press.

Hadley, Elaine. 1995. *Melodramatic Tactics: Theatricalized Dissent in Nineteenth-Century England*. Stanford: Stanford University Press.

Henderson, James P. 1990. Induction, Deduction and the Role of Mathematics: The Whewell Group vs. the Ricardian Economists. *Research in the History of Economic Thought and Methodology* 7: 1–36.

Herbert, Christopher. 1991. *Culture and Anomie: Ethnographic Imagination in the Nineteenth Century*. Chicago: University of Chicago Press.

Home, Henry, and Lord Kames. 1800. *Principles of Equity*. 4th ed. Edinburgh: Adam Neill.

Hume, David. [1888] 1978. *A Treatise of Human Nature*. Edited by P. H. Nidditch. Oxford: Oxford University Press.

"iniquity, n.". *OED Online*. January 2019. Oxford University Press. Accessed January 19, 2019. http://www.oed.com.ezproxy.lib.uconn.edu/view/Entry/96048?redirectedFrom=iniquity.

Krugman, Paul. 2017. Why We're in a New Gilded Age. In *After Piketty*, ed. H. Boushey, J. Bradford De Long, and M. Steinbaum, 60–71. Cambridge, MA: Harvard University Press.

Mayhew, Henry. 1851. From *Low Wages, Their Causes, Consequences and Remedies* (November/December 1851). In *The Unknown Mayhew*, eds. E. Yeo and E. P. Thompson, 463–475. New York: Pantheon Books.

———. 1985. *London Labour and The London Poor*. Edited by Victor Neuberg. London: Penguin.

Piketty, Thomas. 2014. *Capital in the Twenty-First Century*. Translated by Arthur Goldhammer. Cambridge, MA: Harvard University Press. Originally published as *Le capital au XXI siècle*. Paris: Éditions du Seuil, 2103.

———. 2017. Toward a Reconciliation between Economics and the Social Sciences: Lessons from *Capital in the Twenty-First Century*. In *After Piketty*, ed. H. Boushey, J. Bradford De Long, and M. Steinbaum, 543–565. Cambridge, MA: Harvard University Press.

Polanyi, Karl. [1944] 2001. *The Great Transformation: The Political and Economic Origins of Our Time*. Boston: Beacon Press.

Report of the Speech of Henry Mayhew, Esq., and the Evidence Adduced at a Public Meeting Held at St. Martin's Hall, Long Acre, on Monday Evening, Oct. 28, 1850, Convened by the Committee of the Tailors of London. 1850. London: Printed for the Committee.

Snyder, Laura J. 2006. *Reforming Philosophy: A Victorian Debate on Science and Society*. Chicago: University of Chicago Press.

Taithe, Bertrand, ed. 1996. *The Essential Mayhew: Representing and Communicating the Poor*. London: Rivers Oram Press.

Thompson, E.P. 1967. The Political Education of Henry Mayhew. *Victorian Studies* 11 (1): 41–62.

———. 1971. Mayhew and the *Morning Chronicle*. In *The Unknown Mayhew*, ed. E. Yeo and E.P. Thompson, 11–50. New York: Pantheon Books.

Thompson, Noel W. 1984. *The People's Science: The Popular Political Economy of Exploitation and Crisis 1816–34*. Cambridge: Cambridge University Press.

Williams, Karel. 1981. *From Pauperism to Poverty*. London: Routledge & Kegan Paul.

Winter, Sarah. 2016. Scottish Enlightenment Concepts of Equity in the Nineteenth-Century British Novel. In *The Language of the Imagination: The Scottish Enlightenment and Literary Culture*, ed. Kenneth Simpson, Ronnie Young, and Ralph McLean, 245–268. Lanham, MD: Bucknell University Press, Rowman & Littlefield.

Yeo, Eileen. 1971. Mayhew as a Social Investigator. In *The Unknown Mayhew*, ed. E. Yeo and E.P. Thompson, 51–95. New York: Pantheon Books.

Yeo, Eileen, and E.P. Thompson, eds. 1971. *The Unknown Mayhew*. New York: Pantheon Books.

INDEX[1]

[1] Note: Page numbers followed by 'n' refer to notes.

Printed by Printforce, the Netherlands